Social Inclusion

Also by Peter Askonas

WELFARE VALUES (*editor with Stephen F. Frowen*)

Also by Angus Stewart

CONTEMPORARY BRITAIN (*editor*)

Social Inclusion

Possibilities and Tensions

Edited by

Peter Askonas
Heythrop College, University of London

and

Angus Stewart
Lecturer in Sociology
London School of Economics and Political Science

First published in Great Britain 2000 by
MACMILLAN PRESS LTD
Houndmills, Basingstoke, Hampshire RG21 6XS and London
Companies and representatives throughout the world

A catalogue record for this book is available from the British Library.

ISBN 0–333–79198–3 hardcover
ISBN 0–333–91835–5 paperback

First published in the United States of America 2000 by
ST. MARTIN'S PRESS, INC.,
Scholarly and Reference Division,
175 Fifth Avenue, New York, N.Y. 10010

ISBN 0–312–23166–0

Library of Congress Cataloging-in-Publication Data
Social inclusion : possibilities and tensions / edited by Peter Askonas and Angus
Stewart.
p.   cm.
Includes bibliographical references and index.
ISBN 0–312–23166–0 (cloth)
1. Economic development. 2. Multiculturalism. 3. Marginality, Social. 4. Social
integration. 5. Political planning. I. Askonas, Peter, 1919– II. Stewart, Angus,
M.A.

HD75 .S624 2000
338.9—dc21

99–056426

This book is printed on paper suitable for recycling and made from fully managed and sustained
forest sources.

10   9   8   7   6   5   4   3   2   1
09   08   07   06   05   04   03   02   01   00

Printed and bound in Great Britain by Antony Rowe Ltd, Chippenham, Wiltshire

Contents

Part III Agendas of Inclusion

Part IV Concluding Thoughts

Acknowledgements

This book arose out of a conference on 'Stakeholding: Structures for a New Society', held at Heythrop College, University of London, in April 1997. The Editors would like to thank the college for its hospitality and all the participants from whose enthusiasm and encouragement the genesis of the present volume sprang.

The Editors would also like to thank Yvonne Brown and Margaret Savage for invaluable secretarial assistance and Fraser Muir and Alma Gibbon for IT input. Peter Askonas remembers with gratitude Jim Millen, Professor of Chemistry, University College, University of London, one of the great intellects concerned with interdisciplinary dialogue, who followed and encouraged every phase of the book. Angus Stewart is most grateful to Sam Whimster for his encouragement and insightful comments. As usual, his greatest debt is to Elizabeth Weinberg, who has given sound advice, wise counsel and extensive practical support. For his part, he joins with her in dedicating this book and its aspirations to Amy, Calum, Daniel and Jonathan, whose generation carry forward the project of inclusion.

Notes on the Contributors

Peter Askonas is Co-founder and Honorary Vice-President, Christian Association of Business Executives (CABE). He is Visiting Tutor, Theology of Society, Heythrop College, University of London.

Zygmunt Bauman is Professor Emeritus of Sociology, University of Leeds. His most recent book is *Globalization* (Polity Press, 1998).

Richard Collins is Head of Education at the British Film Institute and the author of a number of books on media. His most recent book is *From Satellite to Market: New Communication Technology and European Public Service Television* (Routledge, 1998).

Diana Coyle is Economics Editor, *The Independent*, and author of *The Weightless World* (Capstone, 1997).

Bernard Crick is Professor Emeritus of Politics and Fellow of Birkbeck College, University of London. He is Chair of the Advisory Group to the Department of Education on 'Teaching of Citizenship and Democracy'.

Simon Deakin is Reader in Economic Law and Fellow of Peterhouse, University of Cambridge. He is Director of a programme of research in corporate governance at the ESRC Centre for Business Research in Cambridge.

John Gray is Professor of European Thought in the European Institute, London School of Economics. His most recent book is *False Dawn: Delusions of Global Capitalism* (Granta, 1998).

Ruth Lister is Professor of Social Policy in the Department of Social Sciences, Loughborough University. A former Director of the Child Poverty Action Group and member of the Commission on Social Justice, her publications include *Citizenship: Feminist Perspectives* (Macmillan, 1997).

Jonathan Perraton is Lecturer in Economics and Deputy Director of the Political Economy Research Centre, University of Sheffield. He is joint editor of *Global Transformations: Politics, Economics and Culture* (Polity Press, 1999).

Raymond Plant is Professor of European Politics, University of Southampton and a Labour Member of the House of Lords.

Peter Ratcliffe is Senior Lecturer in Sociology at the University of Warwick. He has researched and written widely in the area of 'race'/ethnicity, especially in the context of housing and urban inequality.

Peter Robinson is Senior Economist, Institute for Public Policy Research, London.

Richard Sennett is Professor of Sociology, London School of Economics. He trained as a cellist, then studied sociology at Harvard. His research interests are Social Theory, Urban Studies and Sociology of Labour. His most recent book is *The Corrosion of Character* (John Wiley, 1998).

Giles Slinger is a consultant at A.T. Kearney, London. Previously Research Fellow, ESRC Centre for Business Research, Cambridge, he has published a number of papers on stakeholder theory.

Angus Stewart is Lecturer in Sociology and Course Director, Master's Programme in Political Sociology, London School of Economics. A former Editor of the *British Journal of Sociology*, his research interests include power relations in late modern societies, citizenship and the constitution of political identities.

Christopher Stoney is Lecturer in Management and Organizational Behaviour at Imperial College Management School, London. He has published on stakeholding, international corporate governance and strategic management.

Charles Taylor is Professor Emeritus of Philosophy, McGill University, and the 1999 Gifford Lecturer on the theme of 'Living in a Secular Age'.

Diana Winstanley is Lecturer in Human Resource Management, Imperial College Management School, London. She has published a number of books on human resource management, management development and business ethics and conducted a number of research projects for the Department of Health.

1
Social Inclusion: An Introduction

Angus Stewart

Possibilities of achieving social justice and social cohesion in a world subject to chronic and apparently irresistible forces of economic and cultural change are central to the contemporary political and social agenda. This situation arose most immediately from the collapse of state socialism in the former Soviet Union and its Eastern European satellites, and from a recognition of the inability of unregulated market forces to generate and sustain necessary structures of cohesion, given the relentless erosion of stable social contexts by the steady advance of a global economy. The vacuum created by the discrediting of collectivist and liberal market models provides the critical context of the current search to identify new models of social order and justice. The rise of novel variants on familiar responses to processes of social change gives this attempt new dimensions and added urgency.

This attempt has various expressions. One has focused largely upon issues of social marginalization and exclusion within a market-driven society, advancing a range of proposed solutions under the general rubric of 'welfare to work'. While such solutions contain an implicit understanding of political priorities and possibilities, other expressions have involved a more explicit and systematic analysis of the causes which generate widespread social destabilization and exclusion, the major developed example of such analysis being the stakeholder project.[1]

What these expressions share in common is the search for solutions to the tensions involved in the coexistence of competing values and interests in late modernity. These tensions arise from the diverse ideologies and interests of a pluralistic world and as such provide the inescapable conditions for any attempt to reconcile competing conceptions of necessity, justice and order. The tensions involved are both intellectual – conflicting ways of analyzing the nature and possibilities of social organization – and practical, that is, between economic and political institutions on the one hand and the achievement of justice and social order on the other. The centrality of such tensions to current debate is evidenced in critical assessments of the Clinton administration's systematic erosion of public provision in the USA, and of the character and limitations of New Labour's understanding of social inclusion in the UK. Assessment of such arguments centres on the following proposition: from the point of view of policy and practice, projects of social inclusion can either seek to ameliorate the consequences of economically-driven modes of action and organization (the clear intention behind New Labour's Social Exclusion Unit) or they can be open to more fundamental changes in social organization and social relationships. These possibilities call upon distinctive arguments regarding both the nature and causes of social exclusion and the possibilities for an inclusive society.

Against this background, two elements give this book its specific character. The first involves the attempt to look systematically at the nature of social inclusion itself. This entails a group of interrelated questions such as: is inclusiveness as a social norm merely a utopian dream, an ideological construct or an achievable model? If social inclusion is a response to exclusion, who is being excluded, on what terms and why? Is the primary referent of social inclusion new forms of social organization, geared to maximizing the meaningful involvement of all citizens, or does it correspond to identifiable realities at the level of *how things are?* The second element involves the combination of a systematically reflective enquiry with practical considerations, on the one hand, with a commitment to explore these considerations in terms of possible structures and institutional developments, on the other.

As the sub-title indicates, this volume addresses these elements by focusing thematically on 'tensions and possibilities'. The tensions identified are those arising from the reality of different perspectives, interests, attitudes and policies, representing the expression of different value stances. Such tensions are necessarily many: between competing world views regarding the nature of political and economic activity, between divergent modes of reasoning about social process, between competing values, between strategies for meaningful social change and between conflicting human needs, such as predictability and security as against creativity. Each contribution, whether primarily reflective or practical, represents an engagement with one or more of the relevant tensions.

As the range of contributions makes clear, there is a wide diversity of conceptions or discourses of social inclusion. Within that context, the following remarks are intended to offer a sensitizing guide to the central issues raised by current agenda of social inclusion.

Social exclusion and inclusion: a preliminary approach

Within the substantial body of material exploring the causes, characteristics and possible remedies for social exclusion, a number of questions can be identified as being of central importance:

The first is **the question of context**; specifically, within what context(s) is social exclusion proposed to be generated and are such contexts understood as being amenable to resistance, amelioration or transformation by projects of social inclusion? Here, the most frequently identified general context in terms of both the emergence of qualitatively new realities generating social exclusion and/or limiting possibilities for social inclusion is **globalization**. A number of the contributions engage with a range of possibilities here, either by way of a critical analysis of the major variants of the globalization perspective (Perraton) or by developing systematic arguments concerning the implications of particular 'readings' of globalization for inclusionary projects (Gray, Bauman, Coyle, Collins, Stewart[2]). The major possibilities are:

1. Globalization refers to a historically novel context of systematic economic interconnectedness which represents a given in terms of the analysis and pursuit of social inclusion;
2. The scope and significance of globalization are significantly if not greatly exaggerated, providing a powerful and potent social myth to legitimate particular kinds of political project and to delegitimate others on the grounds of their 'unrealistic' and therefore utopian character; and
3. While the term globalization may usefully refer to distinctive, important and novel contemporary economic processes, these do not involve a blanket and integrated transformation; therefore any analysis of their implications requires careful specification.[3]

The second context within which it is necessary and useful to locate thinking about social inclusion as we move into the twenty-first century is that of debates about the **possibilities of political**

projects of inclusion. Most immediately, these debates have focused on the meaning and feasibility of the Third Way as a distinctive political project in relation to the perspectives of Right and Left.[4] Thus, Ruth Levitas has argued that fundamentally different inclusionary projects are embedded in three quite distinctive discourses of exclusion.[5] The first of these is a redistributionist one (RED), the historical origins of which may have shown a central preoccupation with the causes and characteristics of poverty, but which has subsequently been broadened out into a general analysis of the relationships between social exclusion and diverse, societally generated inequalities of power and resources. The relevant inclusionary project here is one which focuses upon a comprehensive model of citizenship, refurbished from Marshall's original argument to take account of inequalities of gender and race as well as class.[6]

In its emphasis upon the structural generation of processes of social exclusion, RED stands in fundamental contrast to a second discourse, a moral underclass discourse (MUD), which identifies the cause of social exclusion with the moral and cultural characteristics of those who are excluded, the so-called underclass. This discourse is realized in a narrow but powerful political project which valorizes paid work while devalorizing unpaid work and identifies welfare benefits as the principal source of moral corrosion and social breakdown.

Both the redistributionist and moral discourses stand in contrast to a third discourse which is dominant in both the EU and the UK. This is the social integrationist discourse (SID) which prioritizes economic efficiency and social cohesion and links the two by a consistent emphasis upon the integrative function of paid work. The associated political project valorizes labour market participation as the overwhelming key to social inclusion, thereby obscuring massive inequalities in terms of reward and conditions of work, inequalities not only of class but also of gender.

Levitas notes that current public discourse involves elements of all three of these discourses, although in the case of the dominant discourse this largely only applies to SID and MUD.[7] This very elasticity of the term 'social exclusion' may be a source of analytic difficulties, but it is unquestionably a source of strength in terms of political rhetoric. Social inclusion thus provides part of the landscape of very different political projects. The dominant discourse in particular represents the attempt to resituate fundamentally the political spectrum by marginalizing or eliminating the issue of equality from the political agenda. Indeed, one of the clear lines of distinction within the various positions on social inclusion is between those who continue to see general social inequalities as of central relevance to any adequate understanding of inclusionary possibilities and those who do not. (In this volume these positions are articulated by Ruth Lister and John Gray respectively.)

Two further issues can be identified as centrally important in considering the political context of social inclusion. The first concerns the question of **state power**. For those who view social inequalities as the critical terrain upon which to debate and practice inclusionary projects, redistributive strategies require organized state power for their implementation. On the other hand, the implementation of quite different political projects focused on economic efficiency and social cohesion equally require a strong state.[8] In either case, what is left out of the equation is the question of the effectiveness of centralized state mechanisms in creating an inclusive political community. For example, the proposition that welfare state provision is inhibitory of economic growth does not stand up to empirical scrutiny, a point noted by Jonathan Perraton below. But it is equally the case that the delivery of social citizenship (which is to say state-centred citizenship) as an effective instrument of the redistribution either of resources or power has proved very difficult. Thus, while the New Right project might reasonably be characterized as the use of state power to implement a market dominated society and a particular ethical order, the alternative from the Left requires mechanisms which are themselves exclusionary through the exercise of categorization and control.

The complexities of any redistributionist strategy further derive from another issue central to specifying the political context of inclusion in late modernity. This is **the question of difference**. Whereas the politics of redistribution expresses a universalism of structural inequalities and corresponding political projects (focusing above all upon the divisions and dynamics of class), the adequacy and coherence of contemporary agenda of social inclusion require their engagement with the politics of difference. The pluralism of modern societies means that such differences are potentially mobilizable in a wide variety of forms, of which gender, 'race' and nationalism are among the most prominent. (The relationship between the 'differences' of multi-culturalism and projects of social inclusion are explored in Peter Ratcliffe's contribution, while the papers by Stewart and Lister consider possible relationships between the politics of redistribution and the politics of difference.)

The range of issues arising from a consideration of the political context of proposed inclusionary projects can be summarized in the form of two dichotomies:

1. Social Cohesion vs Social Justice; and
2. State Power vs Alternative Forms of Social Power.

As is almost invariably the case, such dichotomies may most usefully sensitize us to relevant problems rather than providing ready-made answers. The first of these may and should alert us to the capacity that particular discourses and practices of social inclusion possess for obscuring or revealing questions of general social inequality as relevant to the pursuit of meaningful social inclusion, but the effective pursuit of social justice equally depends upon the strategic negotiation of questions of social cohesion. (The tragic consequences of the absence of a meaningful and flexible interdependence between the two has been graphically illustrated in the continuing passion of Northern Ireland.)

Indeed, as Charles Taylor and Richard Collins argue below, to translate the dichotomy of justice and cohesion into that of rights and communalism is to recognize that the issues involved do not permit of any easy resolution, democratic or otherwise. The norm of social inclusion has been actualized historically by the coupling of polity and culture in the form of national societies. The emergence of multinational societies and the globalization of media can be and are seen as threatening the resultant communities of difference. To the extent that this threat is real – or indeed is perceived to be real – the potential consequences greatly exceed those of a loss of cultural diversity.

A key issue in the discussion of social inclusion therefore concerns the minimum requirements of social cohesion necessary to provide a framework within which justice and distinctive conceptions of the good life may be pursued. As we enter the twenty-first century, our world is stratified by inequalities of hitherto unknown proportions, whether within the affluent societies of the 'West' or even more strikingly across the globe as a whole. As Zygmunt Bauman and Richard Sennett note below, exclusionary monopolistic homogeneities, whether material or symbolic, and pervasive insecurities, whether of employment, safety or environment, chronically stimulate embattled fragmentation leading in turn to multiple homogeneities of conformity and mutual suspicion.

The position concerning actual and possible forms of political organization is, if anything, more complicated. The exclusionary possibilities arising from state agency in the context of particular inclusionary projects have already been noted.[9] Equally, assessments of the scope and significance of globalization particularly concern the proposed consequences for state-inspired inclusionary initiatives. (In the present volume, Gray argues for the necessity of all meaningful inclusionary projects engaging with the transformations of globalization – and predicts that they will have to!) To these important perspectives, a further reality must be added: Whatever their degree of internal inclusion, *national states are themselves fundamentally mechanisms of territorial exclusion.*[10] This chronic reality of the spatial organization of political power in the modern world has been given a renewed emphasis and intensity in the brutalities of ethnic cleansing in the former Yugoslavia.

Given the complex relationship that has existed between the modern state and processes of inclusion/exclusion, the range and logic of discussions of social inclusion necessarily implicates questions regarding **alternative organizations of power**. Here, three possibilities are of particular importance: *supranational institutional forms, democratic restructuring of state power* and *various forms of collective agency.* With regard to the first, it has to be said that the contemporary reality can appear much more one of potential and aspiration than actuality. Both the examples of the EU and GATT involve powerful manifestations of 'rich club' exclusionism, highly structured in terms of both gender and race, rather than inclusionary projects transcending the limitations of state-centred processes. Similarly, the inclusionary possibilities represented by an international community focused on the UN appear greatly constrained by the diverse pluralisms of the modern world and the exclusionary agenda of a US hegemony which 'walks tall' but appears systematically enfeebled by both personal and institutional subservience to self-fulfilling electoral concerns.

And yet: there are opposing possibilities. Thus, for example, the EU, for all its bureaucracy and present unaccountability, is the continuing site of a genuinely democratic and inclusive agendum, one which represents possibilities of genuine political debate and which seeks to use concerted political power to subordinate the imperatives and consequences of deregulated market forces.

On balance, certainly, the present realities require a sombre but not pessimistic assessment of possibilities of inclusion 'beyond the nation-state' and its characteristic political configurations, whether of 'culture(s) of contentment', of inequality and marginalization or of reactive and repressive fundamentalism. Nevertheless, the future coherence and viability of inclusionary projects in late modernity depends upon the painstaking development of collaborative international arrangements, whether with respect to the regulation of capital flows generative of chronic social exclusion, or of a serious engagement with the endless cycles of Third World debt or democratically driven agenda for the negotiation of international disputes and environmental control. Within the EU, there are diverse potentials, ranging from the economic laager of an inward-looking trading bloc supported by the complexities of a bureaucratic 'superstate' to a multiplicity of immanent communities of citizenship, including that of a democratic European citizenship.[11]

Realistically, of course, states are going to continue as important sites of political conflict and policy implementation for the foreseeable future.[12] Consequently, any comprehensive analysis of social inclusion requires a consideration of any and all means by which processes of decision making from consideration and consultation, through negotiation to implementation can incorporate the widest diversity of interests and differences as possible. Bernard Crick restates and reaffirms his compelling argument 'in defence of politics' as both the most sociologically most realistic and ethically most desirable manner of negotiating conflict and commonality of purpose in plural societies, while recognizing that there is no 'hidden hand' determining that such political resolutions will be realized. (The centrality of politics and citizenship to any adequate conception of social inclusion is also emphasized below by Plant, Lister and Stewart, who lay particular stress on the importance of the possibilities of active citizenship.)

The distinctive character of citizenship implicated in different discourses points to a further important issue to be considered when assessing models and practices of inclusion. This concerns the degree to which any discourse or model prioritizes **agency as a critical aspect of social inclusion**. Broadly speaking, arguments about social inclusion can be divided between those which see integration into structures of market and/or state as a sufficient criterion of social inclusion, regardless of any inequalities which may continue to characterize such structures, and those which emphasize the importance of self-determination in contexts of mutuality and interaction as a critical, indeed irreducible, aspect of inclusionary projects, with consequent implications for existing structures of power. (The importance of agency in relation to projects of social inclusion is thematically emphasized in the present volume by Stewart, Lister, Plant, Askonas and Winstanley in particular. From a variety of perspectives and in a variety of contexts, all stress the point that *inclusion is a matter not only of an adequate share in resources but equally of participation in the determination of both individual and collective life chances*.) Of course, this emphasis is not without its problematic aspects and consequent need for careful specification. The importance of active involvement as a dimension of social inclusion has to be located within the centrality of plurality as a hallmark of modern societies. The alternative is mobilization around a homogenizing agenda whether of state, market or race.

The discussion of social inclusion requires recognition of the complexities of agency in late modernity, a point stressed in the present volume by Peter Askonas among others.[13] His argument emphasizes the constraints upon agency from diverse structures of domination – most notably the market – generated by human interaction but apparently possessed of an unstoppable momentum and resilience of their own.[14] (Gray, Stewart and Bauman explore variations on the same proposition.) The case can be – and is – made that in a very real sense 'we are all included now!' Such inclusion takes many forms: the transactions of global capitalism; an endless succession of Foucauldian regimes of power/knowledge; vulnerability to diffuse and imitative terrorism, systematically generated but arbitrary in effect; or multiple forms of risk in late modernity.

These many and varied contexts of potential domination are the complex and irreducible context within which the pursuit of social inclusion must be located. But this reality throws into relief the importance of political will and moral responsibility, fundamentals emphasized throughout the present volume. Assessing these possibilities requires consideration of two important factors: first, the multiple processes generating globalization and risk as ubiquitous features of late modernity are accompanied by a potential for communication and cooperation. Perhaps more importantly, the erosion of tradition which is definitive of late modernity literally requires the chronic legitimation of both processes and outcomes.[15] Such legitimation may be argued to require a degree of involvement unnecessary in more traditionally defined social orders.[16]

The discussion of social inclusion necessarily encompasses a wide range of ideas and practices concerning not only legitimation but also regulation and accountability. Indeed, the explication of such ideas and practices has provided a major focus for the clarification of distinctive discourses of inclusion. (Such possibilities are represented here by the contributions of Diana Winstanley and Christopher Stoney, and Giles Slinger and Simon Deakin respectively.) Beyond the detail of diverse models, it is possible to identify a critical consideration for the discussion of social inclusion. Inclusion, whether in the workplace or in the welfare agency – and, by extension, the national state or the international community – requires, as argued by Sennett below, the practice of 'mutual recognition' and mutual exchange.

About the book

The organizational rationale of the book is as follows: there are four parts, each of which generally builds upon the preceding. Each of the contributions is intended to represent a different statement of the possibilities and tensions surrounding current discussions of social inclusion.

Part I offers a variety of perspectives on the analysis of social inclusion. John Gray sets out a radical critique of the concept of social inclusion as specified within contemporary political theory. He critically engages with the dominant discourse of social inclusion, an attempted synthesis of social solidarity and post-egalitarianism, exploring the relationship between inclusion and egalitarianism and contesting the greater compatibility of the former with market globalization. Ruth Lister offers an alternative view, proposing that the project of social inclusion must prioritize issues of social justice as against social cohesion; consequently it must engage with those diverse dimensions of social inequality and exclusion which impede possibilities of inclusion. Angus Stewart then highlights the need to locate discussions of social inclusion in the specific historical context of late modernity. Mapping frameworks of inclusion, Stewart indicates that the central requirement of any distinctive politics of inclusion is the need to combine the continuing pursuit of social justice with a recognition of and respect for pluralistic diversity.

The formidable obstacles to any project(s) of social inclusion are delineated by Zygmunt Bauman, who argues that contemporary social exclusion is generated above all by processes of competition and comparison rooted in electronically mediated 'visibilities'. In a world increasingly divided between an extraterritorial elite and an unavoidably local rest, a vicious circle is established in which a fear of heterogeneity intensifies accelerating homogeneity. This sombre vision concludes with a contrast between two scenarios involving dramatically opposed solutions to the inescapable reality of cultural diversity. The critical paradox that the central mechanism for the implementation of social inclusion in modern societies – that of democracy – itself possesses a powerful dynamic of exclusion is the focus of Charles Taylor's succeeding discussion. Taylor notes the degree to which democratic polities, unlike their pre-modern predecessors and authoritarian contemporaries, require a high level of civic commitment, grounded in the shared sentiments of either civic republican or nationalist belief and practice. Such consensual identity is directly problematized by the combined realities of democracy and pluralist diversity. Taylor locates the limited solution to these endemic realities in the inescapable necessity for political negotiation and compromise.

Peter Askonas concludes this part with another radical assessment of social inclusion, arguing that theology has the capacity to develop both a coherent philosophy and a consequent praxis of social inclusion. Proposing the fundamental centrality of the concept of *social becoming* to any genuinely radical idea of inclusion, Askonas argues that only such a concept can implicate the requisite dimensions of human-ness and responsibility.

Part Two explores major contexts of exclusion and inclusion. The opening contributions offer contrasting analyses of current economic realities and possibilities. Jonathan Perraton considers the tensions offered to inclusionary projects by those processes of economic globalization which have become such a central aspect of contemporary social theory. Critical of both radical and sceptical accounts of globalization, Perraton argues that the increased power of capital represents a relative rather than absolute change and that globalization has neither a simple logic nor a putative end-state. Diana Coyle's contrasting contribution sets out the case for a qualitative transformation of the modern world in terms of the emergence of 'the weightless economy' and the consequent redundancy of previous political assumptions and policies. Within this perspective, Coyle argues that the nature of dominant economic processes makes unpredictability an endemic feature of contemporary social and existential reality in the face of which national governments are simply powerless. The necessary flexibility to respond to such a transformed world can only be the provenance of individuals who may be assisted in their 'reflexivity' by governmental action but who are ultimately arbiters of their own destiny.

The proposition that those developments and processes referred under the heading of globalization have significantly narrowed the scope for independent economic and social policies at the level of the nation state is systematically contested by Peter Robinson. Analysing the relationship between employment and social inclusion, Robinson argues that the most important factors affecting overall levels of employment in any one country are the particular structure of each economy and the policies followed by national governments. Macroeconomic policy and redistribution both have a role to play in the promotion of social inclusion.

Of course, inclusion is far from being a matter of economic processes alone. A related but distinctive context of inclusion is analysed by Peter Ratcliffe. Exploring the critical question for pluralistic, polyethnic societies as to the compatibility of minority identity with the idea of inclusion, Ratcliffe emphasizes the multiplicity of meanings attached to the terms 'social exclusion' and 'inclusion'. In identifying the limitations of a discourse which equates inclusion with integration, this contribution takes up another concern of this volume: the critical role of individual and collective agency in processes of social inclusion. In a concluding assessment of the possibilities of creating social inclusion through a fusion of universalism and particularism, Ratcliffe emphasizes that the complexities of inclusion require chronic and sober commitment.

The critical question of the relationship between the general and particular is further explored by Richard Collins in his discussion of the constitution of identities and communities in an era of the globalization of media. Collins explores those versions of social inclusion which have been elaborated as either pragmatic or ethical defences of the need to resist the socially corrosive effects of media globalization. Since unqualified arguments in favour of common culture and collective identity offer no safeguards against the suppression of pluralist diversity, Collins sets out the case for a practicable model of social inclusion, which is both communal and associative.

Part III focuses on practical agenda of inclusion. The case for the continuing, indeed enhanced, relevance of praxis is set out by Raymond Plant in his argument for the increased role of politics in late modernity. Engaging with the (neo-) liberal *zeitgeist* in which contemporary economic developments such as globalization, capital flows and deregulation are viewed as constraining (to the point of redundancy) the possibilities of significant political intervention, Plant argues the contrary case: as a result of the operation of market forces, *large-scale political problems concerned with identity, inclusion, security and belonging have become definitive of a contemporary political agenda for which 'market forces' offer no meaningful solution.* Stressing the necessity for public debate and ethical resolution, Plant concludes by characterizing the politics of late modernity as ideally dialogical, focussing procedurally upon shared interests and general concerns in a context of acknowledged diversity.

This emphasis upon the centrality of politics in the pursuit of social inclusion is taken up by Bernard Crick. In his meditation upon democracy, politics and citizenship, Crick reaffirms his seminal statement 'in defence of politics' as the preferred mode of conducting affairs in an inclusive society.[17] The significance of widespread and robust public debate has not diminished with the collapse of a bipolar world. The preoccupation of professional politicians with electoral advantage to the potential exclusion of leadership on intractable issues in a risk dominated world makes the necessity of active citizenship greater than ever. Preparation for democratic citizenship must be recognized as the essential foundation for an inclusive society.

Peter Askonas' contribution stresses the potential of voluntarity as a significant driving force for advance towards inclusion. Askonas, noting the pressures towards a fatalistic endorsement of the economistic fate of humankind, introduces a contrast into the argument by proposing a transcendent dimension in human striving for fulfillment through recognition of and reciprocal respect for the other. This is exemplified in accounts of down-to-earth voluntary activity in the UK.

The proposition that optimal engagement with the potential of social inclusion requires a commitment to fundamental individual, collective and institutional change is carried forward by Diana Winstanley and Chris Stoney. Mapping the core principles of inclusiveness in the workplace, they emphasize the importance of attachment and reciprocity as bases of community membership. Any agenda of inclusion requires placing appeals to mutuality within the asymmetrical balance of rights and responsibilities between employers and employees. This contribution highlights the degree to which any and all projects are necessarily rooted in conflicts over values and interests.

This practical focus on inclusionary projects is further elaborated by Giles Slinger and Simon Deakin in a discussion of takeover regulation. Their contribution identifies two distinct approaches to stakeholder regulation, one based on rights and the other on cooperation. Whereas the former seeks to codify and enforce the interests of all those affected by economic relations, the latter aims to create and maintain a social rather than juridical framework. Their discussion incorporates a range of possibilities and tensions which have a resonance for the analysis of social inclusion going far beyond the particular focus of their argument. This includes questions of structured interest and conflict, asymmetries of power and consequent differential vulnerability and the institutional and attitudinal prerequisites of authentic co-operation as opposed to manipulated cohesion.

That the complexities of social inclusion find their critical expression in the changing realities of human experience is highlighted in Richard Sennett's discussion of the logic of social inclusion and its endemic erosion in contemporary capitalism. All the necessary elements of the practice of social inclusion, Sennett argues – mutual exchange, ritual and the 'generation of witnesses' whose vital function it is to judge the adequacy with which relations of dependency are fulfilled elements – are critically called in question by the practices of contemporary capitalism. Prioritizing autonomy (and therefore dispensability) as opposed to dependence and the recognition of worth, contemporary capitalism – and by extension, welfare agency organized along business lines – inculcates an ethos in which the mutual need which binds human beings together is chronically eroded.

Part IV offers concluding thoughts from the editors on the analysis of and prospects for social inclusion.

Notes

1 See Hutton (1999).
2 See, also, Gray (1998), Bauman (1998), Coyle (1997), Held *et al.* (1999).
3 This third position is adopted by Perraton in the contribution below. See, also, Perraton (1997 and in Held *et al.*, 1999). Representative examples of the first and second positions respectively are Ohmae (1990) and Hirst and Thompson (1996) and Weiss (1998). On the significance of myths of globalization, see also Scott (1997).
4 See Giddens (1984).
5 See Levitas (1998, chap. 1).
6 For Marshall's original, now classic discussion of citizenship, see Marshall (1963). Also Stewart (1995).

7 One of the purposes of Levitas' study is to argue and document the case that 'the developing discourse of New Labour' shifted it significantly away from RED towards an inconsistent combination of SID and MUD; *op cit.*, p. 28.

8 See Gamble (1988).

9 One might reasonably propose that, given the inescapable plurality of human society in general and of all modern societies in particular, the resultant diversity of interests means that in the implementation of any political project there are bound to be various kinds and degrees of 'exclusion'. Thus, for example, Stuart Hall has criticized the New Labour Project on the grounds that it purports to evade this reality ('there are no losers') behind what Hall sees as the subterfuge of populist rhetoric. Hall (1998).

10 See Brubaker (1992).

11 See, for example, the recent discussion by Habermas (1998).

12 Mann (1995).

13 How best we may understand the relationship between structure and agency has become a, if not the, central issue in social theory in recent decades. Giddens' structuration theory has become the standard point of reference. See Giddens (1984). For a critical assessment, see Mouzelis (1995).

14 A Marxist perspective would doubtless express such a perception in terms of alienation. Habermas' discussion of system and lifeworld represents the outstanding, if highly contentious, articulation of the same perception in contemporary social thought.

15 Giddens defines this development as 'the democratization of democracy' (1998; p. 70ff). Perhaps its critical hallmark is the ubiquitous conflict, discursive and practical (not to say on occasion violent), over the one and true interpretation of holy writ, whether religious or secular.

16 Of course, the proposed legitimacy of any modern political project in no way excludes a resort to various degrees of coercion, both material, political and psychic, as numerous and escalating examples from the Killing Fields to Waco testify. But, the argument would still remain that such examples rest upon the need for initial legitimation and the continued engaged support of at least an active minority.

17 Crick (1992).

References

Bauman, Z. (1998) *Globalization* (Cambridge: Polity Press).

Brubaker, W.R. (1992) *Citizenship and Nationhood in France and Germany* (London: Harvard University Press).

Coyle, D. (1997) *The Weightless Economy* (Oxford: Capstone).

Crick, B. (1992) *In Defence of Politics*, 4th edn (London: Penguin).

Gamble, A. (1988) *The Free Economy and the Strong State* (Basingstoke: Macmillan).

Giddens, A. (1984) *The Constitution of Society* (Cambridge: Polity Press).

Gray, J. (1998) *False Dawn* (London: Granta).

Habermas, J. (1998) *The Inclusion of the Other* (Cambridge, Mass: MIT Press).

Hall, S. (1998) 'The Great Moving Nowhere Show', *Marxism Today*, Special Issue (Nov/Dec).

Held, D., McGrew, A., Goldblatt, D. and Perraton, J. (1999) *Global Transformations: Politics, Economics and Culture* (Cambridge: Polity Press).

Hirst, P. and Thompson, G. (1996) *Globalization in Question* (Cambridge: Polity Press).

Hutton, W. (1999) *The Stakeholding Society* (Cambridge: Polity Press).

Levitas, R. (1998) *The Inclusive Society? Social Exclusion and New Labour* (London: Macmillan).

Mann, M. (1995) 'As the Twentieth Century Ages', *New Left Review*, vol. 214 (Nov/Dec), pp. 104–24.

Marshall, T.H. (1963) 'Citizenship and Social Class', *Sociology at the Crossroads* (London: Heinemann).

Mouzelis, N. (1995) *Sociological Theory: What Went Wrong?* (London: Routledge).

Ohmae, K. (1990) *The Borderless World* (London: Collins).

Perraton, J. *et al.*, (1997) 'The Globalization of Economic Activity', *New Political Economy*, vol. 2, pp. 257–77.

Scott, A. (ed.) (1997) *The Limits of Globalization* (London: Routledge).

Stewart, A. (1995) 'Two Conceptions of Citizenship', *British Journal of Sociology*, vol. 46(1), pp. 63–78.

Weiss, L. (1998) *The Myth of the Powerless State: Governing the Economy in a Global Era* (Cambridge: Polity Press).

Part I
Perspectives on Inclusion

2
Inclusion: A Radical Critique
John Gray

Introductory remarks

In recent years governments of the centre-left have modified the egalitarian ideals of classical social democracy. Some – in Britain and Germany, amongst others – have opted for a project of social inclusion as a more or less systematic alternative to egalitarianism. The shift from equality to inclusion has gone with an analysis of globalization according to which it renders many of the values and projects of the traditional Left politically unviable. Inclusion is an attempt to conserve some of the core aspirations of social democracy in an historical context in which many of its classical objectives have ceased to be achievable.

My purpose is not to defend social democracy. I share with many of the advocates of social inclusion the conviction that egalitarian goals have been rendered politically unfeasible, not so much as a direct consequence of ongoing globalization but more because of the socially divisive consequences of the workings of late capitalism in a context of globalization. This is a view that the emergence of social democratic governments across most of Europe has done nothing to falsify. It still remains a vanishingly remote prospect that these governments will be able to restore a social democratic regime of full employment, income redistribution and a comprehensive welfare state. Most likely they will oscillate between a defensive strategy of salvaging the surviving remnants of previous social democracies and acting as the political vehicle for further neoliberal market reform. The social democratic governments of Europe show no signs of solving the central problem of centre-left politics today, which is how to advance (or indeed conserve) social democratic values in a global context in which social democratic policies have ceased to be effective.

The vogue for inclusion is an attempt to conserve something of social democracy's values at a time when classical social-democratic egalitarianism is no longer politically advantageous. Additionally in the UK, the shift to inclusion has been an element in a hugely effective political strategy. Yet along with many of the newer values and objectives of centre-left parties and governments, an inclusive society is not easily reconciled with the workings of a global free market. Global *laissez-faire* is indifferent to social cohesion. Further, if national governments adhere to its ground rules, they are inhibited by global *laissez-faire* from acting to repair the social injuries it has caused. A global free market constrains narrowly the range of strategies and policies national governments, or regional institutions such as the European Union, can adopt. For that reason alone, inclusion is – perhaps unwittingly – a radical project. This illustrates a more general truth. The political effect of market globalization is not to compel convergence at the centre. It is to kindle new varieties of radicalism.

Market globalization does not engender stability – social, political or economic. Its political concomitant is not 'the end of politics' in 'democratic capitalism' but instead the volatile politics of economic insecurity. Over the past decade, in many societies, globalization has triggered powerful political movements of religious fundamentalism and produced a resurgence of the radical Right. It is a reasonable wager that, over the coming decades, globalization will trigger the reemergence, in unfamiliar but recognizable forms, of the radical Left.

The shift from egalitarianism to inclusion on the centre-left has been justified by the claim that electoral support for classical social democratic values has dwindled to the point that strong egalitarian policy positions have become a political liability. At the same time the political costs of egalitarian policies have increased as globalization has advanced. When production is highly mobile it is free to exit from states whose governments are committed to high levels of taxation. When capital markets are unregulated capital will seek maximal profits. In a globalized economy capital and production will avoid economic and political environments characterized by high levels of taxation, state spending and regulation. There are of course many offsetting factors, such as political stability, the rule of law, and levels of education in the workforce, which induce transnational corporations sometimes to accept higher wages than they could pay elsewhere; but the tendency of footloose capital to seek low-tax, low-regulation environments is real enough.

Plainly, the egalitarian objectives of classical social democracy are no longer politically realizable. Hence the appeal of a successor project: inclusion. I think this analysis is largely correct.[1] My argument will therefore be two-fold. First, the political unfeasibility of egalitarian values under a regime of globalization applies equally to inclusion. Secondly, and as a consequence, if social inclusion is to be promoted or safeguarded, then governments must be ready to contemplate imposing political restraints on globalization. The preconditions of social-democratic equality and post-social-democratic or social-liberal inclusion are not as different as their respective protagonists imagine. Indeed they are much the same.

For the purposes of my argument, John Stuart Mill and Joseph Raz can be considered paradigm social liberals, and Anthony Crosland and R.H. Tawney paradigm social democrats. The difference between social liberalism and social democracy is that while both are strongly committed to social cohesion, social liberals do not share the commitment of social democrats to distributive equality. In this regard, recent shifts in centre-left thinking (notably in Blair's New Labour) may be characterized as a move from social democracy to social liberalism. Inclusion stands to social liberalism as distributive equality stands to social democracy. My argument here is that both are unrealizable in the context of a global free market.

Governments that are serious about their commitment to social inclusion must be willing to alter the institutional framework of unfettered capital mobility with which globalization has been widely (though mistakenly) identified. Like traditional social democratic values, the ideal of social inclusion is incompatible with the project of a global free market. This is not a tension between values in regard to which a compromise can be pursued. It is a conflict of objectives about which political choices can and must be made.

The argument stated

I will develop my argument in two parts. The first is normative and philosophical, the second empirical and social-theoretical. First I will consider how inclusion and equality are related, arguing that they are overlapping but distinct and sometimes conflicting values. Secondly I will distinguish different meanings of globalization and argue that the particular institutional framework within which globalization has occurred over the past decade or so is inimical both to equality and to inclusion.

I call this a radical critique of inclusion, partly because it entails that the preconditions of inclusion and of social democratic equality at the level of the global economy are pretty well identical. The institutional framework and the ground rules of global laissez-faire must be altered if either inequality is to be significantly reduced or social inclusion advanced. Globalization may be an inexorable historical process (I am confident that it is); *but its institutional framework and political concomitants are highly contingent.* It is a grave error to identify globalization with the ephemeral politic-economic consensus of the 1990s. Market globalization works to radicalize political life – and not necessarily always for the better (*pace* the radical Right in continental Europe). The politics of inclusion are not an alternative to radicalism in an age of globalization. There is no such alternative.

When equality was replaced by inclusion in the rhetoric of centre-left parties something important was undoubtedly gained in terms of electoral advantage; but in normative terms something was definitely lost. In day-to-day political struggles eclecticism and inconsistency have familiar advantages. But over the longer haul it can also be useful to know where one is going. This essay aims to be a contribution to such understanding.

I will argue that, though there can be large areas of practical agreement between egalitarians and inclusionists, they adhere to distinct ideals. In terms of British and European traditions, one is social-democratic and the other social-liberal. Where these ideals clearly diverge in their practical implications we must choose. At the same time, where they overlap or converge both are largely irreconcilable with the workings of a global free market.

Equality vs inclusion

Equality and inclusion are distinct values. Often they overlap, but sometimes they are competitors. Policies that promote social inclusion are commonly understood as somehow necessarily advancing an ideal of equality. This is a mistake. Sometimes they do, but that is an unintended consequence. Supporters of social inclusion do not pursue an ideal of egalitarian justice, but an ideal of common life. This will surely condemn many inequalities. But not all. Inclusion is indifferent to some inequalities that egalitarians condemn. Policies promoting inclusion will sometimes generate inequalities that are regarded by egalitarians as unfair but are viewed by advocates of inclusion as fair. In this latter case equality and inclusion are not just different. They are rivals.

Rivalry between equality and inclusion arises in several contexts and for a number of reasons. One reason is that concern about social inclusion focuses not only on the bottom, in regard to the so-called underclass of unskilled and marginalized persons, but also at the top, in respect of overclass groups that opt out of public services and civic obligations. For the ideal of social inclusion the revolt of the elites is as much a problem as welfare dependency; but recognizing this does not entail embracing an egalitarian ideal of justice.

Policies that aim to stem middle-class and elite opt-out from public services will normally have a reasonable chance of success only if they depart from classical social democratic egalitarian principles in some crucial respects. Some pragmatically-minded egalitarians might find such departures acceptable; but they are bound to regard them as compromises. For an advocate of social inclusion they need not be. Inequalities that are tolerated or generated by inclusionary policies aimed at encouraging the middle classes to opt back into public services may be fair, provided we understand fairness not in terms of a small set of egalitarian principles but as a complex network of values that tracks local understandings of justice.

The intuitive core of the idea of inclusion looks simple enough. It is the idea that every member of society should participate fully in it. The social ideal that inclusion expresses is an ideal of common membership: no one is denied access to activities and practices that are central in the life of society. An inclusionary society is a cohesive society.

On social cohesion

Some Old Right conservatives cherish cohesive societies for their own sakes. They think that traditions and institutions carry authority merely by existing.[2] For them a good society is one whose component groups and ways of life cohere in a kind of organic unity. In this conservative view social cohesion is a good in itself and social inclusion – if the ideal is given any credence – means assimilation to practices and social structures that are taken as given.

That is a view no social liberal or social democrat can accept. Aside from anything else it stands at a large remove from social reality. We live in a world in which many practices are contested and need to justify themselves to those who are affected by them. This is partly because society is nowadays more deeply plural than it has been in the past. None of us is the radically situated human subject of communitarian theory.[3]

Each of us belongs not to one but to several ethical communities, whose demands are often conflicting. No way of life can claim to be self-justifying when those over whom it seeks to exercise authority belong also to other ways of life. In late modern societies, marginal and hybrid subjects – people who belong in part to many forms of life but wholly to none – are common. In these circumstances ways of life must justify themselves to their practitioners. They must show themselves sensitive to their needs and responsive to the developing sense of fairness in the larger society. Even those who belong only to a single way of life have the option of migrating to another. In our historical context no tradition is self-validating. Traditions gain and keep adherents only insofar as they promote and protect their well-being. The idea that social cohesion is valuable in itself has ceased to be credible.

There is another reason why social cohesion cannot mean a flat acceptance of one's station and its duties. Today continuous technical innovation has thrown the social division of labour into a flux. Of course structural inequalities in life-chances have not disappeared. Indeed some inequalities in life-chances have increased. Low-skill groups risk being trapped in a cycle of poverty; even within better-off groups, new inequalities are arising with the development of winner-take-all labour markets. The overall effect of an ongoing stream of new technologies is to destroy existing industries and occupations along with their associated ways of life. No one nowadays can hold to his station and duties, for no one has a fixed station or the duties that might go with such a position.

Other economic changes have greatly altered social institutions. The extension of employment opportunities to women has transformed family life unevenly – but at the same time radically and irreversibly. In many respects these have enhanced the options and advanced the interests of women. Ethnic and cultural minorities have also benefited from economic change. The breakdown of established hierarchies, which the Old Right bemoans, may have involved some real cultural losses; but it has clearly carried with it some substantial social gains. In these circumstances of continuing technical and economic change, social cohesion cannot mean stabilizing the positions of people in an immobile or stationary condition of society. It can only refer to a particular way of coping with change.

There is a more positive reason for rejecting the conservative understanding of social cohesion. Cohesive societies may be repressive. They may achieve stability by practices of subordination and hierarchy that few, if any, late modern societies can accept or tolerate. When societies are cohesive in this way it is partly their cohesiveness that makes them unacceptable. Such societies remain cohesive by disabling individual autonomy. They thereby injure the well-being of their members.

In late modern contexts, a highly repressive society is not less but perhaps more undesirable for being highly cohesive. In saying this, I do not mean to suggest that individual autonomy is a universal human value, a necessary ingredient in good human lives. I mean that in historical contexts in which autonomy is a widespread aspiration, social cohesion which is achieved at the cost of autonomy has little value and is unlikely to be sustainable for long. Social cohesion is a necessary (but not a sufficient) condition of individual flourishing.

What is social cohesion? We should define it weakly, so that many different societies can achieve it. If we do, it is reasonable to stipulate that social cohesion encompasses a general consensus on basic values, a lack of widespread alienation and anomie and an absence of marginalized and disaffected social groups. On this understanding, it is individual human subjects rather than forms or ways of life that are the final repositories of value in the human world. This is a truth with particular application in our circumstances, in which forms of social life are not fated but are more open to individual choice than they have been in most previous historical contexts. Social institutions and ways of life have value only insofar as they contribute to the well-being of those affected by them. How forms of life enter into individual well-being is a complicated matter. Sometimes they do so as empirically necessary conditions, sometimes as essential ingredients. Either way, it is individual well-being that is the bottom line.

Nevertheless, the most plausible forms of liberal theory recognize that individual well-being is essentially social. By this I mean more than that individuals unavoidably depend on society – in one way or another – for their material sustenance. *I mean that in order to flourish most people need social support for their values and identities.*[4] Consider how employment and unemployment impact on individual well-being in late modern societies such as ours. In a society in which employment is a precondition of social standing long-term unemployment means more than a loss of income. For most people long-term unemployment is a threat to autonomy and self-esteem. This does not mean that job-holding or indeed work deserves the central role it has acquired in late modern societies. Nor is it to endorse the view that human lives should be understood on the model of careers. It is simply to note that in a society in which social status depends upon occupation few people can preserve their autonomy if they are shut out from access to employment.

In the theory of social inclusion, individual well-being is the bottom line, and it is understood as being *essentially social*. In New Right thinking, individual choice is ascribed an overriding value, and it is theorized as being entirely an attribute of individual human subjects. In contrast with this view, social liberals – along with other advocates of inclusion – think of personal autonomy as having both individual and social connotations and dimensions.[5]

To be autonomous means something different from being independent or self-directed. A concentration camp inmate, someone living in a totalitarian regime or a mafia boss in a postcommunist city can be self-directed. By contrast, to be autonomous means having a decent range of choiceworthy options. That presupposes a public environment of a definite kind. If I cannot go to a restaurant without fearing assassination, if I cannot saunter in city streets because of pervasive crime, if the city in which I live is poorly planned and badly serviced, then I cannot be highly autonomous however rich or powerful I am. Personal autonomy is an attribute of individuals; but it can exist only as a collective good. For this reason, a society that values personal autonomy will seek to ensure access to work for all its members.

The relation of inclusion and equality

Let us return to how inclusion and equality are related. I take egalitarianism to be a variant of the view that principles of justice constrain the pursuit of collective and individual well-being. Different egalitarian theories specify different equalities as being demanded by justice. Some favour equality of resources or initial assets, some equality of welfare or well-being, some talk of compensating for the effects of brute luck. The familiar distinction between equality of outcome and equality of opportunity fails to capture the diversity of egalitarian theories, partly because it fails to specify which outcomes and opportunities are to be equalized.

A view of equal opportunity in which it applies over most of people's lives is an improvement on one in which it is restricted to their formative years. Since it has to do with life-chances, and they are determined by other factors in addition to schooling, equal opportunities cannot mean only equal access to education. Life-chances are not – or should not be – once-for-all, make-or-break opportunities. They apply to each phase of the life-cycle. For these reasons, a conception of equal opportunity that is maximal, comprehensive and lifelong in its applications marks a genuine advance. Even so, there is far more to any coherent ideal of equality than can be captured in any conception of equality of access to the labour market. While it is true that access to work is at the heart of inclusionary social policy, the goal of an inclusionary employment policy cannot merely be to get the maximum number of people into paid work. It must address their need to reconcile work with family and personal life. Human beings have vital needs that are not met by participation in the labour market. Poverty and disability injure individual well-being in ways that may have nothing, or little, to do with equal opportunity.

The notion that the transfer state can be replaced entirely by a 'social investment state', which is often associated with theories of equality of opportunity, is an illusion. A social investment state is one which seeks to avoid the waste of talent that happens when education fails to draw out the skills of underclass groups, or lack of decent housing and healthcare stands in the way of people making use of their skills. In these examples, a commitment of resources to individuals who are at risk of wasting their lives is justified on the ground of the social return it gives. But some resources are committed in public services, even as things stand, with no expectation of a return. They are not investments but acts of human solidarity. A 58-year-old unskilled labourer for whose labour no market demand exists needs income and social recognition, not work. The severely disabled need resources to enable them to have lives worth living. That may or may not involve their participation in the labour market. No development of public services will ever remove the need for transfers of these kinds. The prospect of a welfare state that can be justified solely on investment principles is a mirage.

A welfare state based on an ideal of inclusion would nevertheless differ from one based on egalitarian principles. What the main egalitarian theories have in common that distinguishes them from ideals of social inclusion is the claim that purely relational properties can have fundamental ethical importance. From the standpoint of the ideal of social inclusion only individual well-being has that significance. It is the impact of inequality on social cohesion and thereby on individual well-being that explains the moral importance we attach to it. The implausibility of concerning ourselves with merely relational properties of social life is suggested by the example of a society in which the differences between people are small but in which no one can alter the social position in which he or she was born. Contrast such a quasi-egalitarian caste society with a much more unequal society with considerable social mobility. It is manifestly the latter that meets our concerns about inequality. The reason is not that it corresponds better with some theory of justice but rather that individual well-being is likely to be better protected in such a society. Hierarchy and subordination need justification not because they violate some principle of equal distribution but because their impact on well-being is injurious. Similarly with any kind of social exclusion. The ideal of social inclusion is not distribution-blind. It is unavoidably distribution-sensitive; but it is not a distributional ideal. It differs fundamentally from any egalitarian morality in attaching only an instrumental importance to distribution.

Inclusion requires that every member of society have access to its central goods. This requirement incorporates at least two components – fair opportunities and the satisfaction of basic needs. While both are necessary for individual flourishing, they are not the same, and neither is sufficient. Both are distribution-sensitive in that some distributions will be condemned by them; but neither is essentially distributive.

Egalitarian distributional criteria are irrelevant to the satisfaction of basic human needs. What justifies universal public services are the human needs they meet and the role these services have in cementing a common life. Consider a paradigm case, meeting basic medical needs in the NHS. Of course the distribution of medical resources is relevant to how well basic needs are met. It is unacceptable if people's chance of being treated depends on the accident of where they live. Even so, the wrongness of such random distributions of medical resources does not arise from any departure from equality that they entail. They would be unacceptable for a utilitarian who cared nothing for equality. They result in an allocation of resources that is inefficient from the standpoint of the purpose of the NHS – meeting basic medical needs. To be sure, any public health service will have to decide priorities in meeting medical needs. Yet the justification for such priorities is not a principle of distribution but rather a concern with individual well-being. Disabling or life-threatening illnesses are treated before trivial conditions because they pose a greater threat to the well-being of the individuals who suffer from them. We care about unequal access to medical care not because it is unequal but because it means that greater needs are not getting priority. What justifies caring for the sick is not the difference between them and those who are healthy but the harm that illness does to their well-being.

It must be a failing for an egalitarian that some empirical work suggests that universal public services may fail to redistribute to the less affluent. For someone interested in promoting inclusion it need not be a disadvantage. Once basic needs have been met, distribution is irrelevant.

The fundamental indifference of inclusion to distributional concerns is illustrated by the issue of reversing middle-class opt-out from public services. What is undesirable about that trend is that it can produce a society in which people have radically different experiences of satisfying their basic needs. A society in which formative life-experiences diverge widely not because of differences between individuals but because different groups have access to very different institutions and services is a divided society. It therefore falls short (in that regard at any rate) of the ideal of inclusion.

For anyone who wishes to see an inclusive society it is highly desirable that middle-class people stay in public services or, if they have abandoned them, return to them. But providing incentives for them to do so will not typically result in an egalitarian distribution of resources (or outcomes). Selective state schooling may be an effective incentive to middle-class parents to refrain from educating their children in the private sector. It can also be defended as fair on meritocratic ground. I know of no way, however, in which it can be justified by egalitarian principles. For egalitarian social democrats allowing selection in state schools is a departure from justice. Yet it may be necessary if we are to promote inclusion. For advocates of inclusion, nothing of importance need be lost in such a policy. Here we see the two ideals diverging sharply and clearly. This is only a particular instance of a more general truth. Universal public services promote inclusion rather than equality in distribution.

Of course basic needs cannot be met without some attention to distribution. For one thing, some basic needs are partly constituted by the way most people live. The level of income needed if an unemployed person is to live tolerably is not determined by biological needs alone. It must be high enough to allow the unemployed to participate in some degree in most of the activities in which employed people engage. If it is insufficient for that purpose it will exclude the unemployed from the rest of society. Because poverty is partly a relative condition, the relief of poverty itself entails some reduction in inequality between the majority and the bottom. The difference between the affluent majority and the poorest social groups will inevitably and rightly be narrowed by any successful programme of poverty relief. Again, while it is true that universal public services redistribute from the less to the more affluent, the reverse also occurs. For largely environmental reasons, the poor have worse health than other people; but for that very reason they use some universal social services more than other people do. Universal public services may compensate in some degree for differences in life-chances in the larger society.

Finally, basic needs are not always fully satiable. When that is so, social conventions about fairness may be decisive in allocating resources.[6] Where medical needs are not entirely satiable, it may be judged fairer to allocate a scarce medical resource to a person whose ill-health is the result of brute luck rather than to someone whose personal choices have caused it (this may be true, even where the relevant medical needs are fully satiable but only at prohibitive cost). This shows that an inclusive society cannot avoid being concerned about distribution. It does not show that an inclusive society must be committed to equality, or to any other principle in which distribution is fundamental.

Now consider fair opportunities. However fair opportunity is understood, it is quite distinct from any intelligible ideal of equality of rewards. Indeed, when it is combined with the marketization of rewards that has developed lately in some societies, fair opportunity can produce very large inequalities in incomes. From an inclusionary standpoint such large inequalities will matter only if they lead to opt-out from public services and civic obligations as in the revolt of the elites. Where this is so, a concern for inclusion will condemn too large a gap between the majority and the top. Large economic inequalities will be socially divisive if they are widely judged to be unfair.

There is little evidence, however, that large differences in marketized reward are themselves judged to be unfair. It is the means whereby they arise rather than the size of such differences that seems to be offensive. It is when they are acquired in quasi-monopolistic situations – as in the newly privatized utilities – that they are condemned. Moreover, such monopolistic practices plausibly violate fair opportunity. The assumption of recent political philosophers that the sense of justice of most people in contemporary societies can be reconstructed as a system of distributional principles applying in all domains of social life appears to be ill-founded. Today, as in the past, the sense of justice is largely domain-specific. Its content varies widely in different social contexts and across societies.

By contrast with theories of distributive justice, the ideal of inclusion accepts as its starting point the complex understandings of fairness that are to be found in society. (To that extent, inclusion is a relativistic notion.) Large economic inequalities are not condemned if they arise against a background of fair opportunity and basic human needs have been met. If we think of justice not as a matter of distributive principles applying throughout society but instead as a complex body of norms about local justice that vary from domain to domain and society and society, then justice will condemn economic inequalities only when they undermine an inclusive society.

The ideal of inclusion, then, is distinct from any ideal of equality; but it acts as a constraint on inequalities at both the bottom and the top. We are now in a position where we can consider the substantive question animating this inquiry: Is an inclusive society achievable in current circumstances?

Globalization versus the global free market

At the beginning of this essay I noted the argument that globalization has increased the economic cost of egalitarian policies to the point of making them politically unfeasible. Before proceeding to consider how globalization bears on the project of an inclusive society it is essential to make some distinctions.

'Globalization' can mean many things.[7] Among its diverse meanings, two must be distinguished. In one of the senses in which it is commonly used, 'globalization' refers to an historical process of increasing interconnection between economic and social life throughout the world that has been going on for centuries. In another, it refers to a particular political and economic framework in which that process has very recently occurred – the framework of a global free market. In the latter sense, globalization signifies not a long-standing process of development but a specific – and in all likelihood, I have argued,[8] short-lived – economic regime.

As Giddens has put it: 'Globalization can . . . be defined as the intensification of world-wide social relations which link distant realities in such a way that local happenings are shaped by events occurring many miles away and vice versa.'[9] When this process began is debatable; but it has been underway at least since the projection of European power through colonialism in the fifteenth and sixteenth centuries. By the end of the nineteenth century, a well-developed international economy was in existence. The motor of globalization in this sense is the interaction of technological innovation with the development of capitalism. The telegraph cable powered an acceleration of globalization comparable with that produced in the last decades of the twentieth century by information technologies.

This meaning of globalization, in which it signifies worldwide industrialization through the banalization of new technologies and the global extension of capital, is to be distinguished clearly and sharply from the other, quite different sense of the term, in which it refers to a global liberal economic regime. Though worldwide industrialization and the current regime of global *laissez-faire* are commonly conflated, the two are by no means identical or coterminous. Globalization as an historical process powered by new technologies and capitalist expansion antedates a global free market by centuries. It will persist long after the current regime of global *laissez-faire* has become a fading historical memory.

The most significant feature of globalization as an historical process is that it has continued through a number of different international economic regimes. In its topical, demotic, political sense, globalization denotes a world economy organized as a single, universal free market. It is this sense of globalization that is usually invoked when it is argued that in our current and foreseeable circumstances the egalitarian project of classical social democracy has ceased to be politically viable. That argument is fundamentally sound. The egalitarian goals of old-fashioned social democracy (including its more recent Rawlsian variants) presupposed economies that were largely closed. The distributional unit of social-democratic policy was the nation-state. When capital and production enjoy unfettered mobility worldwide the distributional goals of social democracy cease to be feasible.

This does not mean that all redistributional activities of govern-ments become impossible. Quite clearly, many such activities continue. Nevertheless, footloose capital is increasingly able to seek low-tax, low-regulation environments, and economies that are otherwise comparable tend to converge on similar tax and regulatory poli-cies. Free flows of capital in a regime of global *laissez-faire* are incompatible with the egalitarian values of classical social democracy.

Global *laissez-faire* versus an inclusive society

Global *laissez-faire* is no less inimical to the project of an inclusive society. This is partly because *laissez-faire* in world financial markets has highly destabilizing effects on economic and social life. Sudden inflows of capital followed by its equally abrupt exit have an econ-omic and social impact that can endure for many years. They are especially (but not uniquely) destabilizing in regard to those vari-eties of capitalism that have in the past been legitimated by high levels of secure employment. This can be illustrated by considering some neglected aspects of the so-called Asian economic crisis.

In one sense, the fact that global *laissez-faire* fractured first in Asian markets was an historical accident. In another sense it illu-minated one of the deeper instabilities of global capitalism. Asia's capitalisms are extremely diverse; but they have in common the fact that in all of them shareholder value is subordinated to the generation of employment as the central legitimating activity of firms. Over time unregulated global capital markets will render this distinctive feature of Asian capitalisms unsustainable.

The organization of global capitalism as a universal free market accentuates and accelerates the systemic contradiction in late capitalist societies between the imperatives of the economy and the central legitimating institutions of bourgeois life. The impact is clearest on the canonical bourgeois institution of the career.[10] The tendency of the most radically deregulated capitalisms is to reproletarianise sections of the working classes while debourgeoisifying parts of the middle classes.

In a global free market this tendency is projected (via deregu-lated capital markets) into every economy. In a global free market, very distant social contexts become continuously interconnected; but at the same time, particular societies are increasingly savagely segmented. Elites become more mobile, while an immobile underclass is reproduced. Such segmentation does not promote the convergence to the political centre commonly associated with regimes of 'democratic capitalism'. It tends to issue in a volatile politics of economic insecurity, in which ethnic nationalism and religious fundamentalism are often prominent strands. These effects are not accidental defects in global *laissez-faire*. They are integral aspects of its workings. As Bauman has put it:

> Neo-tribal and fundamentalist tendencies, which reflect and articulate the experience of people on the receiving end of globalization, are as much legitimate offspring of globalization as the acclaimed 'hybridization' of top culture – the culture of the globalized top. A particular cause for worry is the progressive breakdown in communication between the increasingly global and extra-territorial elites and the more 'localized' rest.[11]

It is worth stressing that this segmentation of society by globalized market forces would be an integral feature of a worldwide free market even if – impossibly – such an unmanaged global economy were free of dislocating booms and slumps. The currency fluctuations that erupted in east Asia in 1997 destabilized the real economies of several countries, notably Indonesia, Malaysia, Hong Kong and South Korea. In Indonesia, they have led to deep social divisions and a shift in regime that is not yet complete. Even if these crises had not occurred, the day-to-day workings of deregulated world markets impose a degree of economic insecurity on all countries exposed to them that is inimical to cohesion and, therefore, to inclusion. Reconciling bourgeois values with the social consequences of continuous technical innovation is a problem for all late modern societies. But it is an especially intractable dilemma for societies in which a highly individualistic mode of capitalism aggravates the insecurities produced by the stream of new technologies. If capital relocates from Africa to Latin America, entire industries and their dependent communities can be extinguished. In a regime of universal *laissez-faire*, that risk hangs permanently over everyone.

On the level of the world economy, as on a national level, free markets tend to make cohesion in society harder to maintain. In a global free market, groups whose skills cannot be profitably employed easily become marginal in their own societies. The social effects of free markets observed in the mid-nineteenth century by Marx are reproduced and magnified on a worldwide scale. In the worst cases, such as postcommunist Russia after the economic collapse of August 1998, entire societies can be immiserated and reproletarianized.

Concluding remarks

In the context of a global free market, an inclusive society is not an achievable ideal. Global *laissez-faire* contains no mechanism whereby social exclusion can be stemmed. This is partly because a global free market contains no effective mechanisms for macroeconomic management, and partly because national governments which adhere to the ground rules of global *laissez-faire* are narrowly restricted in the economic policies they can adopt. It is not merely that an unmanaged global market is prone to dislocation and imbalance. Even if currency crises and similar disturbances could be avoided, the systemic logic of a global free market requires the elimination of unproductive enterprises regardless of social cost. For this reason, as with the national free markets of the past, the social impact of unregulated globalized market forces is unavoidably exclusionary.

Social dislocation is an integral aspect of the normal functioning of deregulated global markets. During periods of overall economic expansion the political effects of such dislocation can normally be contained. During economic downturn they become more problematic. In some countries, fundamentalist movements and far-right nationalist parties have been the political beneficiaries of high rates of unemployment. If global markets remain volatile, the radicalization of political life may lead to the ground rules of global *laissez-faire* being challenged from the Left. If this comes to pass, the ideal of inclusion may be invoked against global market forces. In a familiar irony, an idea that had arisen with a political consensus on the hegemony of global market forces will be deployed to resist them.

The shift in centre-left parties from advocacy of social-democratic equality to the defence of social inclusion may have helped resolve some difficult issues in electoral strategy. The ideal of inclusion may be more philosophically defensible than social-democratic egalitarianism. Nevertheless, inclusion has no advantage over equality as a political response to the social and political dilemmas of globalization. Social inclusion and market globalization are opposing political ideas. It is not difficult to envisage circumstances in which recognition of this is made unavoidable.

Notes

1 I have argued this in my monograph, *After Social Democracy* (1996), reprinted in my book *Endgames* (1997).
2 For an example of this Old Right view of social institutions, see Scruton (1980).
3 I refer to Sandel (1982).
4 For the best account of the role of social forms in individual well-being, see Raz (1986, ch. 12).
5 Ibid., ch. 14.
6 I have considered some of the difficulties surrounding non-satiable basic needs in my book, *Beyond the New Right* (1993), esp. pp. 105–8.
7 I have considered the various meanings of globalization more extensively in my book, *False Dawn* (1999), chap. 2.
8 See *ibid.*, chap. 8 and Postscript.
9 Giddens (1990), p. 64.
10 See Diana Coyle, Part II below.
11 Bauman (1998).

References

Z. Bauman, *Globalization* (Cambridge: Polity Press, 1998).

A. Giddens, *The Consequences of Modernity* (Cambridge: Polity Press, 1990).

J. Gray, *After Social Democracy* (London: Demos, 1996).

J. Gray, *Beyond the New Right: Markets, Government and the Common Environment* (London: Routledge, 1993).

J. Gray, *Endgames: Questions in Late Modern Political Thought* (Cambridge: Polity Press, 1997).

J. Gray, *False Dawn: The Delusions of Global Capitalism* (London: Granta, 1998).

J. Raz, *The Morality of Freedom* (Oxford: The Clarendon Press, 1986).

M. Sandel, *Liberalism and the Limits of Justice* (Cambridge: Cambridge University Press, 1982).

R. Scruton, *The Meaning of Conservatism* (Harmondsworth: Penguin Books, 1980).

3
Strategies for Social Inclusion: Promoting Social Cohesion or Social Justice?

Ruth Lister

Introduction

An 'inclusive society' stands as a widespread aspiration at the turn of the century. Yet there is no clear consensus as to what is meant by an inclusive society and by the concept of social exclusion which underpins it. Nor is there necessarily agreement on the objectives and values that would inform any route map towards such a society. Is the over-arching principle that guides us social cohesion or social justice? Is the aim equality of opportunity in an unequal labour market and wider society or to go further and also to reduce the more fundamental inequalities that propel the forces of exclusion? What model of citizenship would frame the construction of an inclusive society? In particular, how would it reconcile ideals of equality and universality with recognition of and respect for diversity and people's attachment to particular identities and groups? More broadly, how would this model of citizenship position itself in the context of global inequalities and movements of peoples as asylum-seekers and migrants?

These are among the questions which this chapter attempts to address before sketching out a role for a proactive social policy that will strengthen citizenship and help to build 'the inclusive society'.

The concept of social inclusion/exclusion

Various paradigms of social exclusion, reflecting different national conceptions of citizenship, inform policy-making (Silver, 1994). While the concept is a relatively new one in the UK, the term originated in France over two decades ago, from whence it was adopted by the European Commission in 1989 in preference to poverty (Cousins, 1998).

While some dismiss the notion of social exclusion as simply a euphemism for poverty, it does arguably have a value, for it captures something different. It is a more multidimensional concept than poverty, embracing a variety of ways in which people may be denied full participation in society and full effective rights of citizenship in the civil, political and social spheres. Different dimensions of exclusion can interact and compound each other. For example, black people are not only more vulnerable to poverty than white people but the exclusion that they experience can be exacerbated by racism which undermines their effective rights as citizens. Racism, and other forms of discriminatory and oppressive behaviour and attitudes such as sexism, homophobia and disablism, can, at the same time, operate as mechanisms of exclusion even in the case of those who have adequate material resources. Thus poverty and social exclusion, while often related, are not necessarily so.

The notion of social exclusion also encourages a focus on processes rather than simply outcomes. In doing so, it pays due regard to *both* agency *and* structure, one or other of which can be lost sight of when attention is fixed, either benevolently or critically, on individual experience or behaviour. The word 'exclusion' implies that something or someone is excluding someone else and encourages us to examine the mechanisms involved. A more dynamic approach also opens up space for the agency of those excluded and for intervening in the 'trajectories' that can lead into or out of poverty and exclusion (Walker, 1998). It has been suggested that social exclusion is primarily about social relations of participation, integration and power whereas poverty is about the distribution of material resources (Room, 1995). One danger with the concept of exclusion is that, if used uncritically, it can obscure the associated poverty that stems from an unequal distribution of resources and the wider relations of inequality and polarization which frame it. As a number of commentators have observed, the key relationship tends to be a horizontal one of 'in' or 'out' rather than a vertical one of 'up' or 'down' (Duffy, 1998).

The notion of exclusion can, in fact, be deployed in very different ways depending on whether the primary objective is social cohesion or social justice. Ruth Levitas (1998) has summed up these different approaches in what she calls the three discourses of SID, MUD and RED. RED refers to a redistributive, egalitarian discourse that embraces notions of citizenship and social rights, which she associates with critical thinkers and activists, but not with the mainstream stance adopted by the European Commission and the UK Government. The primary objective here is social justice in contrast to the other two discourses, which are activated by the primary objective of social cohesion and distinguished by a lack of concern about wider inequalities. MUD is a moralistic discourse, which deploys the divisive and stigmatizing language of the 'underclass' and 'dependency culture' to portray those excluded as culturally distinct from mainstream society. It emphasizes individual behaviour and values. SID, a 'social integrationist discourse', increasingly dominant in both the UK and the wider EU, is focused primarily, and sometimes exclusively, on exclusion from paid work. Levitas sums up the differences between the three discourses according to 'what the excluded are seen as lacking' namely money (and we might add power) in RED, morals in MUD and work in SID. While all share, to varying degrees, a belief in paid work as a mechanism for social inclusion they differ, she argues, 'in their capacity to recognize, let alone valorize, unpaid work', with significant gendered implications (Levitas, 1998: 27).

Paid work – the key to inclusion?

Increasingly, paid work lies at the heart of Western governments' attempts to build a more inclusive society. The European Commission has emphasized the centrality of employment to its 'vision' of 'an active, inclusive and healthy society ... because it is a Europe at work that will sustain the core values of the European social model' (1998: 8). In the UK, the Green Paper, *A New Contract for Welfare*, underlined that 'the Government's aim is to rebuild the welfare state around work' (DSS, 1998: 23). The point had been elaborated in an earlier speech by the then Social Security Secretary, Harriet Harman:

> work is central to the Government's attack on social exclusion. Work is the only route to sustained financial independence. But it is also much more ... It is a way of life ... Work is an important element of the human condition. Work helps fulfil our aspirations – it is a key to independence, self-respect and opportunities

for advancement . . . Parents don't just work to support their families financially, they also work to set an example to their children . . . Work rather than worklessness is the difference between a decent standard of living and benefit dependency. *And between a cohesive society and a divided one.*

(Harman, 1997, emphasis added)

Few would probably question that paid work has an important role to play in any strategy for tackling social exclusion. Research has demonstrated the relationship between changing labour market positions and poverty, the importance to individuals of employment and the adverse and isolating effects of worklessness (see, for instance, Jackson, 1994; Bryson, Ford and White, 1997; Clasen, Gould and Vincent, 1998; McKendrick, 1998). A broad consensus has emerged in the UK around the central importance of good quality jobs in tackling social exclusion.

Yet, as the quotation from Harriet Harman exemplifies, there are a number of assumptions underlying a SID-style social inclusion strategy which need to be unpacked and questioned. These are that:

1 paid work necessarily spells social inclusion;
2 worklessness necessarily spells social exclusion;
3 the only form of work of value to society is paid work; and
4 an inclusive society can be built on the foundations of paid work alone.

In response to the equation of paid work with social inclusion, which has come to dominate policy-thinking, A.B. Atkinson has observed that 'employment does not ensure social inclusion; whether or not it does so depends on the quality of the work offered. "Marginal" jobs may be no solution' and 'if the expansion of employment is obtained at the expense of a widening gap between those at the bottom of the earnings scale and the overall average, then it may not end social exclusion' (Atkinson, 1998: i & 9). Low pay has been a growing problem in the British labour market. The introduction of a minimum wage is therefore an important breakthrough, even if its impact will be blunted by the low rates proposed.

A British study of what happened over a five-year period to a group of people unemployed in 1990–92 found that three out of four of the jobs they moved into were temporary, part-time, self-employed, or at a considerably lower skill level than their previous employment (White and Forth, 1998). The labour market which unemployed people face is primarily one of marginal jobs. Moreover, movement out of such jobs is limited, so that fewer than a quarter of those taking part-time jobs had moved into full time work by the end of the five-year period. Although, by definition, a job could be said to mean that its holder is no longer excluded from the labour market, the quality of his or her inclusion has also to be considered. If previously unemployed people are stuck in low grade, peripheral sectors of the labour market, they will continue to occupy a marginalized position, which is inconsistent with full and genuine inclusion.

It is not an unreasonable assumption that worklessness spells social exclusion. Most notably in the UK it is associated with very low incomes, which themselves make it difficult to enjoy the living conditions and participate in the activities taken for granted by the wider society. Long-term unemployment in particular can mean social isolation and loss of self-esteem. Nevertheless, cross-national research indicates that even long-term unemployment does not necessarily have to lead to social as opposed to labour market exclusion. This partly reflects different policy regimes so that, for instance, in Germany and Sweden relatively generous social security benefits combined with active labour market policies help to counteract unemployment's exclusionary impact (Silver, 1995; Clasen, Gould and Vincent, 1998). Arguably, though, the more social inclusion is defined purely in terms of paid work, the more those not in paid work will come to feel excluded. This is particularly so, if politicians use exclusionary language such as that of the 'dependency culture' or the 'underclass' to describe them (Lister, 1996).

On the other hand, in some cases, exclusion may be resisted by unemployed people themselves through the creation of alternative social networks and activities (Jordan *et al.*, 1992; Jordan, 1996; Clasen, Gould and Vincent, 1998). These include community-based and voluntary activities which can be seen as strengthening 'social capital'. Some have argued that, as such, their value should be recognized as a form of 'active citizenship' involving work, albeit of an unpaid variety (MacDonald, 1996; Zadek and Thake, 1997). Likewise, feminists and others have criticized a definition of work, which confines it to activities for which payment is made, thereby discounting the unpaid work of reproduction and care carried out in the home, mainly still by women. In the context of a social inclusion strategy predicated on the work ethic, the result can be a devalorization of the hard work of caring for children and older people. So, for instance, when the abolition of lone-parents' benefits was justified by the Labour Government with reference to the paid work opportunities opened up through the New Deal, this was interpreted by many lone parents as a denial of the importance of the unpaid work they do caring for their children. Research suggests that complex 'gendered moral rationalities' influence lone parents' own views of the role of paid work in good parenting (Duncan and Edwards, 1999). The Government does claim to recognize the importance of caring responsibilities, in particular through its child-care and family-friendly employment policies for working parents, its strategy for carers and proposals for second pension credits for those caring for young children or adults. Moreover, the Office for National Statistics is now developing household accounts which include an estimate of the value of unpaid care and voluntary work. Yet, welcome as these initiative are, the Government has so far failed to address, at the heart of its welfare reform agenda, what Levitas identifies as 'a profound contradiction between treating paid work as the defining factor in social inclusion, and recognizing the value of unpaid work' (Levitas, 1998: 145).

This leads to the conclusion that, important as paid work is, it does not on its own guarantee the inclusive society. To an extent, this is acknowledged implicitly by the British Government's establishment of a Social Exclusion Unit at the heart of government, reporting directly to the Prime Minister. Although its announcement located it very much within the context of paid work and education as the central weapons in the planned attack on social exclusion (Mandelson, 1997), its remit is wider than that and has included rough sleepers and those living on 'worst estates' as well as truancy and school exclusions. The danger here is that a focus on discrete problem groups could encourage the belief that these groups are themselves the problem (Bennett, 1998). It is therefore essential that the problem of social exclusion and strategies to promote social inclusion are located within a broader analysis of inequality and polarization both inside and outside the labour market.

Inclusion, equality and citizenship

Instead, in the UK, the New Labour Government's espousal of social inclusion as an objective has been underpinned by a shift in philosophy from traditional left notions of equality in favour of those of equality of opportunity. The shift was summed up by the Chancellor, Gordon Brown, in an exchange with Roy Hattersley (former Deputy Leader of the Labour Party), as a rejection by New Labour of 'equality of outcome as neither desirable nor feasible, imposing uniformity and stifling human potential; instead it espouses a view of equality of opportunity that is recurrent, lifelong and comprehensive' (*The Guardian*, 2 August 1997). Brown's conceptualization of life-long equality of opportunity for 'everyone to have their chance to realize their potential to the full' is an attractive one (1996). However, equality of opportunity, even thus defined, within the context of profoundly unequal economic and social structures and power relationships, is likely to remain a chimera, as massively unequal starting points affect the ability to grasp the opportunities opened up. Moreover, not everyone can 'succeed' on the meritocratic terms laid down. An inclusive society must value those who do not as well as those who do, with implications for social policy (White, 1997).

This is one reason why egalitarians argue that equality of opportunity is not in itself enough. This does not mean that, in practice, they necessarily argue for 'equality of outcome' in a literal sense; instead, from the perspective of practical politics, the argument is generally about degrees of (in)equality.[1] The case for reducing inequality is as strong as it has ever been. In the UK, the Joseph Rowntree Foundation Inquiry into Income and Wealth has demonstrated that 'inequality was greater in the mid-1990s than at any time in the forty years from the late 1940s' and that inequality growth 'was exceptional compared with international trends' (Hills, 1998: 5). Moreover, apart from any moral issue about the acceptability of such massive inequalities, research suggests that inequality is bad for national prosperity, health and social cohesion (Glyn and Miliband 1994; Wilkinson, 1996). Thus, a strategy for social inclusion that prioritizes social cohesion, through SID-inspired policies, over social justice, through RED-inspired policies, could ultimately be self-defeating.

In response to Brown's deployment of the old argument that equality imposes uniformity, Hattersley pointed out that 'true diversity is only possible in a society which avoids great discrepancies in wealth and income' (*The Guardian*, 6 August 1997). Without wanting to dispute Hattersley's position, which derives from that of R.H. Tawney, there is a wider issue about the relationship between equality and diversity which neither Hattersley nor Brown addressed. The inequalities that were the subject of debate between the two were, implicitly, those of income, loosely associated with social class.

There are, though, other dimensions of inequality, which can also be exclusionary in their impact, most notably those of gender, 'race', religion, disability and sexuality. These may or may not translate into material inequalities and will interact with them in different ways. They differ, though, in that they raise, first and foremost, issues of 'recognition' of the differences between groups rather than of redistribution from one group to another in the name of greater equality. Proponents of radical democracy argue that democratic participation is undermined not just by socioeconomic inequality, but also by a failure to recognize the cultural or symbolic demands borne of difference and diversity. In the words of Nancy Fraser, the 'struggle for recognition is fast becoming the paradigmatic form of political conflict in the late twentieth century' (Fraser, 1995: 68/1997: 11).

Fraser contrasts this with a traditional materialist 'imaginary centred on terms such as "interest", "exploitation" and "redistribution" (*ibid.*: 69/11).The task, she argues, is to develop a '*critical* theory of recognition, one which identifies and defends only those versions of the cultural politics of difference that can be coherently combined with the social politics of equality'. Her underlying premise is that 'justice today requires both redistribution *and* recognition' (*ibid.*: 69/12). The dilemma, she suggests, is that recognition claims tend to promote 'group differentiation', whereas redistribution claims tend to do the opposite. While the tension is a real one, it can be overstated. In a response to Fraser, Iris Marion Young places greater emphasis on the interrelationship between the two forms of injustice and politics. She argues that 'we should show how recognition is a means to, or an element in, economic and political equality' and that 'so long as the cultural denigration of groups produces or reinforces structural economic oppressions, the two struggles are continuous' (Young, 1997: 156, 159; see also Phillips, 1999). A good example is disability politics. The disabled people's movement has asserted disabled people's right to speak as disabled people. It has demanded *equal* citizenship rights and economic justice through the assertion of disability as a *different* social and political category rather than through its negation in the name of equality.

A social justice agenda for the inclusive society can, therefore, incorporate both equality and difference demands, even if tensions between them may remain. An attempt to do so, even if only at the level of aspiration, is the Northern Ireland Peace Agreement, which declares that power:

shall be exercised with rigorous impartiality on behalf of all the
people in the diversity of their identities and traditions and shall
be founded on the principles of full respect for, and equality of,
civil, political, social and cultural rights, of freedom from discrimination for all citizens, and of parity of esteem and of just
and equal treatment for the identity, ethos and aspirations of
both communities.

(Governments of UK and Ireland, 1998: 2)

The tensions are perhaps rather more acute in the context of an
orthodox social cohesion agenda, which tends to prioritize unity
over diversity and to gloss over conflicts of interests. Moreover, the
promotion of a politics of recognition can be disruptive, as some
of the public protests by disabled people against benefit cuts and
inaccessible public transport have demonstrated. Such actions can
be understood as acts of 'dissident citizenship', conceptualized by
Holloway Sparks as 'the practices of marginalized citizens' for
whom institutionalized forms of opposition have proved inadequate
(Sparks, 1997: 75).

What this all adds up to is the need to rethink the model of
citizenship which underpins an inclusive society. Although citizenship has traditionally been understood as a force for inclusion, in
the civil, political and social spheres, it operates simultaneously as
a force for exclusion both within and at the borders of nation-
states. In the name of universalism, it has excluded women and
'minority' groups from full and effective citizenship within nation-
states, or has included them on terms that have served to marginalize
them. From an internationalist perspective, citizenship has been
identified as 'a conspiracy against outsiders' in a world divided into
a series of states to which citizenship is attached (Hindess, 1998: 67).
The implementation of increasingly exclusionary immigration and
asylum controls and associated welfare entitlements are strengthening this conspiracy in the context of globalizing forces which
are widening the economic gulf between countries of emigration
and immigration.

A more genuinely inclusive model of citizenship needs to incorporate the claims of diverse groups without sacrificing its universalistic
principles (Lister, 1997). This has implications for social policy, some
of which are explored below. An inclusive model will also be internationalist and multilayered, taking on board notions of global
citizenship and its associated responsibilities, both towards other

countries and to those who move between countries. As J.K. Galbraith writes, as part of his vision of 'the good society', 'the responsibility for economic and social well being is general, transnational' (1996: 2). The notion of global citizenship translates on to the transnational political stage, social and economic policy issues of justice and re-distribution (UNRISD, 1995; Deacon, 1997).

Social policy in the inclusive society

Global economic trends also impose constraints on the ability of governments to use social policy to build an inclusive society. These constraints should not, however, be exaggerated and should not be used as an alibi for inaction (Joseph Rowntree Foundation, 1995; Hirst and Thompson, 1996). The centrality of social policy to the task of building an inclusive society is acknowledged, in principle if not in practice, by the European Commission in its *Social Action Programme* (1998). This centrality means that social policy has to be integrated with economic policy and not be left simply to pick up the pieces. Likewise, economic as well as social policy has to be informed by the principle of inclusion so that, for instance, demand-side measures to promote employment together with community-based regeneration strategies are given higher priority. Economic policies which generate employment have to underpin social policies designed to enhance employability. In this final section, I will start by sketching out briefly some of the social policy implications of an employment based approach before moving on to a broader agenda.

Education is widely seen as a key weapon in the attack on social exclusion and as central to promoting equality of opportunity. In the words of the Commission on Social Justice 'a good education is the most effective way to overcome inequalities of birth and status, to enable people to create and seize new opportunities, and to pro-mote social improvement and mobility' (Commission on Social Justice, 1994: 120). Howard Glennester is more cautious, warning that edu-cation cannot provide a short-term fix, but that 'carefully thought out interventions targeted at low performers, both adults and children, especially in poor areas could over the long haul, make a differ-ence' (Glennester, 1998: 148). Among the Commission's priorities were investments in pre-school education and in 'lifelong learning'. The importance of opening up educational opportunities for adults has been emphasized in relation to lone parents in particular as a stepping stone to employment (Select Committee, 1998). Another key area is provision for the 14–19 age group (Pearce and Hillman, 1998). 'Inequalities of birth and status' continue to shape educational outcomes in the UK, with private schooling still buying privilege in higher education, which raises questions about the justifiability of its charitable tax status. Less frequently discussed is education's potential pedagogic contribution to the creation of a more inclusive society. It can, for instance, encourage children to value diversity in its various forms so that they grow up citizens attuned to an inclusive and internationalist culture and it can prepare children for full democratic participation as citizens (Crick, 1998).

Any employment-based strategy has to break down the main barriers to employment, which exclude disadvantaged groups from the labour market or marginalize them within it. Again education and training are important here, particularly in building ladders out of the kind of marginal jobs open to many unemployed people and in opening up opportunities for lone mothers (White and Forth, 1998; Select Committee, 1998). More effective, comprehensive, anti-discrimination legislation, extended to cover discrimination on, for instance, grounds of sexuality and age, would address both recognition and injustice claims. Much more could be done both by employers and through the income maintenance system to support disabled people, including some severely disabled people, who want employment. Stronger employment rights and a decent minimum wage, uprated annually in line with the average rise in wages, are also important components of a more inclusive labour market.

One of the main barriers to employment for those with caring responsibilities is the lack of alternative care provisions and the difficulties faced by parents and carers who try to combine paid work with those responsibilities. Until recently, such matters have been treated as essentially private concerns in the UK, in contrast with, for example, France and the Scandinavian countries. The Labour Government's childcare strategy, which accepts that there is a public interest in these matters, is therefore welcome. As the Government acknowledges, the expansion of good quality pre- and out-of-school care is a priority, if parents of younger children, and especially lone parents, are to be able to take paid work. It is also important for children's own inclusion in the wider society. The adoption of the EC parental-leave directive will mean that statutory parental leave and leave for family reasons will be available for the first time in the UK. However, if it is to be of real value there will need to be some form of payment.

This is particularly important if men are to be encouraged to take the leave. In heterosexual couples, the division of labour and responsibility in the domestic 'private' sphere helps to shape the access of both women and men to the public sphere. It does so by constructing the access that each has to time, which is a resource like money. As Nordic governments have recognized, and the European Commission has argued, social policy has a role to play in trying to shift this division of labour so as to create a more equitable division of paid and unpaid caring work between women and men (Lister, 1997, 1999). Relevant policies include the reservation of part of the parental leave for men, limits on working hours (as introduced to a limited extent under the Working Time Directive), and the opportunity for either parent to work a shorter working day.

A parallel set of policies needs to be developed to support those who are attempting or who want to combine paid work with care of older or disabled people, as signalled in the Labour Government's strategy for carers. The implementation of such policies would need to be sensitive to the needs and preferences of those receiving care and again should encourage a more equitable division of caring responsibilities between women and men.

The role of social policy in supporting those with caring responsibilities raises the issue discussed earlier of the value accorded to the work involved in discharging those responsibilities relative to that accorded to paid work. This, in turn, prompts the wider question of the nature of social citizenship obligations and their relationship to social rights of citizenship. The employment-based model of social inclusion privileges paid work as *the* citizenship obligation. Apart from the question of whether public policy should acknowledge and support other forms of work as representing the discharge of citizenship obligations, there is also the issue of how it should treat those who consciously reject the work paradigm. Stuart White has raised the worry that this paradigm is

> fundamentally illiberal. It supposes that citizens will all be absorbed into conventional forms of economic participation and will orient their lives around such participation. The strategy is inattentive to groups like travellers who aspire to a way of life

in which conventional paid employment is less central . . . The challenge is to work out how travellers and others can be empowered to go their own way without at the same time being given an unjust 'free ride' on the efforts of their fellow citizens.

(White, 1998: 6)

For some, though not White himself, the answer to this conundrum is a basic income scheme under which every citizen (or resident) would receive a tax-free income with no strings attached.[2] Such a scheme has many attractions and more than any other social policy measure would challenge the hegemony of the paid work social inclusion paradigm. However, there is a danger that it could have exclusionary as well as inclusionary consequences. Unless combined with the kind of measures contained in the British Labour government's New Deal, it could consign some people to a life on a benefit which is likely to be pretty minimal, eked out with irregular earnings where such opportunities exist. It would then be all too easy for the rest of society to write them off, even more so than they do now. It is doubtful whether most members of society are ready for a 'no strings attached' benefit of this kind. So long as the work ethic maintains its grip, any basic income is likely to be introduced at a level inadequate to meet the needs of those who have no other income or to have requirements attached, which would undermine its basic principle of unconditionality.

As the Commission on Social Justice argued, it would be a mistake to write basic income off as a possible longer-term option, which might become more appropriate if opportunities for paid work close down. In the shorter term, though, a participation income might represent a more politically viable proposition. This would provide a modest basic income, but subject to a condition of active citizenship for those of working age able to work. This would include not just paid work or training and availability for it, but also caring work and, in some versions, voluntary and community work.

It could be combined with a revitalized, more inclusive, social insurance scheme on the lines recommended by the Commission. Such a scheme would, unlike the present one, reflect women's, and not just men's employment patterns. It would include, for instance, protection for those earning below the national insurance lower earnings limit who are currently outside the scheme; a part-time unemployment benefit; and better recognition of family responsibilities.

The stronger and more extensive the social insurance scheme, combined with higher child benefits, the less the social security system has to rely on means tests, which are divisive and which serve to exclude rather than to include. This points towards Continental European models, inspired by principles of solidarity, which, even though under strain, by and large have been more successful in combating social exclusion and inequalities than the residualist Anglo-Saxon model exemplified by the US (Hirsch, 1997). Cross-national research suggests that adequate social insurance benefits are important in minimizing the social exclusion experienced by unemployed people (Clasen, Gould and Vincent, 1998).

The question of adequacy is itself an important one in combating the social exclusion associated with worklessness more generally. To the extent that it is lack of money which excludes people from enjoyment of the living standards and from participation in the activities taken for granted by the wider society, benefit levels have to be part of the equation. Moreover, research suggests that inadequate benefit levels can make effective job-seeking difficult, can discourage people from taking their chances in an insecure labour market and can undermine education's contribution to tackling social exclusion (Robinson, 1997; Ford, 1998; Lister, 1998). The social security system needs to provide benefits high enough to guarantee genuine security and to meet human need for all legitimate residents, including asylum-seekers. As such it constitutes a core element of social citizenship rights, which promote individual autonomy and the ability to exercise political and civil citizenship rights.

Funding a decent social security system, which contributes to the prevention of poverty, will require redistribution, the unmentionable 'r' word in contemporary British politics. To the extent that the language of redistribution is still used it refers to opportunities rather than to resources. Yet, as argued earlier, the massive inequalities in income and wealth which scar our society (aggravated by the previous government's redistribution to the rich) mean that redistribution of income and wealth through the tax–benefit system still has an important role to play in creating an inclusive society, at the top as well as the bottom. In a polarized society, not only are those in poverty excluded, but the rich and powerful can effectively exclude themselves from the common bonds of citizenship. The principle of progressive income and wealth taxation, as an expression of responsibility to each other as citizens, needs to be rehabilitated.

In addition to redistribution, addressing the exclusion of those living in poverty requires, at the same time, a variant of the politics of recognition. The social exclusion of those in poverty is compounded by their political exclusion, one element of which is their exclusion from debates about poverty and from the development of anti-poverty strategies. A politics of recognition in this context is about the assertion not of group differences but of equality of status and respect, together with according value to poor people's own interpretation of their needs and rights so that they become actors in the political and policy process and not just its objects (Lister and Beresford, 1999). What is needed is a 'participatory infrastructure' which would provide channels through which those excluded from the formal political process can make their views known and can debate them, as was the case in the development of the Irish National Anti-Poverty Strategy. More broadly, this points to a social policy which promotes inclusion as citizens through user-involvement in welfare state institutions and anti-poverty or exclusion initiatives. User-involvement represents a more active form of social citizenship in which welfare state users are constructed as active participants rather than simply the passive bearers of rights or recipients of services. It is easier to promote at local level where community based initiatives can be important in promoting inclusive social relations. A network of Community Development Trusts could promote and support such initiatives (Commission on Social Justice, 1994).

Conclusion

The case for listening to the 'voice' of those in poverty and other excluded groups and promoting user-involvement in welfare services and anti-exclusion initiatives is inspired by a belief in the importance of process as well as outcome. Strategies for creating an inclusive society must themselves be inclusive in their development and implementation. Exclusion has to be tackled at both the material and the symbolic level and across a range of dimensions of inequalities. The promotion of paid work has an important role to play in strategies for social inclusion but, if it is treated as the sole badge of inclusion, the effect will be to serve to exclude those who for whatever reason are not part of the paid workforce. While social cohesion and social justice are not necessarily incompatible, the promotion of a narrow social cohesion model of inclusion, which ignores inequalities of resources and power, runs the risk of becoming detached from principles of social justice. These principles, interpreted in an international context, mean also that a genuinely inclusive society has to look outwards as well as inwards, taking a more inclusionary stance towards those seeking entry and playing its role in achieving a more just global distribution of resources.

Notes

1 For a discussion see Phillips (1999) and Franklin (1997) in which Miller (1997) suggests as a test the degree of inequality (in)compatible with genuine social equality or equality of status.
2 White's objection is that by detaching rights from responsibilities it permits the very 'free-riding' that concerns him (White, 1997).

References

Atkinson, A.B. (1998) 'Social Exclusion, Poverty and Unemployment', in A.B. Atkinson and J. Hills (eds), *Exclusion, Employment and Opportunity* (London: Centre for Analysis of Social Exclusion).

Bennett, F. (1998) 'Comment: Unravelling Poverty', in C. Oppenheim (ed.), *An Inclusive Society: Strategies for Tackling Poverty* (London: IPPR).

Brown, G. (1996) 'New Labour and Equality', *The Second John Smith Lecture* (Edinburgh: 19 April).

Bryson, A., Ford, R. and White, M. (1997) *Making Work Pay: Lone Mothers, Employment and Well-being* (York: Joseph Rowntree Foundation).

Clasen, J., Gould, A. and Vincent, J. (1998) *Voices Within and Without: Responses to Long-term Unemployment in Germany, Sweden and Britain* (Bristol: Policy Press).

Commission on Social Justice (1994) *Social Justice. Strategies for National Renewal* (London: Vintage).

Cousins, C. (1998) 'Social Exclusion in Europe: Paradigms of Social Disadvantage in Germany, Spain, Sweden and the United Kingdom', *Policy and Politics*, vol. 26(2), pp. 127–46.

Crick, B. (1998) *Education for Citizenship and the Teaching of Democracy in Schools* (London: Qualifications and Curriculum Authority/Citizenship Advisory Group).

Deacon, B. with Hulse, M. and Stubbs, P. (1997) *Global Social Policy* (London: Sage).

DSS (1998) *A New Contract for Welfare*.

Duffy, K. (1998) 'Combating Social Exclusion and Promoting Social Integration in the European Union', in C. Oppenheim (ed.), *An Inclusive Society: Strategies for Tackling Poverty* (London: IPPR).

Duncan, S. and Edwards, R. (1999) *Lone Mothers, Paid Work and Gendered Moral Rationalities* (Basingstoke: Macmillan).

European Commission (1998) *Social Action Programme 1998–2000* (Luxembourg: European Commission).

Ford, R. (1996) *Child Care in the Balance* (London: Policy Studies Institute).

Ford, R. (1998) 'Lone Mothers, Work and Welfare', *New Economy*, vol. 5(2), pp. 83–8.

Franklin, J. (ed.) (1997) *Equality* (London: IPPR).

Fraser, N. (1995) 'From Redistribution to Recognition? Dilemmas of Justice in a "post-Socialist" age', *New Left Review*, vol. 212, pp. 68–93.

Fraser, N. (1997) *Justice Interruptus* (New York & London: Routledge).

Galbraith, J.K. (1996) *The Good Society* (London: Sinclair-Stevenson).

Glennester, H. (1998) 'Tackling Poverty at its Roots?' in C. Oppenheim (ed.), *An Inclusive Society: Strategies for Tackling Poverty* (London: IPPR).

Glyn, A. and Miliband, D. (1994) *Paying for Inequality* (London: Rivers Oram Press).

Governments of United Kingdom and Ireland (1998) *The Agreement* (Belfast: Governments of United Kingdom and Ireland).

Harman, H. (1997) *Speech to Mark the Launch of the Centre for Analysis of Social Exclusion* (London School of Economics, 13 November).

Hills, J. (1998) *Income and Wealth. The Latest Evidence* (York: Joseph Rowntree Foundation).

Hindess, B. (1998) 'Divide and Rule. The International Character of Modern Citizenship', *European Journal of Social Theory*, vol. 1(1), pp. 57–70.

Hirsch, D. (1997) *Social Protection and Inclusion, European Challenges for the United Kingdom* (York: Joseph Rowntree Foundation).

Hirst, P. and Thompson, G. (1996) *Globalisation in Question* (Cambridge: Polity Press).

Jackson, P.R. (1994) 'Influences on Commitment to Employment and Commitment to Work', in A. Bryson and S. McKay (eds), *Is it Worth Working? Factors Affecting Labour Supply* (London: Policy Studies Institute).

Jordan, B. (1996) *A Theory of Poverty and Social Exclusion* (Cambridge: Polity Press).

Jordan, B., James, S., Kay, H. and Redley, M. (1992) *Trapped in Poverty?* (London: Routledge).

Joseph Rowntree Foundation Income and Wealth Inquiry Group, Income and Wealth (1995) (York: Joseph Rowntree Foundation).

Levitas, R. (1998) *The Inclusive Society? Social Exclusion and New Labour* (Basingstoke: Macmillan).

Lister, R. and Beresford, P. (1999) 'Where are "the Poor" in the Future of Poverty Research?' in J. Bradshaw and R. Sainsbury (eds), *Researching Poverty*, Vol. 2 (Aldershot: Ashgate).

Lister, R. (1996) 'Introduction: In Search of the "Underclass"', in R. Lister (ed.), *Charles Murray and the Underclass. The Developing Debate* (London: Institute of Economic Affairs).

Lister, R. (1997) *Citizenship: Feminist Perspectives* (Basingstoke: Macmillan).

Lister, R. (1998) 'Fighting Social Exclusion . . . With One Hand Tied Behind Our Back', *New Economy*, vol. 5(1), pp. 14–18.

Lister, R. (1999) 'What Welfare Provisions do Women Need to Become Full Citizens?', in S. Walby (ed.), *New Agendas for Women* (Basingstoke: Macmillan).

Macdonald, R. (1996) 'Labours of Love: Voluntary Working in a Depressed Local Economy', *Journal of Social Policy*, vol. 25(1), pp. 19–38.

Mandelson, P. (1997) *Labour's Next Steps: Tackling Social Exclusion*, 14 August, published as Fabian Pamphlet 581 (London: Fabian Society Summer Lecture).

McKendrick, J. (1998) 'The "Big" Picture. Quality in the Lives of Lone Parents', in R. Ford and J. Millar (eds), *Private Lives and Public Responses: Lone Parenthood and Future Policy* (London: Policy Studies Institute).

Miller, D. (1997) 'What Kind of Equality Should the Left Pursue?' in J. Franklin (ed.), *Equality* (London: IPPR).

Pearce, N. and Hillman, J. (1998) *Wasted Youth. Raising Achievement and Tackling Social Exclusion* (London: IPPR).

Phillips, A. (1999) *Which Equalities Matter?* (Cambridge: Polity Press).

Robinson, P. (1997) *Literacy, Numeracy and Economic Performance* (London: Centre for Economic Performance).

Room, G. (1995) 'Poverty and Social Exclusion: The New European Agenda for Policy and Research', in G. Room (ed.), *Beyond the Threshold* (Bristol: Policy Press).

Select Committee on Education and Employment (1998) *Pathways into Work for Lone Parents, 7th Report* (London: The Stationery Office).

Silver, H. (1994) 'Social Exclusion and Social Solidarity: Three Paradigms', *International Labour Review*, vol. 133(5/6), pp. 531–78.

Silver, H. (1995) 'Fighting Social Exclusion', in R. Wilson (ed.), *Social Exclusion. Social Inclusion* (Belfast: Democratic Dialogue).

Sparks, H. (1997) 'Dissident Citizenship: Democratic Theory, Political Courage and Activist Women', *Hypatia*, vol. 12(4), pp. 74–110.

UNRISD (1995) *States of Disarray: The Social Effects of Globalization* (Geneva: United Nations Research Institute for Social Development).

Walker, R. (1998) 'Unpicking Poverty', in C. Oppenheim (ed.), *An Inclusive Society: Strategies for Tackling Poverty* (London: IPPR).

White, M. and Forth, J. (1998) *Pathways through Employment* (York: Joseph Rowntree Foundation).

White, S. (1997) 'What do Egalitarians Want?' in J. Franklin (ed.), *Equality* (London: IPPR).

White, S. (1998) *The Economic Strategy of the 'New Centre-Left': A Contribution to the Nexus On-Line Discussion of the Economics of the Third Way* (Internet: Nexus Web Site).

Wilkinson, R. (1996) *Unhealthy Societies – The Afflictions of Inequality* (London: Routledge).

Young, I.M. (1997) 'Unruly Categories: A Critique of Nancy Fraser's Dual Systems Theory', *New Left Review*, vol. 222, pp. 147–60.

Zadek, S. and Thake, S. (1997) 'Send in the Social Entrepreneurs', *New Statesman* (20 June), p. 31.

4
Never Ending Story: Inclusion and Exclusion in Late Modernity

Angus Stewart

Let us begin with a paradox, which we may usefully label Grover's Paradox, after one of the seminal thinkers of our time, who for many years has fearlessly confronted many fundamental puzzles regarding the nature of human existence in the setting of Sesame Street. On one such occasion, while exploring the dialectical possibilities afforded by the swinging kitchen doors, the dark blue philosopher concluded that, 'When I am in, I am also out; in and out, go together, like left and right.'

Putting the matter more formally, Grover's Paradox points to a critical aspect of the terms inclusion and exclusion and of the substantive processes to which they refer: their relational character. Recognizing this leads to the further recognition that, throughout history, all the main axes of inclusion have been simultaneously axes of exclusion. That such continues to be the case in the contemporary world is easily indicated by a brief survey of the main current axes. Let me propose these as those of market, state, gender, race and religion. In each and every case, the basis of inclusion serves as a basis for exclusion.

Thus, in the case of that consumer freedom 'expressed' through the market, all are in principle free to dine at the Ritz, including the homeless who would occupy the neighbouring pavements, were it not for the fact that their presence would impinge upon the freedom of guests to dine untroubled by such a disturbing spectacle. In a world more and more subject to increasing commodification, everyone – from individuals to whole societies – is included in processes in which literally everything is for sale, from swimming pools to gene pools, provided they have the capacity to pay. If not, they are excluded, not merely from the acquisition and consumption of particular sensations and possibilities, but from what they are daily informed by a myriad of means is the embodiment of 'the good life'.

Similarly, in the case of the dominant mode of rule in the modern world, that of a state power conceived as a territorially segmented concentration of legitimate domination,[1] the inclusiveness of state-centred citizenship derives its very *raison d'être* from the fact that it simultaneously embodies exclusion.[2] Moreover, this relational character of inclusion and exclusion concerns not only the external relations of states but is also the predominant characteristic of their internal political organization. The hegemonic realization of state domination does not depend only upon the practical exclusion of large numbers of subjects from the political community, but also upon the symbolic identification of 'those who are to be excluded'.[3]

Yet again, if one accepts that gendering is a fundamentally social process, bearing complex and highly mediated relations with the material 'givens' of sexual differentiation, then clearly the historical realization of particular gender regimes involves a further institutional and cultural patterning of inclusion and exclusion.[4] So too do the power-informed convolutions of the social structuring of race and ethnicity rest upon a multiplicity of finely calibrated inclusions, the articulation of which critically depends upon diverse conceptions of the 'excluded other'. Finally, a plethora of examples, from the homicidal conflicts of Northern Ireland to the fundamentalist inspired law of return in Israel, provide irrefutable evidence that not merely religious differences but also 'shared' religions provide fertile ground for the exclusionary practices of inclusive communities.

In the late modern world, therefore, the warp and weft of inclusion and exclusion provide the typical broadcloth of social relations as much as at any time in recorded history. The historical significance of such a banality takes on sharper focus if we note additionally that the century which is shortly to end is at one and the same time the third century of the Enlightenment and that which has seen the rise and fall of the two most violently 'inclusionary/exclusionary' political regimes in world history. The possibilities and tensions referred to in the subtitle of the present volume may be argued to be most graphically captured in this contrast between the optimistic, emancipatory aspirations of the Enlightenment project and the brutal realities of twentieth century history.[5]

These broad historical strokes indicate that the value of any enquiry into the complicated realities of social inclusion depends upon the degree to which that enquiry is grounded in a particular historical context. In the present historical conjuncture, the most 'meaning-full' context within which to consider the possibilities for a coherent political project of social inclusion is provided by the constraints and possibilities embodied in the structures, identities, cultures and practices of late modernity.

The dominant ethos of late modernity

To proceed in this way requires recognition of the reality that the dominant intellectual ethos is defined by the exhaustion of 'grand narratives' and a postmodernist consensus about the inescapability and relativism of all regimes of power and emancipation.[6] Even among those committed to exploring and enacting projects of social inclusion, the dominant ethos has been such as to lead to the aban-donment of general models of social transformation, such as those articulated around ideas of egalitarianism, in favour of much more limited arguments concerning the disadvantaged situation of particular social constituencies. Alternatively, there are literally global arguments concerning the potential destruction of the human environment due to unregulated commercial exploitation or nuclear hazard arising from regional political fragmentation. In general terms, the imprint of the dominant ethos can be most clearly identified in a pervasive retreatism with respect to political and social purpos-iveness in favour of various forms of 'naturalistic realism', such as that expressed in a rhetoric of unstoppable global market forces or of an inescapable Darwinian utilitarianism currently paraded in the hard sell of genetic determinism.

Central to the defining core of this dominant ethos is the propo-sition, frequently a taken-for-granted assumption, that structured exclusion is inevitable. This proposition is equally central to dis-cussions of the consequences of the 'creative destruction' of capitalism, whether with respect to individuals, communities, regions or even whole societies, to characterizations of the futility of resistance in a social universe composed of a collage of incomparable regimes of power and knowledge, to arguments concerning the inevitable limi-tations upon democratic participation whether in a workplace or interest group by the 'realities' of economic or political efficiency, to pleas for 'tolerance' towards members of minority groups or towards those whose sexuality is not legitimated by the operative value system.[7] In each of these examples there is either an argument regarding the inevitability of certain forms of social exclusion or an implicit endorsement of degrees of social exclusion finding expression in calls for the toleration of difference and a complementary moderation of inclusionary demands.

This fatalistic and therefore passive stance towards the inevitability of exclusion and the consequent limitation upon projects of inclusion finds its complement in pessimistic readings of the dominant material and cultural tendencies of the age. Such readings retain the dialectical emphasis regarding the interplay between universalism and particularism characteristic of the dilemmas and debates surrounding the Enlightenment project. The contemporary reading, however, has an altogether bleaker hue. The Jekyllian tension between an abstracting but liberating universalism and a differentiating but identity-affirming particularism is now transformed into its Hydean opposite. The aspirations of the Enlightenment project towards a common universe for humankind are proposed to have found their terminus in the consumerist universalism of a globalizing homogeneity, while the contrapuntal plurality of traditional communities of recognition and endorsement emerge as the proliferating particularisms of mutually exclusionary, invented and frequently combatative traditions (as in Barber's contrast between 'McWorld' and communities of 'jihad'; Barber, 1996).

It is important to examine critically the fatalistic mythology generated within this cultural and political ethos. Such an examination involves two questions: the first concerns the basis of social order, the second the nature of political praxis in an inclusive society. Whatever the differences involved, the diverse conceptions of social inclusion have one element in common: a particular conception of social relations. Fundamentally, two such conceptions can be identified: the first views social relations as based on the principle of **the social contract**; the second proposes as the basis of social relations the very different principle of **the social compact** (Sklar, 1996: 156).

Social contracts have been integral to and definitive of modern market society. In such societies contracts embody 'economic relationships, exchanges, promises or commitments enforceable by law' (*ibid.*). The capacity to enter into such contracts has been the hallmark of full adult status and, as such, has been interwoven with the granting of full membership of the widest political community

(Marshall, 1950). 'Contracts are how business gets done in a capitalist economy' and, as Hayek argues, they form the basis of the market order. To the extent that social relationships generally are organized upon such a contractual model, they will reflect the possibilities and constraints inherent in such an economic order. Within the terms of Hirschman's useful distinction of different action possibilities in relation to social organization – possibilities of exit, voice and loyalty – power relations within a social order grounded in contractual relations are expressive of different abilities to exit or to mobilize individual and collective voice, as represented, for example, in possibilities of selling one's labour elsewhere or to effectively bargain over the distribution of reward (Hirschman, 1970; Offe, 1985).

In contrast to the emphasis on the relationship between discrete individuals of the social contract model, the model of the social compact focuses upon communality and the generation of power through communal action. Compacts involve the recognition of social relationships of *interdependence* and *mutuality* and prioritize solidarity and collective empowerment. Social compacts constitute and facilitate immanent communities of meaning and purpose. The goals which are generated within the framework of such communities are ultimately enforceable by moral or social persuasion rather than the formalities of law, although, as Hutton for example has extensively and correctly argued, legal regulation and institutional reform have an essential role to play in creating those contexts of action and meaning which facilitate relations of compact (Hutton, 1995).

Inclusion and exclusion in the social contract model

Within the terms of the social contract model, the axis of social inclusion/exclusion and the index of social integration revolves above all around *individual capacity* to enter into social contracts. This capacity is understood in terms of the resources and transferable skills available for contractual relations. The more widespread such capacity, the greater the degree of individual empowerment and the greater the degree of social inclusion. Conversely, the more limited such capacity, the more limited the degree of individual empowerment and the greater the degree of social exclusion.

This was the model at the centre of the New Right political agenda in the UK and the US during the 1980s. The causes of social exclusion were seen as arising from policies of state regulation and state provision and from the associated power of special interests. In combination, these policies and their institutional embodiment in the social democratic political project were seen as creating economic rigidity and welfare dependency, thereby limiting individual autonomy and choice on the one hand, and collective well-being on the other. Through the implementation of policies designed to remove these obstacles, the effectiveness of the market, the key institutional mechanism of social allocation, would be maximized, its working unimpeded by a flexible labour market. Individual autonomy and choice (conceptualized in the literature on power relations as 'power to') would widely spread through the acquisition of transferable skills and the diffusion of home and share ownership.

In the United Kingdom, the social contract model continues to be the dominant model at the centre of New Labour thinking and action in relation to social inclusion. Thus, the rationale of New Labour's 'welfare-to-work' policy is entirely consistent with an understanding of social inclusion in terms of labour market capacity. Similarly, the central emphasis upon preparation for the world of work in New Labour's educational thinking, not merely in terms of the acquisition of marketable skills but in the valorization of 'value added' as the overriding criterion for a meaningful educational process, offers a parallel endorsement of the contract model.

As a model of social order, the social contract model is defective in two main respects:

1 First, the model ignores the degree to which the acquisition of capacities to enter into contractual relations is not individual but *significantly structural and cumulative over generations*. To the extent that this is so, the contractual model is as much if not more a model of social exclusion as it is one of social inclusion.

2 In its emphasis upon empowerment through the market, the model ignores the second face of power, 'power over'; the unfettered operation of the market inevitably leads to great concentrations of capacity, concentrations of 'power to' which confer upon their holders the ability to dictate the terms upon which other social actors may exercise their stakes.[8]

Inclusion and exclusion in the social compact model

Within the terms of the social compact model, the central emphasis is upon collective rights and obligations determined through membership of communities and organizations. In Hirschman's terms, within this model power relations are expressive of entitlements of voice and the generation of parallel commitments of loyalty and obligation; in this way, participation, trust and legitimacy are inextricably bound up with one another. Thus, in a discussion of a stakeholding perspective which has provided an important focus for discussions of social inclusion and exclusion, the authors propose that:

> Stakeholders collectively exercise rights of voice which establish accountability and control. To be a stakeholder is to be *recognised* as having an interest in the decisions and actions of particular organisations and to claim as a result the rights of consultation, information and participation in decision making, while accepting that membership carries with it obligations.
>
> (Kelly, Kelly and Gamble, 1997: 240; emphasis mine)

The meaning and force of this conception of stakeholding rests on its proceeding from compact and not contract. Its practical significance rests upon the requirement for participation in decision-making.

The important emphasis in the social compact model on collective purposes and obligations requires clarification. The model does not require consensus on either purposes or means; rather its focus is upon collective empowerment through a shared participation in the determination of rights and obligations. Such participation is proposed to generate continuing loyalty to collective structures as a means of enhancing a plurality of individual and collective capacities and goals.

Central to the social compact model is a participatory conception of social inclusion. The effectiveness and viability of social relationships are seen to derive from that combination of voice and loyalty generated by means of what has been variously termed 'deliberative democracy' (Miller, 1993) or 'dialogic democracy' (Giddens, 1994). Both these terms refer to possibilities for addressing the central dilemma of social inclusion in modern societies: the need to reconcile demands for justice and the pursuit of adequate degrees of social cohesion with social plurality as an inherent and desirable social characteristic, a plurality necessarily involving very different conceptions of the good life.[9] Discussions of deliberative democracy must consequently recognize – and address – the connection between issues of 'power to' (the generation of collective capacity) and issues of 'power over' (on the one hand, the pursuit of viable structures of authority and, on the other, the avoidance of structures of domination, whether in the form of unfettered market relations, bureaucratic organizations or centralized state power.)

The conception of social exclusion in the social compact model is the logical and practical complement of the conception of social inclusion. Social exclusion therefore refers here to an absence of any meaningful participation in deliberative democracy.[10]

Political praxis in the inclusive society

The coherence of comprehensive projects of social inclusion depends upon the extent to which such projects involve an exemplary mode of political praxis. In late modernity there are two such modes, one expressive of the politics of 'the just society', the other expressive of the politics of the good life.

An inclusionary praxis of justice is directed towards an immanent political community generated by common action and expressive of collective rights and obligations. Such praxis seeks to overcome any and all obstacles to full participation in the political community, as in inequalities such as those of income, work situation, gender or minority status (whether of ethnicity or religion) which can be identified as sources of social exclusion. The praxis of social justice is egalitarian to the extent that it is directed towards the removal of inequalities that clearly obstruct full and meaningful participation in the determination of social outcomes; that is, *social justice concerns not just outcomes but process*. A meaningful equality of opportunity depends upon an absence of those inequalities which clearly preclude the possibility of participation in the processes of deliberative democracy.

In contrast, an inclusionary praxis of the good life is directed towards the realization of specific ethical communities, communities defined by the sharing of particular complexes of values. Given the plurality of the modern world, there are inevitably a wide diversity of such communities, both national and international. A praxis of social inclusion directed towards the realization of the good life is therefore expressive of the politics of difference. Since diverse ethical communities are necessarily and designedly exclusive, the crucial issue raised by an inclusionary praxis of the good life is how to reconcile diversity and justice, since the generalized equality of opportunity which governs the praxis of justice must

Bases of Social Order

		Social Contract	Social Compact
Modes of Political Praxis	Praxis of Justice	Liberal Society	Inclusive Society
	Praxis of the Good Life	Postmodern Orders	Communitarianism

Figure 4.1 **Frameworks of Social Inclusion**

necessarily be in tension with the specific differences expressive of the praxis of diverse conceptions of the good life.[11]

Combining these factors produces the possibilities indicated in the matrix of Figure 4.1, Frameworks of Social Inclusion. The top left-hand box, Liberal Society, specifies a model of social order in which the predominant form of social relations is that of social contract, while the predominant mode of political praxis is that concerned with the pursuit of social justice. The bottom left-hand box, Postmodern Social Orders, also involves the social contract model of social relations but in combination with a predominant mode of political praxis concerned with the pursuit of the good life. The bottom right-hand box, Communitarianism, represents the combination of a predominant model of social relations expressive of social compact with a mode of political praxis also concerned with the pursuit of the good life. Finally, the top right-hand box, that of Inclusive Society, represents the combination of a predominantly social compact form of social relations with a predominant mode of political praxis concerned with the realization of social justice.

There is a further broad distinction involved in the figure. This lies between the social types exemplified above the horizontal axis which represent different possibilities of engaging with systematic forms of inequality, and those types exemplified below the horizontal axis which represent different possibilities of engaging with the social pluralism, the 'differences' characteristic of modern societies. Overall, the typology seeks to engage with the critical dichotomy in modern politics between the politics of redistribution and the politics of identity.

Ideal types of inclusion

Contemporary political projects principally identifiable in terms of the type Liberal Society involve the acceptance of the autonomy of macro-level economic structures and processes.[12] They further involve an endorsement of the social contract model as the predominant mode of social relations and articulate policies in terms of their ability to optimize participation in such contractual relations. Here, examples of social exclusion deriving from an inequality of resources are identified as forms of exceptionalism, the product of obstacles (including inappropriate motivations) to full participation in market processes. Such examples are understood as potential or actual threats to the efficient functioning of the contract society and therefore to the realization of social cohesion. In a parallel manner, examples of racial discrimination, whether in terms of the labour market or disproportionately higher levels of physical assault, are also viewed as forms of exceptionalism, ultimately random expressions of individuated exclusionary acts rather than as symptoms of institutionalized racism. The understanding of social inclusion here is primarily in terms of social efficiency and social cohesion. Within such an understanding, single mothers are to be 'assisted' back into the labour market as the arbiter of real social inclusion, and the emphasis is upon the need to extend toleration to ethnic minorities rather than to ensure the effective implementation of a comprehensive system of justice. This context of meaning and practice requires that a praxis of justice be understood as primarily concerned with the allocation of the resources and the production and implementation of the rules necessary for efficient social functioning and adequate social cohesion.

If the ideal type Liberal Society is defined by the combination of the contractual self and a political praxis of liberal justice, the type Communitarianism is, in contradistinction, defined by the combination of relations of social compact and a praxis directed towards the good life. Consequent political projects set out both a critique of and remedy for the limitations and the proposed socially destructive consequences of the practical priorities embodied in the Liberal type.[13] Within this perspective, whereas relations of social contract exude 'a politics of self-interest undertaken by a freely choosing, rational agent . . . reborn, within the present order, as a sovereign consumer', relations of social compact emphasize the importance of historically and socially-situated selves inescapably constituted by their membership of networks of obligations and debts as much as they are bearers of rights. (Elstain, 1995: 104) Here, social inclusion is a comprehensive principle: social reality is argued to be constituted by a myriad of both ascribed and achieved communities of recognition and meaning, whether of kinship, class, ethnicity, place or purpose, the last viewed as rooted in one of the preceding. Equally, social exclusion is also a comprehensive principle in that it is not conceived as a function of inequalities of status and condition but rather as the product (whether by design or circumstance) of exclusion from those immanent communities of meaning which provide the context for individual human fulfilment and which are realized through the acceptance of mutuality.

A political praxis directed towards the social realization of the good life also provides part of the specification of the ideal type Postmodern Orders, which in the context of the pluralism of modernity valorizes a politics of difference. However, political projects identifiable in terms of this type are seen as contextualizing such projects within an uncontested framework of relations of social contract. As Habermas has proposed, the focus of such projects is upon issues generated by a concern with diverse 'grammars of life' as against a concern with issues of redistribution, a politics of difference as against a politics of inequality[14] (Habermas, 1987: viii, sect. 3). Universalist responses to inequalities of class, ethnicity or gender are rejected or subordinated to particularistic responses concerned with the removal of obstacles to specific definitions of the good life. This type involves a rejection of the adequacy of those forms of equality associated with the type Liberalism in producing the preconditions for the realization of specific forms of the good life. Thus, for example, various feminist projects stipulate not merely the inability of liberal justice to engage meaningfully with institutionalized forms of gender inequality, but propose the chronic complicity of this very 'universalism' in perpetuating such forms.

The ideal type Inclusive Society seeks to illuminate the conditions of and possibilities for social inclusion: here inclusion is specified primarily in terms of meaningful participation in processes of deliberative democracy. Here, political projects seeking to maximize social inclusion necessarily implicate a social compact, emphasizing the pursuit of common purposes and the sharing of collective rights and obligations. To that end, the type proposes a political praxis of social justice as the necessary complement to such relations of compact: the social realization of these relations depends upon a chronic pursuit of a comprehensive equality of opportunity to participate in collective determinations of social outcomes. This involves the recognition that a politics of inequality remains central to projects of social inclusion in two ways: first, in relation to the way in which diverse inequalities, such as class, gender and/or ethnicity, can be demonstrated to present obstacles to practical participation in substantive processes of deliberative democracy and, secondly, in relation to the way in which inequalities of power, such as those of capital control and state domination, necessarily provide important items for any democratic political agenda. Central to any political project conceived within these terms, therefore, is a contestation of the 'natural' and, by implication, unstoppable, character of critical aspects of the political terrain, whether they be the global economy, diverse political, social and civic inequalities or sociological 'laws' setting clear limits to democratic accountability and inclusive forms of participation.

Praxis of the good life

What then, within such a perspective, becomes of a praxis of the good life, of that politics of difference which forms such a striking feature of contemporary political discussion and analysis? From the perspective proposed here, an authentic engagement with the plurality of the world means that inclusionary projects, whether of government, movement or social network, will necessarily involve a praxis of the good life. There are clear limits upon the degree to which processes of deliberative democracy, insofar as they concern the communicative rationalization of competing normative claims can, in and of themselves, generate substantive ideals of the good society.[15] Evaluative judgements about the good society necessarily draw on a range of sources which can never be made fully conscious nor be fully rationalized. It is a central concern of the communitarian perspective to emphasize precisely this reality. However, the possibilities for a coherent conception of social inclusion set out here do not require that this limitation necessitates the adoption of a communitarian perspective. The specification of practical projects of social inclusion through processes of deliberative democracy within whatever context requires engagement with *the inescapable tension* between differing conceptions of the good life and competing claims of social justice.[16] The reality at this point in late modernity is that a praxis of justice concerned with the pursuit of practical norms of social inclusion – understood in terms of equality of opportunity for participation in processes of deliberative democracy – will necessarily engage in a critical interrogation of the values expressive of particular conceptions of the good life.

An excellent example of such a critical interrogation is to be found in Benhabib's discussion of the particular conception of social inclusion in modernity implicated in Habermas' notion of the public sphere (Benhabib, 1992: 89–120). Benhabib notes that, while formally matters of justice and those of the good life are distinct from the sociological distinction between the public and the private spheres, in practice there is a frequent conflation of religious and economic freedoms with the freedom of intimacy under the blanket title of 'private questions of the good life'. This conflation has given rise to two important consequences: first, contemporary normative moral and political theory has been gender blind, to the large extent to which it has ignored the issue of difference; that is, the difference in the experiences of male as opposed to female subjects in whatever sphere of social life. Secondly, there has been an absence of concern with the issue of power relations in the private realm. This analytic and practical neglect has meant that the rules determining the sexual division of labour in the private sphere, rules embodying and perpetuating diverse forms of inequality, have been largely placed beyond the scope of a praxis of justice. Thus, the implementation of such a praxis must necessarily be in tension with – indeed, in this instance, conflict with – the reproduction of a particular model of the good life:

> ... [W]hat were hitherto considered 'private' matters of the good life [become] 'public' issues of justice by thematising the asymmetrical power relations on which the sexual division of labour between the genders has rested. In this process, the line between the private and the public, between issues of justice and matters of the good life, is ... *renegotiated*.
>
> (*Ibid.*: 109; emphasis mine)

Both the possibilities and the tensions surrounding the pursuit of social inclusion arise from the necessarily chronic nature of such renegotiations. An understanding of social inclusion in terms of the pursuit of deliberative democracy involves the recognition and acceptance of the *historically situated and therefore contingent* character of prevailing institutional realizations of justice and concomitantly privileged conceptions of the good life obtaining at any point in time. The most important practical implication of such recognition concerns the limitations of the dominant site of political agency in late modernity, the territorial state.

As Connolly has persuasively argued, *'late modernity is a systemic time without a corresponding political place'* (Connolly, 1991: 215 emphasis mine; see also Held, 1993). Central to the specification of that time is a recognition of the globalization of capital, labour and contingency. This recognition brings with it a heightened awareness of 'the gap between the universalist pretensions of modern ideals and nagging doubts that the most distinctive achievements of modernity can ever be universalized to the entire world' (Connolly, 1991: 216). The democratic deficit of late modernity derives from the substantial absence of political sites within which these definitive issues may be democratically addressed. What Connolly identifies as 'the double-bind of late-modern democracy' derives from the twin realities that a state-centred, not to say state-dominated, democracy confines participation and accountability within the limits of territorial organization – limits specified by the widening gap between internal power and both internal and external efficacy – while control over such state-centred democracy via electoral mechanisms is dependent upon effectively denying these very limits[17] (1991: 217).

Social inclusion in late modernity

To specify social inclusion in late modernity in terms of deliberative democracy is to recognize that the constriction of even the potential of such democracy within the straitjacket of territorial organization generates largely exclusionary alternatives: either conceptions and practices of democracy remain tied to 'spaces of place' as embodied above all in the sovereign territorial state and therefore become increasingly implicated in projects of social cohesion directed to dealing with the consequences of social liberalization – what Connolly terms a 'politics of negation and exclusion'; or, alternatively, the attempt to create more effective political sites in the form of supranational bodies produces a widening gap with respect to democratic participation and accountability. The meaningful pursuit of inclusionary projects in late modernity requires a commitment to democratic practices which avoid the Scylla and Charybdis of state-centred democracy and supranational elitism respectively. This commitment can find expression, as Connolly argues, by supplementing and challenging structures of territorial democracy with a politics of non-territorial democratization of global issues (1991: 218).

The specification of inclusion and exclusion elaborated here focuses centrally upon the issues of political agency and efficacy within the context of the differentiation, plurality and globalization of contingency definitive of late modernity. Such a perspective is consistent with a 'participatory' as against an 'integrationist' response to the challenges of late modernity.[18] Whereas an integrationist response to the plurality characteristic of late modernity focuses upon possibilities for social solidarity through a politics of value reform attempting to reconcile personal and political ideals, the participationist view emphasizes the importance of institutional implementations of agency and efficacy as mechanisms of social inclusion. As Benhabib argues,

> the participationist view . . . does not see social differentiation as an aspect of modernity which needs to be overcome . . . the participationist advocates the reduction of contradictions and irrationalities among the various spheres, and the encouragement of non-exclusive principles of membership among the spheres.
> (Benhabib, 1992: 78)

A commitment to social inclusion in terms of a chronic pursuit of a politics of deliberative democracy therefore necessitates the equally chronic pursuit of a distributive justice of complex equality. Such a pursuit both addresses inequalities of class, gender, race and religion as structured obstacles to the effective exercise of political agency and control and confronts institutional forms of domination, whether economic, bureaucratic or cultural. Such a model of social inclusion requires acceptance of the contingent character of institutional arrangements as realizations of particular democratically generated projects and of their chronic availability for democratic critique and reform. It equally requires recognition and acceptance of the reality that all projects of inclusion have the capacity to generate new forms of exclusion available in their turn for democratic critique and reform.

Such are the possibilities and consequent tensions of the never-ending story of social inclusion in late modernity.

Notes

1 Ruggie (1993).
2 Brubaker (1992).
3 The categories of those who are practically excluded and those who are symbolically so are clearly not the same. The marginalization, indeed depression, of the former is a consequence of the realization through policies and practices of a particular set of political priorities. Symbolic exclusion, whether of the 'workshy', 'welfare scroungers', 'political agitators', 'degenerate races', 'predatory homosexuals', 'race fanatics', and so forth, involves a purposive implementation of political processes, of which the practical neutralization of political opposition is only part. The recent 'spectacle' of ethnic cleansing with its novel combination of ancient barbarities, global illumination and international impotence is merely one reminder that symbolic and practical exclusion easily incorporate physical humiliation, violation and extermination.
4 See, for example, Connell (1987).
5 One of the contributors to this volume has gone further than such a contrast, arguing for a direct link between at least one dimension of the Enlightenment project and the genocidal 'exclusions' of the Final Solution. See Bauman (1989).
6 See Lyotard (1984) and Dreyfus and Rainbow (1982).
7 On the 'creative destruction' of capitalism see Schumpeter (1934). The *fons et origo* of the futility of resistance argument in the contemporary era remains Michel Foucault. For a critical analysis of this position, its limitations and arguable dishonesty see, for example, Hoy (1986), especially the essays by Walzer and Taylor. This reality is not diluted, but merely complicated, by the growing literature on the 'late Foucault'. Too late for what, one might wonder?
8 See, for example, the discussion of individual capital concentration in Korten (1999).
9 For a wide-ranging discussion of the relevant issues, see Bohman and Rehg (1997), especially section I, 'The Idea of Deliberative Democracy'.
10 The question of meaningfulness necessarily involves both synchronic and diachronic elements; the former concerns the openness of deliberative processes with respect to a broad equality of opportunity for participation at given points in time, while the latter relates to an absence of any systematic inequality of outcomes over time.
11 Just one example of the complexities arising from the interplay of the praxes of justice and particular conceptions of the good life, respectively, is to be found in the paradoxes of Northern Ireland. Whereas, on the one hand, the Unionist majority boldly proclaim that justice demands the province's homogeneous incorporation within the legal framework of the United Kingdom, on the other hand they make common cause with the Catholic minority in demanding that the province remain exempt from the abortion law as it applies to the rest of the United Kingdom and in so doing set forth the case for the priority of a particular conception of the good life over a universalist determination of collective social justice.

12 Of course, the basis of such acceptance may vary quite widely. Major examples are arguments which propose economic processes as natural phenomena involving inevitable hierarchies of domination and reward, the facilitation of which will optimize social well-being but which equally involve inescapable processes of social exclusion and quite distinctive arguments which view the autonomy as arising from and the perpetuation of the extreme asymmetry of power between multinationals as collective actors on the one hand and states on the other.

13 Sandel (1984); Walzer (1990).

14 This is not to argue that Habermas formally privileges the politics of difference over the politics of inequality. Nevertheless, some of his critics, including some broadly sympathetic ones, have argued that his general position involves an abstraction from the realities of gender inequality both historical and contemporary. See, for example, N. Fraser (1996)

15 For a lucid discussion of this issue in the context of the arguments advanced by Habermas, see White (1988: p. 103).

16 Possible contexts are those of gender, family, workplace, locality, region, ethnicity, state and international arena. The suggestion is that, given the extent of communicative rationalization and the potential for transcending space and time by means of media at this point in the development of modernity, such contexts provide the possibility for the creation of a wide variety of immanent communities.

17 As Connolly notes, 'Who wants to elect representatives who concede the inefficacy of the unit they represent? or who call upon the state to revise priorities that currently provide the stable base of identity and unification for a majority coalition within it? or who compromise the principle of sovereignty through which the sense of the self-sufficiency of established institutions is secured?' (1991: p. 217).

18 For a discussion of integrationist versus participatory responses to modernity, see Benhabib (1992: p. 76 seq).

References

Barber, B. (1996) *Jihad vs. McWorld* (New York: Ballantine Books).

Bauman, Z. (1989) *Modernity and the Holocaust* (Cambridge: Polity Press).

Benhabib, S. (1992) *Situating the Self* (Cambridge: Polity Press).

Bohman, J. and Rehg, W. (1997) *Deliberative Democracy* (Cambridge, Mass.: MIT Press).

Brubaker, W.R. (1992) *Citizenship and Nationhood in France and Germany* (London: Harvard University Press).

Connell, R. (1987) *Gender and Power* (Cambridge: Polity Press).

Connolly, W. (1991) *Identity/Difference* (London: Cornell University Press).

Dreyfus, H. and Rainbow, P. (1982) *Michel Foucault: Beyond Structuralism and Hermeneutics* (Brighton: The Harvester Press).

Elstain, J. Bethke (1995) 'The Communitarian Individual', in A. Etzioni (ed.), *New Communitarian Thinking* (London: University Press of Virginia).

Fraser, N. (1996) *Justice Interruptus* (London: Routledge).

Giddens, A. (1994) *Beyond Left and Right* (Cambridge: Polity Press).

Habermas, J. (1987) *The Theory of Communicative Action*, Vol. II (Cambridge: Polity Press).

Hirschman, A. (1970) *Exit, Voice, and Loyalty* (Cambridge, Mass.: Harvard University Press).

Held, D. (1993) 'Democracy: From City-States to a Cosmopolitan Order?' in D. Held (ed.), *Prospects for Democracy* (Cambridge: Polity Press).

Hoy, D.C. (ed.) (1986) *Foucault: A Critical Reader* (Oxford: Blackwell).

Hutton, W. (1995) *The State We're In* (London: Jonathan Cape).

Kelly, G., Kelly, D. and Gamble, A. (eds) (1997) *Stakeholder Capitalism* (Basingstoke: Macmillan).

Korten, D. (1999) *The Post-Corporate World* (West Hartford, Conn.: Kumanan Press Inc.)

Lyotard, J. (1984) *The Postmodern Condition* (Manchester: Manchester University Press).

Marshall, T.H. (1963) 'Citizenship and Social Class', in *Sociology at the Crossroads* (London: Heinemann).

Miller, D. (1993) 'Deliberative Democracy and Social Choice', in D. Held (ed.), *Prospects for Democracy* (Cambridge: Polity Press).

Offe, C. (1985) *Disorganised Capitalism* (Cambridge: Polity Press).

Ruggie, J. (1993) 'Territoriality and Beyond: Problematising Modernity in International Relations', *International Organisation*, vol. 47 (1), pp. 139–74.

Sandel, M. (1984) *Liberalism and its Critics* (Oxford: Blackwell).

Schumpeter, J. (1934) *The Theory of Economic Development* (Cambridge, Mass.: Harvard University Press).

Sklar, R. (1996) 'Empire to the West: Red River', in J. Hillier and P. Wollen (eds), *Howard Hawks: American Artist* (London: British Film Institute).

Walzer, M. (1990) 'The Communitarian Critique of Liberalism', *Political Theory*, vol. 18 (1), pp. 6–23.

White, S.K. (1988) *The Recent Work of Jurgen Habermas* (Cambridge: Cambridge University Press).

5
What it Means 'To Be Excluded': Living to Stay Apart – or Together?

Zygmunt Bauman

In the last two years or so a tide of multiple murders has swept American schools and children's playgrounds; it shows no signs of ebbing yet. They are just steep rocky protrusions on a flat yet vast plateau of aggression stretching over the world, a murderous tip of the iceberg of violence. All these murders are described by journalists and viewed by their readers as senseless: devoid of motive and purpose. Murder is settling fast in the second place on the list of causes of young adults' death.

Murder is the ultimate, the irretractable form of exclusion. Its rising incidence signals a society in which the urge to separate, to isolate and to exclude must be as overwhelming as it is running deep. Perhaps this is why children killing children defy the cause-and-logic seeking reason: not for the shortage, but because of the surfeit of motives. The tide of hatred and violence is, so to speak, over-determined; the abundance of pressures makes singling out a single cause an exceedingly hard, but also, in the end, a superfluous task.

The understanding of complex phenomena may suffer from the mind's proclivity to simple, single-factor explanation. Svi Shapiro, professor of education from North Carolina, rightly warns against the widespread inclination to resort to evil as the explanation.[1] Yet 'evil' (of nature or nurture, of genes or acquired character) is a tempting explanation, difficult to resist – because it allows us to assimilate the horror without damaging the reassuring vision of an orderly and basically decent world: at all times and places evil people did evil things, and everywhere the evil people's monopoly on evil

73

absolves all the rest (and 'us' above all) from the suspicion of sharing the guilt and responsibility. Alas, the causes of the rising tide
of evil exploits among the young are many, intertwined and mutually reinforcing. There is hardly any reason to be amazed that the
victims of exclusion are the first to learn that excluding others,
and better still excluding them for good and so preventing them
from continuing the exclusive practices of their own, is the prime
tool of self-assertion.

The seeds of exclusion

Exclusion is, one may say, self-perpetuating. Once set in motion, it
acquires momentum of its own and needs few if any further in-
puts. But is it also self-igniting and self-propelling?

No, it is not. The first experience of the newly-born human is
(m)other – the other as the source and warrant, indeed the arche-
type, of *inclusion*: of sharing, caress and succour; of togetherness as
safety and reassurance. But then a long, bumpy road leads from
the comforting security of pristine inclusion to the frightful insecurity of 'mature' exclusion. Comparison and competition are the
milestones on that road. And comparison – compulsive and continuous comparison, of all and everyone with all and everyone
else – is the trademark of the era simultaneously electronic and
consumerist.

Paul Virilio has written recently of the 'social *tele*-proximity' which
elbows out and replaces the 'simply *social*' proximity of yore.[2] 'Tele-
proximity' means relentless thrusting of distant, in fact exterritorial
and spatially un-anchored images, into the life-world of every individual. The contents of the life-world no longer overlap with the
site of true proximity on which the seeds of a community could
sprout. The whole world has been opened for viewing. While the
realm of human bonds remains as local and confined as it always
was, the limits for comparison have been broken.

Electronically mediated images are free-floating; they precede, not
follow human bonds, and more often than not prevent the bonds
from incubating or, failing to do so, make sure that they are still-
born. The non-virtual others are cast as local condensations of global
or extra-spatial images – and thus fitting reference points in the
labour of universal comparison. The status of orientation points
helps to reduce the others to pure visibility – to visible surfaces.
Not that the appearances overshadow the 'true essences' of the

obsessively watched and enviously eyed human; it is, rather, that the visible surface has all but eaten up the 'issue' of 'true' or 'authentic' self and put paid to the very notion of 'true essence'.

It is no more the question of 'putting up appearances', that ancient and perhaps incurable human weakness. It is now the appearances that matter alone; they matter for their own sake. You *are* what you can show to possess, what you wear and what others see that you are consuming. The market, aided and abetted by the World Wide Web of electronic imagery, trades in *visibilities*. What emanates from that market to condense in the living condition of contemporary men and women, from their early childhood on, is (in the words of Benjamin R. Barber) a culture in which 'it is the habit which makes the monk' and in which 'the look has become the ideology of sorts', properly to be called 'videology', a culture of the company logos, of pop-stars, trade-marks and commercial jingles.[3]

As Jeremy Seabrook sums it all up in his own inimitable way,

> As money and what it can buy slowly colonizes greater and greater areas of our daily experience, this is accompanied by a growing dependency upon it . . . If the creation of wealth itself destroys and wastes humanity, that wealth, however vast, will never suffice to repair the ravages it has wrought . . . Money cannot cure what money has caused. . . .
>
> Once the basic cause of poverty is removed (absolute dearth of resources) this must be replaced by the development of an artificially created and subjective sense of insufficiency, for nothing could be more menacing to industrial society than that the people should declare themselves satisfied with what they have . . . The rich become objects of universal adoration.

Admired and adored they might be, which does not mean, though, that the rich are exempt from the universal blight of insufficiency. The rich differ from the poor and the not-so-rich not by being happier, let alone fulfilled, but by being able to select their means according to their goals instead of being forced to cut the goals to the size of means. 'Being rich' means enjoying the harmony between means and ends; being poor (or not rich enough) in the world of ubiquitous comparison means to desire what the means do not allow one to have while having no power to stop them from being desired.

Indeed, 'the poor do not inhabit a *separate culture* from the rich: they must live in the same world that has been contrived for the benefit of those with money. And their poverty is aggravated by economic growth, just as it is intensified by recession and non-growth'.[4] Some youths are lucky enough to get a pair of Nike sneakers in the shop; some others must kill to get them. But the first and the second alike cannot taste the job of the insiders until they parade the sneakers on their feet; and even then for a short time only, until 'new and improved' and certainly more demanding yet and costly conditions of 'inclusion' are set by the joint impact of videology and the commodity market.

But the rich and the poor live in *different spaces*; the space inhabited by the rich is global and virtual, the space of the poor is local and all-too-real for comfort. In the first space, reality is soft and pliable; the inhabitants may shape and re-shape it at will. Yet, there is hardly a hard-and-fast, let alone non-negotiable, borderline between the 'brute facts' of 'tough reality' and the infinite expanses of the flexible simulacra. The second space is full of borders and border guards, and the most tangible of borders are those between reality and fantasy.

Precarious present, uncertain future

Two spaces, indeed, ruled by sharply dissimilar logics, supplying different life experiences, gestating diverging life itineraries, and burdened with opposite definitions of similar behavioural codes. And yet both spaces are accommodated within the same world – and the world they are in is the world of vulnerability and precariousness.

The title of a paper given in December 1997 by one of the most incisive social analysts of our times, Pierre Bourdieu, was: *Le précarité est aujourd'hui partout.*[5] The title said it all: precariousness, instability, vulnerability is a most widespread (as well as the most painfully felt) feature of contemporary life conditions. The French theorists speak of *précarité*, the German of *Unsicherheit* and *Risikogesellschaft*, the Italians of *incertezza* and the English of *insecurity* – but all of them have in mind the same aspect of human predicament. The phenomenon which all these concepts try to grasp and envelop is the combined experience of insecurity (of position, entitlements and livelihood), of *uncertainty* (as to their continuation and future stability) and of un-safety (of one's body, one's self and their extensions: possessions, neighbourhood, community).

To start with the preliminary condition, livelihood. This has already become exceedingly fragile, but grows more brittle yet by the year. German economists write of 'zwei-Drittel Gesellschaft' and expect it to become soon an 'ein-Drittel' one, meaning that everything needed to satisfy the market demand can be produced now by two-thirds of the population. Soon one-third will be enough, leaving the rest of men and women without employment, making them *economically* useless and *socially* redundant. However brave are the faces the politicians make and however audacious their promises, unemployment in the affluent countries has become 'structural': there is simply not enough work for everybody. And technological progress – indeed, the rationalizing effort itself – brings ever fewer, not more jobs.

However brittle and uncertain the life of those already redundant has become does not take much imagination to adumbrate. Yet, psychologically at least, everybody else is also, indirectly, affected. Precariousness, Bourdieu points out, 'haunts consciousness and the subconscious'. In the world of structural unemployment no one can feel secure. No one may reasonably assume to be insured against the next round of 'downsizing', 'streamlining' or 'rationalizing', against erratic shifts of market demand and whimsical pressures of 'competitiveness', 'productivity', and 'cost-effectiveness'.

No one can therefore feel truly irreplaceable; even the most privileged position may prove to be 'until further notice'. In the absence of long-term security, 'instant gratification' looks therefore enticingly like a reasonable strategy. Whatever life may offer, let it offer it *hic et nunc* – right away. Who knows what tomorrow may bring? Delay of satisfaction has lost its allure: it is, after all, highly uncertain whether the labour and effort invested today will count as assets as long as it takes to reach reward; it is far from certain, moreover, that the prizes which look attractive today will still be desirable when they at long last come.

Precarious economic and social conditions train men and women to perceive the world as a container full of *disposable* objects, objects for *one-off* use. The whole world – including other human beings. Today's car mechanics are not trained in repairing broken or damaged engines – only in replacing the ready-made and sealed parts with others on the warehouse shelf. Of the inner structure of the exchanged parts they have little or no inkling; they do not consider it to be their responsibility or to lie within their field of competence.

Since present-day commitments stand in the way of next day opportunities, the lighter and more superficial they are, the lesser is the damage. 'Now' is the keyword of life strategy, whatever that strategy may refer to. Through an insecure and unpredictable world, smart and clever wanderers travel light. They seldom pause long enough to muse that human bonds are not like engine parts – that they hardly ever come ready-made, and are never hermetically sealed.

And so the policy of deliberate 'precarization' conducted by the operators of labour markets is aided and abetted by life policies. The result: falling apart and decomposing of human bonds, communities and partnerships. Commitments of the 'till death us do part' type become contracts 'until satisfaction lasts', temporal by definition and amenable to be broken unilaterally, whenever one of the partners sniffs better value in opting out rather than continuing the relationship.

Bonds of consumption

Bonds and partnerships are viewed, in other words, as things to be *consumed*, not produced; they are subject to the same criteria of evaluation as all other objects of consumption. In the consumer market, the ostensibly durable products are as a rule offered for a 'trial period'; return of money is promised if the purchaser is less than fully satisfied. If the partner in a partnership is seen in these terms, then it is no more the task of both partners to 'make the relationship work' – to see it work through thin and thick, 'through richer and poorer, in health and sickness' – to help each other through good and bad patches, to trim if need be one's own preferences, to compromise and make sacrifices for the sake of lasting union.

What follows is that the assumed temporariness of partnerships tends to turn into a self-fulfilling prophecy. If the human bond, like all other consumer objects, is not something to be worked out through protracted effort and occasional sacrifice, but something which one expects to bring satisfaction right away, at the moment of purchase – and something that one rejects if it does not satisfy, something to be kept and used only as long (and no longer) as it continues to gratify – then there is not much point in trying hard and harder still, let alone in suffering discomfort and unease in order to save the partnership. Precariousness of social existence inspires perception of the world around as an aggregate of products for immediate consumption. But perceiving the world, complete with its inhabitants, as the pool of consumer items, makes the negotiation of lasting human bonds exceedingly hard.

There is one more link between 'consumerization' of a precarious world and the disintegration of human bonds. Unlike production, consumption is a lonely activity; endemically and irredeemably lonely – even at such moments when it is conducted in company with others. Productive efforts require cooperation even if what they call for is just adding up raw muscular forces: if carrying a heavy log from one site to another takes eight men one hour, it does not follow than one man can do the same given eight (or any number of) hours. In the case of more complex tasks which involve a division of labour and call for diverse specialist skills which cannot blend in one person's know-how, the need for cooperation is even more obvious; without it, there won't be any chance for any product to emerge. It is the cooperation which makes the scattered and disparate efforts into productive ones. In the case of consumption, though, cooperation is not only unnecessary, but downright superfluous. Whatever is consumed is consumed individually, even in a crowded hall (in a touch of his versatile genius, Luis Buñuel showed eating, in *Phantom of Liberty*, to be, contrary to pretences, the most solitary – and secret – of activities, guarded from other people's inquisition . . .).

One may object to this assertion, pointing out that sometimes identical consumer desires may bring people together and could even gestate something reminiscent of (albeit short-lived) community. Pop concerts, festivals Woodstock-type or Saturday football gatherings come to mind immediately. We may observe, however, that in such and similar cases the illusion of community is conjured up for the duration of the event because it is the 'mass event', the crowd itself, and not the ostensible reason of gathering, which is the true object of consumption. In a world in which communal emotions are in short supply and more often than not prominent for their absences, there is steady consumer demand for *community substitutes*. The events under discussion meet the demand very well: they display all the trappings of community while remaining, like all other objects of consumption, disposable and meant to be used and used-up in one go. It is the appearance of community (reassuringly ephemeral), rather than the goods named on the bill-boards, that is sold, with huge profits, by the show-business produces of mass culture.

Privacy, shelter or prison

In his study under the telling-it-all title *Building Paranoia*, Steven Flusty noted in the cities of the United States of America the breath-taking explosion of ingenuity and a most frenetic building boom in a field unknown in the metropolitan areas of yore: that of the 'interdictory spaces' – 'designed to intercept and repel or filter would-be users'.[6] Indeed, the designing of 'spaces to bar access to spaces' seems to be the hottest preoccupation of American urban planners and the most profitable branch of the building industry. Flusty deploys his exquisite talent for precise and suggestive metaphors to distin-guish several varieties of such spaces which can best be seen as the contemporary equivalent of the moats and turrets which once pro-tected mediaeval castles (with the proviso, though, that while their middle-ages prototypes guarded the populated areas from an out-side wilderness, the present-day 'interdictory spaces' cut through the populated areas, defining the cut-off bits as wilderness and aban-doning them to the law of the jungle). Among the varieties named by Flusty, there is 'slippery space' – 'space that cannot be reached, due to contorted, protracted, or missing paths of approach'; 'prickly space' – 'space that cannot be comfortably occupied, defended by such details as wall-mounted sprinkler heads activated to clear loi-terers or ledges sloped to inhibit sitting'; or 'jittery space' – 'space that cannot be utilized unobserved due to active monitoring by roving patrols and/or remote technologies feeding to security sta-tions'. These and other 'interdictory spaces' put a final touch on the fairly advanced disintegration of locally-grounded forms of togetherness and a shared, communal living.

The boom in 'interdictory spaces' represents a wider tendency, most visible in American cities but affecting nowadays, to a vary-ing degree, all areas of dense occupation, those remote and mutant descendants of the ancient *polis*. The *polis* was held together by the *agora* or *forum* – that, in Cornelius Castoriadis's characteriza-tion, 'private/public spaces', where interests of private households met the communal standards of public good and the two engaged in a meaningful conversation – so that both the welfare of the community and citizens' liberties could be served simultaneously and in conjunction. It is this private-public space which finds itself today under assault in our cities. Access to some public spaces tends to be ever more qualified and conditional, while remaining public spaces turn into territories for private persons (at least those who have the means to avoid them) to shun.

In a development complementary to that of the spread of 'interdictory spaces', such private/public urban areas where the occupants of different residential areas could and wished to meet face-to-face, to engage in casual and more-than-casual encounters, accost and challenge one another, talk, quarrel, argue or agree, lifting their private problems to the level of public issues and making public issues into matters of private concern – are fast shrinking in size and number. The few that remain tend to be increasingly selective – adding strengths to, rather than repairing the damage done by, the pressures of disintegrating forces. As Steven Flusty puts it,

> Traditional public spaces are increasingly supplanted by privately produced (though often publicly subsidized), privately owned and administered spaces for public aggregation, that is, spaces of consumption . . . [A]ccess is predicated upon ability to pay . . . Exclusivity rules here, ensuring the high levels of control necessary to prevent irregularity, unpredictability, and inefficiency from interfering with the orderly flow of commerce.

The great divide

This is, arguably, the most bewildering paradox of our times, as the tendencies prevalent in sewing together and tearing apart of human bonding are concerned. On the one hand, as the World Wide Web of communication and the net of information flow gets tighter and more dense by the month, the surfers of the Internet spend an ever growing part of their lives in the global (or rather exterritorial), seamless space of universal participation; the material spaces in which the internet-surfers and all the others who reside in their daily mundane existence are ever more starkly split into the mutually-no-go, no-pass and particularly no-stay areas. In sharp opposition to the virtual space of the Internet, the material space of the city is ruled by separation, segregation, isolation and breaks of communication. In that material space, each gesture of inclusion is accompanied by the act of exclusion. The two spaces drift further and further apart, and so do the life experiences and the *Weltanschauungen* of their habitual dwellers.

The overall effect is a growing gap between the spiritual and material worlds; if expressed in sociological terms, the gap is one between the spiritually exterritorial 'spiritual elite' and the unredeemably local, indeed, *glaebe adscripti*, rest. The isolated and fenced-off sectors of urban space in which they dwell serve the elite as mere launching pads for cosmic travels in which most of their life is spent and where most of their world-view formed.

The globals have the best of both worlds: they feel secure in its closely guarded material residence, yet are free to fly (to seek another shelter) in the virtual space the moment their physical location gets too hot for comfort or too short of 'new and improved' temptations and amusements.

For the rest of the urban dwellers, the material part of the city in which they try to entrench themselves or to which they are confined is the most real of realities: the toughest and harshest among them. It dominates their lives and sets limits to their dreams of escape – limits all the more oppressive for the sweetness of the dreams. The world they occupy is marked primarily by borders, barriers and 'no trespassing' signs. A street too far is the forbidden territory; for a reckless or foolhardy vagrant, this is where the jungle starts. In this world, the sight of difference is the portent of danger, horrifying for being unfamiliar and unspeakable. It is also a command to retreat or a call to battle. The locals have the worst of both worlds: they can stroll through the paradise gardens of the virtual world only in their day- or night-dreams, while feeling nonstop utterly insecure and under constant threat of invasion in the real world in which they are incarcerated.

Little wonder that the elite and the rest, the globals and the locals, if they communicate at all, tend to speak nowadays past each other, rather than to engage in a conversation meaningful to both. They speak, after all, from different worlds. In the vocabulary of both, 'community' crops up fairly often – when the past bewailed or the hoped-for future are the topic. 'Community' stands for the congregation of like-minded and solidary people; for human warmth, for standing shoulder-to-shoulder, for the profusion of helping hands, for the neighbours unobtrusive, kind and friendly and the passers-by polite and smiling. It stands, in other words, for that security, certainty and safety without which all freedom to move and to experiment is devoid of charm and the courage is missing for *being* free (as distinct from *having* – being given or burdened with – freedom). This image shines through the word 'community' from whomever's lips it falls. But here the similarity between its different uses ends and the difference begins. The worlds referred to bifurcate and diverge.

The 'community' of the exterritorial (for all intents and purposes, *extraterrestrial*) elite (described recently by Denis Duclos as the 'new global class of salaried bourgeois' which undermines and threatens to displace the traditionally national middle classes) is imagined after the pattern of the soft world of the Internet: an inviting and hospitable land which throws its gates wide open to any one wishing to enter and having paid the monthly subscription.[7] The land of exciting adventure but no wild animals, or rather a sort of safari park explored from the safety of the armoured car. The land where being different, even bizarre, is not a liability but an asset, not a stigma but a sublime aesthetic experience. The land where travellers are brought together and gladly stay together not despite, but because of their differences and idiosyncrasies. The catchword is 'hybridity': cultures, traditions, accumulated experiences of many itineraries and dissimilar profiles meet, mix, fertilize and produce new unheard of, tradition-free styles and forms of life. Everyone in that 'community' is a 'hybrid' of sorts, though each is a hybrid of a somewhat different kind. Not being of a pure stock is the trait which unites all: a true tag of belonging. This trait also sets the community of the 'new global middle class' apart from the rest, stuck as they are in their respective localities and local histories, and thereby constitutes the cultural correlate of the globals' joint social exterritoriality.

The virtuality of global community differs starkly from the reality of local lives. Little of the new appetite for difference and love of cultural exchange and hybridity trickles down from the virtual community into the context of life conducted within local frames. Their effect boils down to the alerting of the 'locals' to the opportunities denied and the dangers impossible to repel: more exactly – to the opportunities which, once denied, turn into threats. What to the global elites is the chance to be enjoyed looks to the locals more like the conspiracy to be unmasked and fought back; a plot aimed at their livelihood, place in society, chances of a better life, and everything they have grown to like and cherish. In other words, what is the sunlit surfing beach for some, is the ominously rising flood-tides for others.

One of the most insightful analysts of urban life, Richard Sennett, has unraveled the links between the life conditions, life experiences and life strategies which stand behind such contradictory perceptions:

> Cries for law and order are greatest when the communities are
> most isolated from other people in the city . . .
>
>   Cities in America during the past two decades have grown in
> such a way that ethnic areas have become relatively homogene-
> ous; it appears no accident that the fear of the outsider has also
> grown to the extent that these ethnic communities have been
> cut off (Sennett, 1966: 194).[8]

In other words: homogeneity breeds fear of heterogeneity, and the
fear of heterogeneity breeds more homogeneity. A vicious circle –
if ever there was one.

> The 'we' feeling, which expresses the desire to be similar, is a
> way for men to avoid the necessity of looking deeper into each
> other (Sennett, 1966: 39) . . . The image of the community is
> purified of all that might convey a feeling of difference, let alone
> conflict, in who 'we' are. In this way the myth of community
> solidarity is a purification ritual (Sennett, 36).

Indeed, if not self-propelling, most definitely a self-perpetuating and
self-exacerbating process, from the moment it has been triggered
off. Communities of 'the like' are built of the desire for sameness.
That desire blinds the eye to the diversity of 'us' while simultaneously sharpening it to the otherness of 'them'.

Learning to live together in diversity

Twenty years ago René Girard considered hypothetically how a
hypothetical community could emerge in equally hypothetical pre-
social times when dissension was plentiful but scattered throughout
the population; when feud and violence, fed by cut-throat struggle
for survival, tore communities apart.[9] Trying to answer that question, Girard came forward with a self-consciously and deliberately
mythological account of the 'birth of unity'. The decisive step, Gerard
ruminated, must have been a selection of a victim in whose killing
all members of the population would take part, thereby becoming
united in murder – as co-perpetrators or accessories after the fact.
Only such a spontaneous act of coordinated action could blend
diffuse and dispersed enmities and condense the free-floating aggression into a clear division between propriety and impropriety,
legitimate and illegitimate violence, innocence and guilt. It could

(and did) bind the lonely (and frightened) beings into *solid* (and confident) community.

Girard's story is, let me emphasize, a fable, an etiological myth; a story which does not pretend historical truth, only aspires to make sense of the unknown Origins – to imbue the mystery of creation with a sort of psychological logic. Like other etiological myths, it does not tell us what actually did happen *in the past*; it is, rather, an attempt to make sense out of the *current* presence of a phenomenon which is bizarre, bewildering and difficult to explain, and to account for its continuous presence and re-birth. The true message of Girard's story is that *whenever* dissent is scattered and unfocused, and *whenever* mutual suspicion and hostility rule, the only way forward or back to communal solidarity, to a secure habitat, is to pick a joint enemy and to unite forces in an act of joint atrocity aimed at a common target.

Girard's is a sad and sordid story. But it goes some way towards 'making sense' of the resurgence of tribal hostility which does not seem reasonable nor relevant once the genuine causes of the current anxiety and fears are pondered. One should beware, however, of going too far, and to assume that its evident sense-making capacity renders Girard's story the only scenario which these anxieties and fears render plausible and feasible. There are other scenarios as well – like the one emphatically restated once more by John Rex; one of the 'public political culture and a political society based upon the idea of equality of opportunity, but often also on a conception of at least a minimum of social rights for all, that is, equality of outcome'.[10] We will be well-advised to remember that none of the alternative itineraries is a predetermined choice, that both are but plausible scenarios, and that the choice between them and the way they are staged depend each time on the actors who play the leading characters, but also on the crowds of anonymous extras and stagehands.

Despite the widespread tendency to self-entrenchment and wall-building, the coexistence of diverse traditions and also cultural variety in our part of the world is likely to increase rather than diminish. Cultural convergence, blending of cultures, assimilation of the weaker by the 'stronger' (that is power-supported) cultures is not however a feasible or likely prospect. It is becoming more and more evident that rather than as a battleground of complete and integrated 'cultures', of an aggregate of distinct *cultural totalities* engaged intermittently in mutual warfare or exchange, the present-day cultural stage is better seen as a matrix of cultural offers capable of end-lessly generating many and varied permutations. *Cultural plurality* does not have to mean *plurality of cultures*, even less (as Alain Touraine recently pointed out) does it have to mean plurality of *culture-defined communities.*[11] Whatever road to integration is chosen, it starts from diversity, leads through diversity and is unlikely to reach beyond it, at least not in a foreseeable future.

The choice between Girard's and Rex's scenarios is far from be-ing a matter of just academic interest. It involves the value which our civilization rightly considered to be the main, perhaps even the only, title to its glory: its past readiness to recognize sense and dignity in alternative ways of life, to seek and find grounds for peaceful and solidary coexistence which are not dependent on com-pliance with one homogeneous and uncontested pattern of life. The choice between scenarios is also deeply *ethical*; that choice determines whether the form of life which the chosen strategy is meant to preserve is worth defending in the first place. The future of humanity depends on our ability and willingness to learn to live with cultural diversity; on whether the issue of inclusion and the postulate of sameness can be set apart and held apart.

The struggle between the two scenarios is and will go on being fought (and over and over again, never conclusively decided) in the realm of the human condition, as defined by the interplay be-tween freedom and security. It is in the end through this condition that people perceive the world, complete with the other people with whom they share it; it is this condition that decides the like-lihood of adopting one or another life strategy and sets the limits to the freedom of choice between them. It is therefore an ethical imperative, arguably the most imperative of ethical imperatives in our life-time, to attend to the play of freedom and security in the human condition and seek the optimal balance between them.

If security without freedom feels like repulsive oppression, free-dom without security prompts one to dream of oppression as the miraculous cure for the pains of vulnerability. Richard Sennett re-minds us of the need of 'social situations that will weaken, as a man matures, the desire for controlled, purified experience'; situa-tions which would induce people to 'learn to tolerate painful ambiguity and uncertainty, and cause them 'to feel incomplete with-out a certain anarchy in their lives, to learn, as Denis de Rougemont says, to love the "otherness" among them'.[12] But calls to do just that would sound hollow, and prospects to make them audible would look nebulous as long as the precariousness, fragility and insecurity of human existence remain for the majority of people the primary and most evident of the 'facts of life', and a distant, yet tangible and not at all fanciful possibility for most or all of the others.

It so happens that learning to live with diversity is also the condition of coming to grips with the true causes of contemporary discontents. The option portrayed by Girard is not just cruel and inhuman – it is also *ineffective*. Only with that option out of the way will we be able to confront the genuine, deep roots of the fears and anxieties of which present-day discontents are born. The choice between exclusion and inclusion is cultural; but it is the social nature of society in which people live that makes the difference between the likely and the 'irrealistic' choices, and it is the political acumen of society which decides what the choice ultimately will be like.

Notes

1 Shapiro (1998), pp. 23–4.
2 See Virilo (1998), p. 20.
3 Barber (1988), pp. 14–5.
4 Seabrook (1988), pp. 1–2, 163, 164, 168–9 (my emphasis).
5 See Bourdieu (1998), pp. 95–101.
6 See Flusty, 'Building Paranoia' in *Architecture of Fear*, pp. 48–9, 51–2.
7 See Duclos (1988), pp. 16–17.
8 Sennett (1966), pp. 194, 39, 36.
9 See Girard (1977).
10 See Rex (1995).
11 See Touraine (1997), p. 292 ff.
12 Sennett (1966), p. 108.

References

Barber, B.R. (1988) 'Vers une société universelle de consommateurs: Culture McWorld contre démocratie', *Le Monde diplomatique* (August), pp. 14–5.
Bourdieu, P. (1998) *Contre-feux: Propos pour servir à la résistance contre l invasion néo-liberale* (Paris: Liber-Raisons d'Agir).
Duclos, D. (1998) 'Une nouvelle classe s'empare des levirs du pouvoir mondial: Naissance de l'hyperbourgeoisie', *Le Monde diplomatique* (August).
Flusty, S. (1997) 'Building Paranoia', in Nan Elin (ed.), *Architecture of Fear* (Princeton: Princeton Architectural Press).
Girard, R. (1977) *Double Business Bind* (Baltimore: University of Baltimore Press).
Rex, J. (1995) 'Ethnic Identity and the Nation State', *Social Identities*, vol. 1.
Seabrook, J. (1988) *The Race for Riches: The Human Cost of Wealth* (Basingstoke: Marshall Pickering).
Sennett, R. (1966) *The Uses of Disorder: Personal Identity and City Life* (London: Faber & Faber).

Shapiro, S. (1998) 'Killing Kids: The New Culture of Destruction', *Tikkun*, vol. 4

Touraine, A. (1977) 'Faux et vrais problèmes', in M. Wieviorka (ed.), *Une société fragmentée? Le multiculturisme en débat* (Paris: La Découverte).

Virilio, P. (1998) 'S'observer et se comparer sans cesse: La règne de la délation optique', *Le Monde diplomatique* (August).

6
Democratic Exclusion (and its Remedies?)

Charles Taylor

Democracy, particularly liberal democracy, is a great philosophy of inclusion. Rule of the people, by the people, for the people; and where 'people' is supposed to mean everybody. This offers the prospect of the most inclusive politics of human history. And yet, there is something in the dynamics of democracy which pushes to exclusion. I want in this chapter first to explore this dynamic, and then to look at various ways of compensating for it.

What makes democracy inclusive is that it is the government of all the people; what makes for exclusion is likewise, that it is the government of all the people. Exclusion is, paradoxically, the by-product of something else: the need in self-governing societies of a high degree of cohesion as well as a common identity. For the people to be sovereign, it needs to form an entity and have a personality.

The revolutions which ushered in regimes of popular sovereignty invented a new form of collective agency. This kind of agency was something unprecedented. The notion 'people' could certainly be applied to the ensemble of subjects of a premodern kingdom, but did not indicate an entity which could decide and act together, to whom one could attribute a will. Why does the new kind of entity with its attribute of common will need a strong form of cohesion? Is not the notion of popular sovereignty simply that of a majority will, more or less restrained by respect of liberty and rights?

Supposing that during a public lecture some people feel the heat oppressive and ask the windows to be opened; others demur. One might easily decide by a show of hands. Note that the audience might be the most disparate congerie, unknown to one another, just brought together by that event. Yet democratic societies have to be bonded more powerfully than a chance grouping. To push then the logic of popular sovereignty, note that it recommends a certain class of decision procedure: a procedure grounded on the majority (with restrictions). It also offers a particular justification; under a regime of popular sovereignty we are free in a way we are not under an absolute monarch, for instance.

We might see this from the standpoint of some individual. Let's say I am outvoted on some important issue, forced to abide by a rule I am opposed to. My will is not being done. Why should I consider myself free? Does it matter that I am overridden by the majority of my fellow citizens, as against the decisions of a monarch? Why should that be decisive? We can even imagine that a potential monarch, waiting to return to power in a coup, agrees with me on this question, against the majority. Wouldn't I then be freer after the counter-revolution? After all, my will on this matter would then be put into effect.

We can recognize that this kind of question is not merely a theoretical one. It regularly arises on behalf of sub-groups, for example national minorities, who see themselves as oppressed. Whatever one says, they cannot see themselves as part of the larger sovereign people, and they therefore see its rule over them as illegitimate, and this according to the logic of popular sovereignty itself. Here is the inner link between popular sovereignty and the idea of the people as a collective agency. This agency is something you can be included in without really belonging. The nature of this belonging becomes clearer if we ask what answer we can give to those who are outvoted and are tempted by the argument above.

Some extreme philosophical individualists believe that there is no valid answer, that appeals to some greater collective are just so much humbug to get contrary voters to accept voluntary servitude. But without deciding this ultimate philosophical issue, we can ask: what is the feature of our 'imagined communities' by which people very often do readily accept that they are free under a democratic régime, even where their will is overridden on important issues? The answer runs something like this: You, like the rest of us, are free just in virtue of the fact that we are ruling ourselves in common, and not being ruled by some agency which need take no account of us. Your freedom consists in your having a guaranteed voice in the sovereign, that you can be heard, and have some part in making the decision. You enjoy this freedom in virtue of a law which enfranchizes all of us, and so we enjoy this together. Your freedom is realized and defended by this law, whether you win or lose in any particular decision. This law defines a community; it defines a collective agency, a people whose acting together by the law preserves their freedom.

Such is the answer, valid or not, that people have come to accept in democratic societies. We can see right away that it involves their accepting a kind of belonging much stronger than the people in the lecture hall. It is an ongoing collective agency, one the membership in which realizes something very important, a kind of freedom. Insofar as this good is crucial to their identity, they thus identify strongly with this agency, and hence also feel a bond with their co-participants in this agency.

Only insofar as people accept some such answer can the legitimacy principle of popular sovereignty work to secure their consent. The principle is only effective via this appeal to a strong collective agency. If the identification with this is rejected, the rule of this government seems illegitimate in the eyes of the rejecters, as we see in countless cases with disaffected national minorities. Rule by the people, all right; but we can't accept rule by this lot, because we aren't part of their people. This is the inner link between democracy and strong common agency. It follows the logic of the legitimacy principle which underlies democratic régimes.

This example points to an important modulation of the appeal to popular sovereignty. It came to be accepted in many circles that a sovereign people, in order to have the unity needed for collective agency, had to already have an antecedent unity of culture, history or (more often in Europe) language of culture. And so behind the political nation there had to stand a preexisting cultural nation. Nationalism, in this sense, was born out of democracy as a benign or malignant growth.

Nationalism gives another modulation to popular sovereignty. The answer to the objector above: something essential to your identity is bound up in our common laws, now refers not just to republican freedom, but also to something of the order of cultural identity. What is defended and realized in the national state is not just your freedom as a human being, but this state also guarantees the expression of a common cultural identity. We can speak therefore of a 'republican' variant and a national variant, to popular sovereignty, though the two in practice often live together and lie undistinguished in democratic rhetoric and imagery. And so we have a new kind of collective agency with which its members identify as the realization/bulwark of their freedom, and/or the locus of their national/cultural expression.

A question can arise for the modern state for which there is no analogue in most premodern forms: what/whom is this state for? whose freedom? whose expression? The question seems to make no sense applied to, say, the Austrian or Turkish Empires – unless one answered the 'whom for?' question by referring to the Habsburg or Ottoman dynasties; and this would hardly give you their legitimating ideas.

The political identity of the modern state

This is the sense in which a modern state has what I want to call a political identity, defined as the generally accepted answer to the 'what/whom for?' question. This is distinct from the identities of its members, that is the reference points, many and varied, which for each of these defines what is important in their lives. There should be some overlap, of course, if these members are to feel strongly identified with the state. The identities of individuals and constituent groups will generally be richer and more complex, as well as often being quite different from each other.

The close connection between popular sovereignty, strong cohesion and political identity can also be shown in another way: the people concerned are supposed to rule; this means that the members of this 'people' make up a decision-making unit, a body which takes joint decisions. Moreover, it is supposed to take its decisions through a consensus, or at least a majority, of agents who are deemed equal and autonomous. It is not 'democratic' for some citizens to be under the control of others; it might facilitate decision-making, but it is not democratically legitimate.

In addition, to form a decision-making unit of the type demanded here it is not enough for a vote to record the fully formed opinions of all the members. These units must not only decide together, but deliberate together. A democratic state is constantly facing new questions, and in addition aspires to form a consensus on the questions that it has to decide, and not merely to reflect the outcome of diffuse opinions. However, a joint decision emerging from joint deliberation does not merely require everybody to vote according to his or her opinion. It is also necessary that each person's opinion should have been able to take shape or be reformed in the light of discussion, that is to say by exchange with others.

To some extent, the members must know one another, listen to one another and understand one another. If they are not acquainted, or if they cannot really understand one another, how can they engage in joint deliberation? This is a matter which concerns the very conditions of legitimacy of democratic states.

If, for example, a sub-group of the 'nation' considers that it is not being listened to by the rest, or that they are unable to understand its point of view, it will immediately consider itself excluded from joint deliberation. Popular sovereignty demands that we should live under laws which derive from such deliberation. Anyone who is excluded thereby has no part in the decisions which emerge and these lose their legitimacy for him. A sub-group, by the same token is no longer bound by the will of that nation. A people must thus be so constituted that its members are capable of listening to one another; or at least it should come close enough to that condition to ward off possible challenges to its democratic legitimacy from subgroups. This demands a certain reciprocal commitment. It is the shared consciousness of this commitment which creates confidence in the various sub-groups that they will be heard. A modern democratic state, then, demands a 'people' with a strong collective identity. Democracy obliges us to show much more commitment to one another than was demanded by the hierarchical and authoritative societies of yesteryear.

Thinkers in the civic humanist tradition, from Aristotle through to Arendt, have noted that free societies require a higher level of commitment and participation than despotic or authoritarian ones. Citizens have to do for themselves, as it were, what otherwise the rulers do for them. But this will only happen if these citizens feel a strong bond of identification with their political community, and hence with those who share with them in this.

From another angle again, because these societies require strong commitment to do the common work, and because a situation in which some carried the burdens of participation and others just enjoyed the benefits would be intolerable, free societies require a high level of mutual trust. In other words, they are extremely vulnerable to mistrust on the part of some citizens in relation to others, that the latter are not really assuming their commitments – for example that others are not paying their taxes, or are cheating on welfare, or as employers are benefiting from a good labour market without assuming any of the social costs. This kind of mistrust creates extreme tension, and threatens to unravel the whole skein of the mores of commitment.

Identity and exclusion

So there is a need for common identity, but how does this generate exclusion? In a host of possible ways.

1 The most tragic of these circumstances is also the most obvious, where a group which can't be assimilated to the reigning cohesion is brutally excluded; what we have come today to call 'ethnic cleansing'. But there are other cases where it doesn't come to such drastic expedients, but where exclusion is at work all the same against those whose difference threatens the dominant identity. I call this 'forced inclusion'; a kind of exclusion, which might seem a logical sleight of hand. It is saying in effect: as you are, or consider yourselves to be, you have no place here; that's why we are going to make you over. Or exclusion may take the form of chicanery, as in the old apartheid South Africa, where millions of Blacks were denied citizenship on the grounds that they were really citizens of 'homelands', external to the state.

All these modes of exclusion are motivated by the threat that others represent to the dominant political identity. But this threat depends on the fact that popular sovereignty is the regnant legitimacy idea of our time. It is hard to sustain a frankly hierarchical society in which groups are ranged in tiers, with some overtly marked as inferior or as subjects.

Hence the paradox that earlier conquering people were quite happy to coexist with vast numbers of subjects who were very different from them. The more the better. The early Muslim conquerors of the Ommeyad empire didn't press for conversion of their Christian subjects, they even mildly discouraged it. Within the bounds of this unequal disposition, earlier empires often had a very good record of 'multicultural' tolerance and coexistence under Akbar, which seem strikingly enlightened and humane compared to much of what goes on today in that part of the world and elsewhere.

The democratic age poses new obstacles to coexistence because it opens a new set of issues which may deeply divide people, those concerning the political identity of the state. In many parts of the Indian sub-continent, for instance, Hindus and Muslims did coexist in conditions of civility, even with a certain degree of syncretism, where later they would fight bitterly. What happened? The explanations often given include the British attempt to divide and rule, or even the British mania for census figures, which first made an issue of who was a majority where. These factors may have their importance, but clearly what makes them vital is the surrounding situation, in which political identity becomes an issue. Will it simply be that of the majority? Are we heading for Hindu Raj? Muslims ask for reassurance. Remember that Gandhi's and Nehru's proposals for a pan-Indian identity don't satisfy Jinnah. Suspicion grows, as do demands for guarantees, and ultimately separation.

Each side is mobilized to see the other as a political identity threat. This fear can then sometimes be transposed, through mechanisms we have yet to understand, into a threat to life; to which the response is savagery and counter-savagery, and the spiral which has become terribly familiar. Census figures can then be charged with ominous significance but only because, in the age of democracy, being in the majority has decisive importance.

2 Then there is the phenomenon we can sometimes see in immigrant societies with a high degree of historic ethnic unity. Commitment with the receiving population has been for so long bound up with the common language, culture, history, ancestry and so on, that it is difficult to adjust to a situation where the citizen body includes lots of people of other origins. The 'locals' feel a certain discomfort with this situation.

In one kind of case, the homogeneous society is reluctant to concede citizenship to outsiders. Germany is the best-known example of this, with its third generation Turkish 'Gastarbeiters', whose only fluent language may be German, whose only familiar home is in Frankfurt, but who are still resident aliens.

But there are subtler, and more ways in which this discomfort can be played out. Perhaps the outsiders automatically acquire citizenship after a standard period of waiting. There may even be an official policy of integrating them, widely agreed on by the members of the 'old-stock' population. But the 'insiders' are still so used to functioning politically among themselves, that they find it difficult to adjust. They don't quite know how to adjust yet; the new reflexes are difficult to find. For instance, they still discuss policy questions among themselves, in their electronic media and newspapers, as though immigrants were not a party to the debate. This example helps to illustrate just what is at stake here. I don't want to claim that democracy unfailingly leads to exclusion. That would be a counsel of despair and the situation is far from desperate. I also want to say that there is a drive in modern democracy towards inclusion, starting with the premise that government should be by all the people.

For a transition period, traditional society may have to forgo certain advantages which came from the tighter cohesion of yore. Québec clearly illustrates this. During recent agonizing attempts by the government to cut back the galloping budget deficits, the Premier organized 'summits' of decision-makers from business, labour and other segments of society. Not only the fact that this seemed worth trying, but the atmosphere of consensus, at least the earnest striving towards an agreement, these all reflected the extremely tightly-knit nature of Québec society as it has come down to us. The decision-makers are still disproportionately drawn from old-stock Québeckers, quite naturally at this stage of development. The operation might not be as easy to repeat twenty years from now.

So much for historically ethnically homogenous societies, but we have analogous phenomena in mixed societies. Think of the history of the United States, how successive waves of immigrants were perceived by many Americans of longer standing as a threat to democracy and the American way of life. Some of this was blind prejudice. But not all. The early Irish, and later European immigrants, couldn't integrate at once into American WASP political culture. The new immigrants often formed 'vote banks' for bosses and machines in the cities; and this was strongly resented and opposed by Progressives and others, concerned for what they understood to be citizen democracy. Here again, a transition was successfully navigated, and a new democracy emerged, although arguably at the price of the fading of the early ideals of a citizen republic and the triumph of the 'procedural republic', in Michael Sandel's language. But the temptation to exclusion was very strong for a time; and some of it was motivated by the commitment to democracy itself.

3 Exclusion can also operate along another axis. Just because of the importance of cohesion, and of a common understanding of political culture, democracies have sometimes attempted to force their citizens into a single mould. The 'Jacobin' tradition of the French Republic provides the best-known example of this. Here the strategy is, from the very beginning, to make people over in a rigorous and uncompromising way. Common understanding is reached, and supposedly forever maintained, by a clear definition

of what politics is about and what citizenship entails. Together these define the primary allegiance of citizens. This complex is then vigorously defended against all comers, ideological enemies, slackers, and, when the case arises, immigrants.

The exclusion operates here against other ways of being; a formula which forbids other ways of living modern citizenship and which castigates a way of living which would not subordinate other facets of identity to citizenship. In the particular case of France, for instance, a solution to the problems of religion in public life was adopted by radical Republicans, one of extrusion. The strength of this formula was that it managed for a long time to avoid or at least minimize the other kind of exclusion, that of new arrivals. It still surprises Frenchmen, and others, when they learn from Gérard Noiriel that one French person in four today has at least one grandparent born outside the country. France in this century has been an immigrant country without thinking of itself as such. The policy of assimilation worked totally with the Italians, Poles and Czechs who came between the wars. These people were never offered the choice of living their own traditional culture, and became indistinguishable from 'les Français de souche'.

It has been argued that another dimension of this kind of inner exclusion has operated along gender lines; and this not only in Jacobin societies, but in all liberal democracies where without exception women received voting rights later than men.

I hope I have made clear what I mean by the dynamic of exclusion in democracy. We might describe it as a temptation to exclude, beyond that which people may feel because of narrow sympathies or historic prejudice; a temptation which arises from the requirement of democratic rule for a high degree of mutual understanding, trust and commitment. This can make it hard to integrate outsiders. It can also tempt us to what I have called 'inner exclusion', the creation of a common identity around a rigid formula of politics and citizenship, which refuses to accommodate any alternatives and imperiously demands the subordination of other aspects of citizens' identities. So, societies based on inner exclusion may come to turn away outsiders, as the strength of the Front National in France, alas, illustrates; societies whose main historical challenge has been the integration of outsiders may have recourse to inner exclusion in an attempt to create some unity amid all the diversity.

Now the obvious fact about our era is that, first, the challenge of the new arrival is becoming generalized and multiplied in all democratic societies. The scope and rate of international migration is making all societies increasingly 'multicultural'; while, second, the response to this challenge of the 'Jacobin' sort, a rigorous assimilation to a formula involving fairly intense inner exclusion, is becoming less and less sustainable.

This last point is not easy to explain, but it seems to me an undeniable fact. There has been a subtle switch in mind-set in our civilization, probably coinciding with the 1960s. The idea that one ought to suppress one's difference for the sake of fitting into a dominant mould, defined as the established way in one's society, has been considerably eroded. Feminists, cultural minorities, homosexuals and some religious groups, all demand that the reigning formula be modified to accommodate them, rather than the other way around.

At the same time, possibly connected to this first change, but certainly with its own roots, has come another.

The difference between the earlier near-total success of France in assimilating East Europeans and others (who ever thought of Yves Montand as Italian?), and the present great difficulty with Maghrébains, doubtless depends upon other factors – for example, greater cultural-religious difference, and the collapse of full employment – but nevertheless must also reflect the new attitude among migrants. The earlier sense of unalloyed gratitude towards the new countries of refuge and opportunity has been replaced by something harder to define. One is almost tempted to say, by something resembling the old doctrine which is central to many religions, that the earth has been given to the human species in common. A given space doesn't just unqualifiedly belong to the people born in it, so it isn't simply theirs to give. In return for entry, one is not morally bound to accept just any condition they impose.

Two new features arise from this shift. First, the perception I attributed to Hispanics in the USA has become widespread, namely, the idea that the culture they are joining is something in continual evolution, and that they have a chance to codetermine it in the future. This, instead of simply one-way assimilation, is more and more becoming the (often unspoken) understanding behind the act of migration.

Secondly, we have an intensification of a long-established phenomenon, which now seems fully 'normal', where certain immigrant groups still function morally, culturally and politically as a 'diaspora', whilst aspiring to full identity with their receiving society. Whereas people muttered darkly in the past about 'double allegiance', I believe now that this kind of behaviour is coming to be seen as normal. It is becoming more and more normal and unchallenged to think of oneself and be thought of as, say, a Canadian in good standing, while being heavily involved in the fate of some country of origin.

And yet exclusion, besides being profoundly morally objectionable, also goes against the legitimacy idea of popular sovereignty, which is to realize the government of all the people. The need to form a people as a collective agent runs against the demand for inclusion of all who have a legitimate claim on citizenship. What are the remedies? I believe that an important first step is to recognize the dilemma. For this allows us to see that it can very often only be dealt with by struggling towards a creative redefinition of our political identity. The dilemma arises because some often historically hallowed definition can't accommodate all who have a moral claim to citizenship.

This appeal to the origins can occur in both 'republican' and 'national' registers.

Sharing identity space

The reflex of many people in liberal societies to this kind of thing is to blame 'nationalism' and not democracy. But this is to take too quick a way with it. To start with, 'nationalism' has many senses. The original idea, for instance in its Herderian form, was a liberating one, and highly consonant with democracy. We don't have to force ourselves into an artificial homogeneity in order to live together in peace. We can recognize different 'national' (Volk) identities, even give them political expression, because each in this act of recognition acknowledges that it is not universal, that it has to coexist with others which are equally legitimate. Herderian nationalism is a universalist idea, all Völker are equally worthy of respect.

What this pushes us towards is the idea which I believe is the key to facing the dilemma of exclusion creatively, the idea of sharing identity space. Political identities have to be worked out, negotiated, creatively compromised between peoples who have to or want to live together under the same political roof (and this coexistence is always grounded in some mixture of necessity and choice). Moreover, these solutions are never meant to last for ever, but have to be discovered/invented anew by succeeding generations.

The idea of nationalism which creates bitter trouble is that defined by Gellner: the 'political principle, which holds that the political and national unit should be congruent'. According to this idea, the problem of how to share identity space can be solved by giving each nation its territory on which it can erect its sovereign state. The utopian, even absurd, nature of the proposal immediately strikes the eye and could only be carried through by massive ethnic cleansing. It is clear that this idea will only 'work' by making certain groups more equal than others. The unreal idea of a definitive solution to the problem of democratic coexistence is blinding people to the effective situation on the ground in almost all democratic states. The hope is once again to arrest history, to fix it in some original moment when our people attached themselves to territory. And, similarly, what offers itself as a solution to the democratic dilemma can only exacerbate it to the point of bitter conflict.

In face of the prospect of having to bring together so many differences of culture, origin, political experience and identity, the temptation is naturally to define the common understanding more and more in terms of 'liberalism', rather than by reference to the identities of citizens. The focus should be totally on individual rights and democratic and legal procedures, rather than on the historical-cultural reference points, or the ideas of the good life by which citizens define their own identities. In short, the temptation is to go for what Sandel calls the 'procedural republic'.

What does the procedural republic have going for it? I have discussed this elsewhere, but I think we can both see and understand the drift away from ethics of the good life towards ethics based on something else, allegedly less contentious, and easier to carry general agreement. This partly explains the popularity of both utilitarianism, and Kantian-derived deontological theories. Both manage to abstract from issues of what kind of life is more worthy, more admirable, more human, and to fall back on what seems more solid ground. In one case we count all the preferences and focus on the rights of the preferring agent.

The act of abstraction here benefits from three important considerations. First, in an age of (at least menacing, if not actual) scepticism about moral views, it retreats from the terrain where the arguments seem most dependent on our interpretations, and most incapable of winning universal assent; whereas we can presumably all agree that, other things being equal, it is better to let people have what they want or to respect their freedom to choose. Second, this refusal to adopt a particular view of the good life leaves it to the individual to make the choice, and hence it fits in with the anti-paternalism of the modern age. It enshrines a kind of freedom. Third, in face of the tremendous differences of outlook in modern society, utilitarianism and Kantian deontology seem to promise a way of deciding the issues we face in common without having to espouse the views of some against others.

Now the first two considerations are based on philosophical arguments – about what can and cannot be known and proved. But the third is a political argument. Regardless of who is ultimately right in the battle between procedural ethics and those of the good life, we could conceivably be convinced on political grounds that the best political formula for democratic government of a complex society was a kind of neutral liberalism. And this is where the argument has mainly gone today. The shift in Rawls' position is a clear example of this. His theory of justice is now presented as 'political, not metaphysical'. This shift perhaps comes in part from the difficulties that the purely philosophical arguments run into. But it also corresponds to the universal perception that diversity is a more important and crucial dimension of contemporary society. This comes partly from the actual growth in diversity in the population through, say, international migration; and partly from the growing demand that age-old diversities be taken seriously, put forward, for instance, by feminists.

So the issue now could be: what conceptions of freedom, of equality, of fairness, and of the basis for social coexistence are – not right in the abstract, but feasible for modern democratic societies? How can people live together in difference, granted that this will be in a democratic régime, under conditions of fairness and equality? The procedural republic starts right off with a big advantage. If in your understanding of the citizen's roles and rights you abstract from any view of the good life, then you avoid endorsing the views of some at the expense of others. Now no-one in their right mind today would deny that this is an important dimension of any liberal society. The right to vote, for instance, is indeed accorded unconditionally; or on condition of certain bases of citizenship.

However, it can look immediately that whatever other reasons there might be for treating people this way, at least it facilitates our coming together and feeling ourselves to be part of a common enterprise. But this retreat to the procedural is no solution to the democratic dilemma. On the contrary, it very often itself contributes to activating it.

The procedural route supposes that we can uncontroversially distinguish neutral procedures from substantive goals. But it is in fact very difficult to devise a procedure which is seen as neutral by everyone. The point about procedure, or charters of rights, or distributive principles, is that they are meant not to enter into the knotty terrain of substantive differences in ways of life. But there is no way in practice of ensuring that this will be so. The mistake here is to believe that there can be some decision whose neutrality is guaranteed by its emerging from some principle or procedure. This breeds the illusion that there is no need to negotiate the place of these symbols, and hence to confront the actual substantive differences of religious allegiance in the public square. But no procedure can dispense from the need to share identity space. Moreover, as against a political solution based on negotiation and compromise between competing demands, this provides no opportunity for people on each side to look into the substance of the other's case.

My argument here has been that a full understanding of the dilemma of democratic exclusion shows that there is no alternative to what I have called sharing identity space. This means negotiating a commonly acceptable, even compromise political identity between the different personal or group identities which want to/ have to live in the polity. Some things will, of course, have to be non-negotiable, the basic principles of republican constitutions – democracy itself and human rights, among them. But this firmness has to be accompanied by a recognition that these principles can be realized in a number of different ways, and can never be applied neutrally without some confronting of the substantive religious–ethnic–cultural differences in societies.

There are not too many things that one can say in utter generality. Solutions have to be tailored to particular situations. But some of the political mechanisms of this sharing are already well-known; for example various brands of federalism, as well as the design of forms of special status for minority societies such as we see today in Scotland and Catalonia, for instance. But many other modalities remain to be devised for the still more diverse democratic societies of the twenty-first century.

In the meantime, it will have helped, I believe, if we can perceive more clearly and starkly the nature of our democratic dilemma, since the hold of unreal and ahistorical solutions over our minds and imagination is still crippling our efforts to deal with the growing conflicts which arise from it.

7

The Ground of Inclusiveness

Peter Askonas

'Ich lebe mein Leben in wachsenden Ringen
die sich um die werdenden Dinge ziehn
Ich werde den letzten nicht vollbringen,
Aber versuchen will ich ihn.'

Rainer Maria Rilke[1]

'I am living my life in expanding circles
Encompass the Things in their becoming;
The last of these I shall not complete,
But its achievement I will assay.'

Introduction

Clarifications: how methaphysics and theology can enrich political analysis

Like John Gray in the opening chapter, I propose to submit the concept of inclusiveness to a radical critique. But it is bound to reverberate in a different tonality. A theologically orientated enquiry does not take place in the harsh, at times chilling, light of empirical analysis used by the social sciences. It is cultivated in the intimacy of inner gazing, with all that this implies by way of misconception, even folly and perplexity in the face of the unutterable. Not that a theology of society worth its salt can be unrelated to the immediacy of economics, sociology and politics and to the extended here-and-now with its impact on human beings; but this dimension of 'now' is enriched by a sense of 'beyond now'.

Like Professor Gray also, and like several other contributors, I start by offering a phenomenology of Inclusiveness. I see it as a web of dispositions: a readiness to respond constructively to the basic human need summed up by the words 'I count'. This implies new supporting structures at different focal points of socioeconomic activity. I suggest, moreover, that inclusiveness must extend over a wider range of contexts than the purely sociological and economic ones. Progression towards an inclusive society can come about only if responsiveness towards 'I count' flourishes throughout the entire gamut of human-ness. My definition aims to dispose of the many purely utilitarian ones now in fashion. It demands much more than a facile egalitarian optimism, or appeal to traditional socialist sentiment.

Inclusion, and hence the Inclusive Society, is not a static, once-and-for-all definable condition. It is part of a dynamic, evolving process. I call it *social becoming*, a key concept in this essay. Note that colloquially *becoming* has strong overtones of *becoming more*. But the alternative of *becoming less* is ever present. Any social philosophy has to take very seriously this two-fold reality and its implicit uncertainty.

Whilst most of my colleagues in our book reason on pragmatic lines, I propose in this chapter to consider the essence of social becoming and of movement towards inclusiveness. What meaning can be perceived in the chain of events which we call social evolution? What is the latter's foundation and its end? Thereby it should become clearer whether inclusiveness does truly correspond to a reality at the basic level of how things are. In turn, this should enable us to judge whether inclusiveness is worth achieving, and whether its achievement is a possibility.

Inevitably such questions postulate epistemological ones. How and by what processes can reflections of this order have any significant impact on the actual unfolding of political processes? What mode of expression is comprehensible today? Can such reflections exercise a normative influence in high modernity?[2] The prevailing sceptical outlook makes this a particularly acute challenge. Nor do I disregard the objections to any philosophical or theological approach which presupposes that metaphysics contributes extra depth to the enquiry. Yet, as I see it, to have, before our eyes, end and meaning is the precondition of a dynamic social model capable of giving shape to what at present is largely shapeless, disordered.

A unifying framework

Politicians of the day project the notion Inclusive Society as if they had discovered a new concept. Yet inclusiveness is nothing new. Only the parameters have been widened. Inclusiveness has been a constituent of the bundle of conditions supporting human survival, from the dim past onwards. In cultural history throughout the millenia this theme has contributed significantly to the evolution of civilization. Inclusiveness has been a catalyst in the emergent world pictures. Particularly since the Enlightenment it has given shape to a welter of social models. Thus throughout the variety of political connotations of society there persists the age old 'Immortal Longing'[3] for some kind of Universal Harmony, perhaps seen as Reign of God, or convergence of *'homini bonae voluntatis'*.[4] Now once again 'Search for a Better – More Inclusive World' has become a major communal and political preoccupation.

Whatever the shape assumed by the overall historical narrative and notwithstanding the current unfashionableness of unifying worldviews, a pattern of continuity can be recognizable, at least *a posteriori*; albeit in fits and starts, false starts included; untidy and unpredictable like all human endeavour. To evaluate the Inclusive Society, we need to empathize with that setting: continuity, at times discontinued, but perennially reappearing.

Exclusion too is a perennial component of human agency. Within unsophisticated societies it would even have been a factor making for internal cohesion, and thereby for survival. But simultaneously to the maturing of inclusiveness, and whilst richer modalities emerge, exclusion becomes more unequivocally negative. Observe the transformation from primitive tribalist exclusion of the intruder, to racialism in modernity where necessity imposed by survival is replaced by more complex and more sinister drives.

Against this background I will consider ambivalence, a reality with defining impact on the shape of any possible sociopolitical model, on the degree of freedom in shaping it, and on the possibility of achieving success. If I stray into 'grand' ideas – some would say vague ideas – I do so as a reaction to the current obsession with scientism and neatly fitting academic minutiae which in the end do not fit well enough to provide meaning. Reader, please be patient with an unavoidably cavalier method.

Social becoming: movement towards the inclusive model, or away from it

'Becoming', in most people's minds points towards progressing, opening up, transition to completion. If we look at the phenomenon 'from the heart' we perceive a basic, but often unarticulated human need, the need for hope for a richer more meaningful condition. Inclusion is very much part of this aspiration. Another approach to **becoming**, especially Social Becoming is to recognize it as an ongoing process. When **becoming more** is actualized, the potential for further becoming expands. New patterns appear. In their turn they can give tangible shape to what has only been latent. Recognition of the possibilities offered by inclusiveness advances as inclusiveness itself does. These might imply a changed capacity for dealing with complexity – dealing with globalization is a prime example – greater harmonized interaction. Or another instance: we can now identify with the sentiments of distant peoples. This, in turn will bring about an expansion of consciousness. Teilhard de Chardin, philosopher and visionary, has coined the term hominization for these processes.[5]

A variety of formulations for 'social becoming' present themselves. Foremost to my mind it is 'a process of straining to reach out beyond personal limitations and towards transcendent reality'. Hand in hand with this idea goes that of 'movement toward a telos (end)'. Or again: 'progression towards accomplishment of identity at an elevated level'; meaning progression unrestricted by quantifiable categories; or simultaneously regression into the subhuman.

Social *becoming* manifests itself as

- movement from compulsion to consent;
- transformation of human dispositions: from the tendency of clinging to passivity, instead of rising to the role of living freely consenting and creative agents;
- a psychological perspective. For example, Alexander Maslow describes a series of advancing stages.[6] Kohlberg, in a similar context, describes human development in progressive ethical categories.[7]
- Lastly, to take account of the metaphysical content, I suggest: Social becoming signifies being increasingly in tune with a unifying current at the core of existence.

We are conscience bound to take cognizance of postmodern scepticism to which these propositions are antithetical. In this language 'social becoming' might read: 'mere surface ripples on a flow of existence, the meaning of which escapes us'. Or: cyclical states of eruption and subsequent stagnation.

It cannot be stressed enough that 'becoming' is bonded to a shadow side. The narratives of 'becoming' have to include becoming less, un-becoming reversal, distortion of purpose, freezing of dynamic social relationship. The latter is illustrated most trenchantly by the structures of totalitarian states. Or to take us right into today's not-so-brave world, un-becoming is exemplified by 'management' of thought and consumer behaviour with consequent blunting of sensibilities.

History can easily be read as a perpetual wavering between *becoming* and *un-becoming*, but simultaneously also as thrust to promote inclusion and restrain exclusion and its negative dynamics. Thus the signs of our times, say power concentration in the marketplace, are evidently symptoms of progressive exclusion and of decline into *un-becoming*. Even so, when looking at a tortuous and largely unpredictable evolution, eventual progression towards yet another of many 'expanding circle' is within the compass of hope.

Rilke's intuition – see the opening lines of the chapter – has much to commend it.

Ambivalence, particularly in the contemporary situation: obstacle to social becoming

A mass of stories of ambivalence can be told, so familiar that a few headings suffice.

- The cost-cutting icon:
  beneficent outcomes – more affordable products for a broader (more inclusive) constituency; better use of (scarce) resources; increased profitability, possibly of benefit for the non-stakeholder, such as alternative investment, fiscal revenues;
  harmful outcomes – job losses, insecurity, lowering of quality, depersonalized service.
- Mobility:
  beneficent outcomes – facilitating close personal contact; widening of horizons; diminishment of divisive prejudice;
  harmful outcomes – footlooseness, both in material and cultural terms.

Then there are the stories with unequivocally negative impact:
- Progressive deterioration of care and exclusion of the aged;
- Increasing disparities of remunerations, out of proportion to social values.

And simultaneously yet other stories with unequivocally positive consequence:

- A growing sense of solidarity with victims of the world's ills.
- Persistence in searching for participative social and corporate models.

These, read together with the negative accounts, illustrate the overall ambivalence of human enterprise.

So, it is reasonable to assert that the totality of these narratives which characterize social and political evolution, is essentially ambivalent too. This ambivalence results in a pattern of perpetual tensions. It can be argued that this tension is itself favourable to social becoming.

Ambivalence is inherent not only in political and economic processes, but in their instrumental agent, humanity or, colloquially, *human nature*. Careful. This terms calls for discernment. Too often it is used with the implication that this *nature* is a given, something uniform and constant, functioning in a particular way once and for all and in any setting: a misconception of popular discourse, of course. We must resist absolute statements on the subject like: it is human nature to behave in this way or that, say to be acquisitive, or 'to obey the law of the jungle', as if these were pervasive behaviour patterns without valid alternatives. Such discourse disregards moral ambivalence, an essential element of human 'nature' properly understood. The resulting arguments are misused to justify certain economic and political theories. It needs firm reminders that human nature includes the tendency to be generous as well as grasping; not just to take but to give; or to create as well as to destroy.

No need here to enlarge on psychological complexity as a major contributing factor. But let me draw attention to two other significant components of human-ness, those of unpredictability and self-contradiction. A human agent faced by a particular situation has a wide-ranging capacity to act either for good or for ill, yet this capacity and the resultant choices can be in contradiction to what might be expected of such-and-such a person. Coexistence of rationality and irrationality in economic and social activity is insufficiently recognized. These are mighty factors influencing events in the public arena where positive (good) acts and negative ('ill') acts are constantly intertwined to the point where they and their motives defy identification, let alone prognosis. (Good is equated here with *becoming*, and ill with *un-becoming*, undoing.) This statement should not be understood to imply moral agnosticism. Just beware of simplistic models and fast-acting prescriptions.

Determinization in economic affairs: one of several processes affecting social becoming

Crucial to 'social becoming' are questions concerning the social and economic agent's freedom, not only when this finds expression in action, but in his/her disposition. The very term 'agent' empha- sizes the pivotal position in a set of actions; he/she is seen as the subject; with seemingly extensive access to deliberate choice. Yet crucial to any initiative in support of inclusiveness is the recogni- tion that this freedom is only part of the picture; and that there is ambivalence and tension at a still more basic level of reality where spontaneous initiatives and determining circumstances concur.

Consequent to the intensification of economic activity there comes a point at which human agency is detached from its source, from the person initiating action. 'The work of human hands' has the appearance of assuming a condition of autonomy. A conglomerate of multifarious, power-spelling acts become mechanisms and struc- tures with virtual lives of their own. In that mode they dictate personal responses and behaviour patterns, somewhat like the Sor- cerer's Apprentice's brooms who have become masters of the one who conjured them into activity. There is an inversion of roles. The person, or persons have made structures – now the structures make the persons. Mark O'Keefe observes pertinently: '. . . social structures become accepted as the manner in which certain actions *must* be carried out or in which certain relationships *must* be shaped [my italics] . . . to suggest that [this kind of] structure be uprooted becomes tantamount to suggesting the introduction to chaos.'[8]

This is particularly the case of many economic structures in postmodernity. Any one person's capacity to make a significant impact, and influence outcomes to be favourable to *becoming*, is weakened, if not eliminated. Who has not experienced feeling squashed by the power of mass production and mass marketing? True, exceptions exist. At one end of the spectrum we find persons who remain free and can assert their autonomy humbly, incon- spicuously, but effectively. At the other extreme there are the few with unusual thrust. They usurp control, at least for a while, though the time comes when they too will have become victims of their own creations; see a Robert Maxwell, driven to foolish irresponsibility by having become a globe of empire-building; see also, even more spectacularly, Napoleon propelled against sound strategy into invading Russia. There is no lack of similar examples.

A particularly invidious instance where economic activity has become subjugated by structural necessity is that of the manufacture and sale of weapons notably to markets which cannot afford them, or to predictably irresponsible users. Concupiscence is only part of the story. The economic imperative is such that few if anyone wants to open this Pandora's box. No publicly-accessible attempt is made to work out costs of restructuring industrial and macro-economic patterning to deal with this canker; nor do we hear of contingency plans for dealing with the economic slack resulting from incisive action. Yet it is hard to accept that assessment of this problem and of its major economic elements is beyond available computing techniques.

What applies in specific cases can be seen to take place comprehensively: 'the market does . . .', 'the market demands . . .'. Also: 'the market creates (opportunities and wealth, for some)'; or 'the market excludes and destroys (others)'. These are statements indicative of a structure which dominates those who brought it into being.

The phenomenon of the market is so significant that it provides generally valid insights. Economists and sociologists explain what the market does, how it functions. What it is remains untouched by postmodern discourse. Yet to understand what things are is a prerequisite for exerting influence over them. I suggest that the market is a function, rather than a being in its own right, as so often perceived. What makes it look like something that is endowed with primary existence, a subject, is its particular mode of being. It is loaded with a sense of weight and power which gives it the appearance of having autonomous being. To accept this absoluteness would mean acceptance – no questions asked – that the market dominates its originators. It determines and there is no escape.

Many see it that way. Nevertheless, this is an incomplete account. It requires a better understanding of whether the category 'being a function' is of the same order, has the same density of being, as the category 'being an autonomous existent' – say a person, a social organism, a specific communal body? I suggest that a function has only contingent, not absolute, existence. It is not an immanent entity *per se* but an outcome. On that reading, notwithstanding that the Market seems to control and determine the subjects who made it happen, its absoluteness is **'almost** but not quite' total. *On this 'not quite' hinges the prospects for inclusiveness.*

Look at it laterally. The Market, an extended set of economic relationships, functions detached from its originators, to the point of just 'being there', as it were in its own right. Just by being there it has an increasingly determining effect on us, the ones who made it happen in the first place. Add economic and political determinacy, the genetic and environmental factors to which the economic agent is subjected, and we have to contend with forbidding implications for the model of a free society in which freedom should play a crucial part. Are, then, notions like economic freedom and choice illusory? Are they not bound to become more and more excluded? Are they phantoms conjured up by some in whose intellectual or political interest it is to cultivate such an illusion; and who in turn delude themselves? Here too, in my view, the same answer applies: '**Almost**, but not quite'.

Determinization and creative initiative: ontological realities

Surely, humankind is driven by a profound need to make sense of its existence. That need is supported by a belief that such shaping, exemplified by the making of an inclusive society, is within range of the possible. Moreover, we want to see ourselves as significant co-actors in the process; not as puppets. Consider now the ubiquitous tension between these needs and ambivalence of freedom and determinacy. I will illustrate this tension by three starkly different yet complementary stories which range from mythological patterns to the most acute of contemporary issues. Each one has universal significance. Each one illustrates tensions between becoming and unbecoming.

First, I have chosen an archetypal metaphor: the Oedipus Saga, in Sophocles' illumination. Here one event determines those following. It is a chain of inescapable necessity. Oedipus himself is anything but a subservient cipher. He is a commanding, turbulent and contradictory personality. Think of a benevolent ruler with a profound sense of responsibility, yet the victim of blinding passion. He senses impending doom. He goes to extremes to avert it, unwilling to be dominated by the forces he has unleashed, but he cannot evade the determining happenings – here called fate – which eventually will activate the chain: Oedipus kills, unknowingly, his father. It had to be so. Sophocles tells of inevitability, and of inevitable undoing which sets in motion acts for which the human being is not entirely responsible. No good saying that everything in this man, and in us all, would revolt against this 'must'; that until the very last moment the human person will strain to find a way out. In that arch-mode of existence of which Sophocles treats, there is a force at work, an inner necessity from which there is no escape. Whatever we postmoderns would say, these dynamics even if we can grasp them only dimly are all-pervasively indomitable – they cannot be shrugged off. They are part of reality. We must not think about *social becoming* without taking account of these.

Next, a huge leap from the ageless representation of the indefinable to the concreteness of our very own biography. Chapter one, based on the history books: a search for understanding and eventual deciphering of particle structure (ambivalent as such, and in terms of consequences). The next chapter: generation of nuclear energy (ambivalent). The next chapter: nuclear weapons production (inevitable, it is said). The penultimate chapter, yet to be completed (to sober reflection, inevitable too): nuclear conflict. Or we might say 'almost' inevitable, since we still allow for the probability of unforeseen circumstances or unforeseeable initiatives. (The denouement is likely to be brought about by either irresponsible absurdity, or else by the redeeming spark of goodwill.) Throughout, a sequence of mutually determining factors has been operative. These factors include free agency and a host of less clearly definable, perhaps intangible dynamics.[9] Inevitability is thereby diluted by possibility.

In the third story the themes are drawn together into a quasi-contrapunctal interaction. Such a relationship can transform purely contingent systems by infusing them with creative freedom. Take the structures of exclusion in Latin America. Are these the necessary and inevitable result of a particular socioeconomic system? Or do they reflect a conglomerate of random decisions, historic circumstances, of a seemingly inevitable darkness in the human heart, of freedom, responsibility?

James Gaffney, a political and philosophical radical, would have it that economic structures are destructive and indeed autonomously so. He uses an analogy, structures of organized crime, and describes them as something more powerful than individual volition, 'a stable, systematic and extensive arrangement which can function even though its component parts are replaceable'. Later he says: 'When social structures reach a certain level of complexity, moral responsibility is shared and diffused to a degree that defies analysis'.[10] In this reading, political ideologies, dominating hierarchies and social division drain the will for change, and perpetuate the status quo of those who control power and wealth.

The most eminent amongst Latin American liberation theologians Gustavo Gutiérrez takes a nuanced position: '. . . sin [his term for exclusion, oppression] is not considered as an individual, private, or merely interior reality . . . it is evident in oppressive structures, in the exploitation of man by man'. The inherent consequences of these structures, as their originating impetus, are virtually automatic. But, even so, he cautions us not to absolutize the process:

> . . . We do not in any way deny the structural reasons and the objective determinants leading to this situation [of oppression]. It does however, emphasize the fact that things do not happen by chance, and that behind an unjust structure there is a personal or collective will responsible.[11]

These questions about the impact of structures which become quasi-autonomous are present also in the thought of Pope John Paul II. In the course of weighing up benefits and damages linked to liberal capitalism, one of his recurring preoccupations, he says,

> One must denounce the existence of economic, financial and social mechanisms which, although they are manipulated by people, function almost automatically . . . [yet] it is the use of the word almost which indicate that structures are not to be treated as wholly deterministic.[12]

Almost is a keyword. **Almost** indicates that in high modernity we have arrived at a critical phase where human identity has to confront the possibility of being eradicated by economic structures, the very opposite of '*I count*'. Instead of my contribution to the common good being a deliberate, free act, I am compelled by mock inclusion to act in such-and-such a way. Being included now demands conformity. Yet acceptance of this enslavement, however powerfully the latter's driving forces, is tantamount to reversal into *social un-becoming*. It must be unacceptable.

Almost is crisis language. It could be code for 'giving up altogether' in the face of what appears inevitable ('Yes, the economic structures which we have created are now irresistible, but let us have a last, hopeless fling at pretending that they are not'). Or it could, and should, signal the shock realization of urgent dissidence

and reordering, not as abstract principle but now, this very moment, in my particular circumstances. Only crisis, indicated by
'**almost**' is the condition in which I realize that I must resist being
mastered by dehumanizing domination through structures of human
making. '**Almost**' will alert me. As a human person I am more than
an economic unit, or a sociological phenomenon. I can call on
inner resources to stand up against being depersonalized and thereby
irremediably excluded. '**Almost**' indicates the sudden concentration
of our intellectual and moral capacities, and the unexpected moment
when effective breakthrough becomes possible.

Christian belief provides an even more existentially dense account
of **almost**. It tells of passage into darkness, into 'the pain of the
world'. This may seem **almost** doom. Yet without it the message of
hope and breakthrough could not be told.

In reflective language **almost** should trigger a search for an understanding in which determinism of structures and mechanisms has
a necessary but still subservient role in shaping future social patterns. The word **almost** does give recognition to the reality of
determining dynamics, but by emphasizing crisis prompts us to resist
their enslaving potential. Simultaneously, crisis opens up interstices
in contingency and determinacy (metaphysical metaphor – what
else could do?) into which spontaneous willing and thereby inde-
terminacy inserts itself. Reflective language. Can it make an impact?
Is there hope that such thoughts will make *'becoming more'* happen?

Reflecting on inclusion and exclusion theologically

This is where a theology has a contribution to make; not as deus
ex machina, a comforting provider of assurance that all will be
well, but as the source for a framework (or several alternative frameworks) for coming to grips constructively with high-modern reality
which is poised to disintegrate into hopelessness.

It may seem odd that I come only at the end of this chapter to
the theological considerations highlighted in the title. From my
viewpoint such emphasis is essential. I place it here to underline
its importance, though a proper theological argument would require
at the very least a separate chapter.

Contemporary theology is not immune to the pluralism of *high
modernity*. Thus many of its practitioners examine with some reser-
vations an epistemology which takes its point of departure exclusively
from faith-inspired and self-confirming concepts. Throughout this

century theologians have seen more and more the necessity of sub-merging themselves in experience. This kind of theologizing means 'learning' from praxis rather than asserting. As part of that process it aims to bring about a transformation of the political. At the same time it endeavours to explicate by appeal to reason, yet with awareness of the limitations to which reason is subjected, a more comprehensive, even unlimited reality.

Yet I propose to go one step further. Having argued in the pre-ceding pages from a pragmatic assessment, I now use for my final reflection a different route. I take my clues unashamedly not from theological textbooks, but from poetry. The resulting speech-mode will be analogical: a groping to condense into familiar language things which by their very nature extend beyond the familiar. The first example draws on one of the authors of the first book of Genesis:

In the beginning God created . . .,

and a few words later:

. . . the earth was formless and empty, and darkness was over the abyss.[13]

The three words 'beginning, God, created' and then the archetypal notion 'abyss'[14] explode with meaning. Tension is palpable. It is the arch tension between being and non-being. Nothing less. What we are told here is that the abyss, metaphor for non-being or noth-ingness, is real. Unless it has reality, how could God, pure reality without beginning and end, confront it? And yet what could there be before 'the beginning' (do not think of big bang) other than God's being? Only nothing.

A second resource. The existential reality of the same paradox is retold by a poet with roots in the broad tradition of western cul-ture, Goethe. In his Faustus drama we find its hero, the relentless seeker and Enlightenment Person, questioning Mephistopheles, spokes-person for the abysmal Nothing:

Who art thou? . . .
I am a part of Part unnamed which first was All.
A part of darkness from which light was born:
That haughty Light which combats us,
Usurping rank and realm of Mother Night . . .[15]

Once again confrontation and tension woven into the matrix of all that is, from 'the Beginning'.

Now to one of the theological giants of our century. Karl Barth speaks about this same paradox. He avails himself of extraordinarily forceful and unashamedly metaphysical language, and in the process employs the word das Nichtige (the Nihil, an equivalent of nothingness, non-being):

> There is opposition and resistance to God's world-dominion. There is in world-occurence an element, indeed an entire sinister system of elements which is not comprehended by God's providence . . . which is itself opposed to being preserved, accompanied and ruled in any sense . . . This opposition, this stubborn element and alien factor, 'das Nichtige'.[16]

This reading forces on us the idea that this stubborn element, which because of its very nothingness must be 'unexpressively abhorrent . . . to the Creators's Being' (Barth, *ibid.*) is necessary to the point of being the precondition for becoming. Necessary as source of confrontation and thereby of tension and as the critical condition from which structures of existence are made to emerge from a chaotic void. Necessary also in a pattern of ambivalence, that of the dynamics of becoming more and the counter-dynamics of being drawn into nothingness.

The reader may wonder why I resort to the metaphysical concept of non-being rather than engage in familiar discourse about sin and evil. After all, one should not be surprised to find the latter words in an essay with a theological intent. These, however, raise theological difficulties of considerable magnitude. The metaphysical idiom, though admittedly abstruse, should provide access for a non-theologically disposed audience. Somewhat more 'inclusive'.

In such terms one can imagine Social Becoming suspended between the poles of being and non-being, and all the while exposed to the conflicting attraction of them both. Hence ambivalence, including ambivalence of inclusion and exclusion. Hence also the destructive impact of structures once they become rigid where rigidity is not of the essence. Hence the destructiveness of freedom when turned upon itself. Hence the beneficent impact of structured order, and, chiefly, of my human freedom when turned towards others.

The model can be challenged: does it not make God utterly remote; relegated into some metaphysical space and unrelated to us?

Or God a chess player, testing the opponent and taking the – for us – inconceivable risk that the opponent turns out to be more powerful? Or that everlasting checkmate will prevail? Where does this leave Social Becoming? Yet how can freedom emerge in God's self-expressing creation without the possibility of 'things going wrong'? Indeed, looking around you may conclude that they did, and continue to go wrong. So is there self-contradiction in God expressing Him/Herself by 'things going wrong'. Yet note that what is suggested here does not mean that 'things go wrong with God', but that God makes space for 'things going wrong', often horrendously wrong. God makes space for the use of freedom, a freedom in tension with determinization to the point of **almost**, and with **almost** giving the cue for the assertion of human dignity.

It would be preposterous to spin this model out into a tidy and aesthetically pleasing one. Nor is there time to engage in the argument whether God is somehow inculpated by 'wrong', or to the 'defence of God' by, say, a Moltmann or Tillich. All I can do is to stress the importance of such a reflective engagement with a fundamental aspect of reality, even if that engagement can be no more than the grappling of the unquiet human mind. Without it the concept of Social Becoming lacks its vital dimension.

'Which angel on the point of a needle?'[17]

A model-builder in high modernity must recognize the multiplicity of alternative, perhaps conflicting models. Yet, whatever the idiom, without a model no meaning (unless you are content with a nihilistic vacuum); without meaning not much hope for identity-discovery and consequent social becoming. What has been indicated here by very broad brush strokes should support the affirmation that social becoming should not be relegated into the realm of utopia. This assertion should hold good in the face of so many accounts of experience in which structures and practises which are intrinsically enriching and should strengthen inclusion, show a tendency to become damaging, some of them unspeakably damaging. We also have a model, or the starting point for models which include ambivalence, uncertainty and fluidity not only as narrow reductions of specific social contexts but as essential elements of how things are and will be. These and yet other elements energize social becoming and the idea of inclusion, because the idea includes exclusion, not as an either – or but as a coexistent. Or, very simply, this model has more to say about social inclusion than that 'it is nice', or 'good' for social cohesion; or because of some other aspect of utility or exteriority.

Notes

1 Rilke (1955).
2 'High modernity', a term coined by Giddens (1991).
3 Kerr (1997).
4 'hominibus bonae voluntatis', that is, 'men of good will', or closer to the original text, 'God's sons', that is, those in harmony with God and all men. See Murray (1959).
5 See 'The Phenomenon of Man', Collins, London, 1964. Teilhard's thesis proposes evolution from simple organisms to humanity and a point of collective reflexion. The ultimate state of the process is the noosphere, a web of thought and higher consciousness encircling the Earth. See also 'The Dune Milieu' (1960), chap. X.
6 Maslow (1970).
7 See his 'Six Stages of Moral Development', 1973.
8 O'Keefe (1990).
9 A major theme of Frederick von Hayek. For example, '... a rule that will be followed at least with sufficient frequency to impress upon such a society an order of a certain kind. But the fact that most people will not follow the rule will leave that order... very indeterminate' (1982).
10 Gaffney (1983).
11 Guitierrez (1988) chap. 9.
12 John Paul II, 'Solicitudo Rei Socialis', Sect. 36, 1987. A useful commentary is 'On Social Concern', McHugh, CSERU (1989).
13 Genesis I. 2.
14 Abyss. Various translations use the words 'shapeless void' or 'the deep'. All convey a primordial, dis-ordered and infinitely sinister metaphysical reality.
15 Goethe *Faust* Part I, transl. ed.
16 Barth (1977), *Church Dogmatic*, III, iii, para. 50.
17 This heading paraphrases a saying malevolently ascribed to Aquinas. 'How many angels on the pin of a needle?' A form of sophistry, contrived probably by a late Scholastic. What concerned Thomas was the potential plurality in something that transcends material substance (for example, 'Summa Theologica' I.Q 52. iii). One might deduce a necessary plurality as the principle of created order.

References

Barth, K. (1977) *Church Dogmatic* (orig. Merde 1961).
Chardin T. de (1995) *The Future of Man*, Engl. translation (London: Collins).
Gaffney, J. (1983) *Sin Reconsidered* (New York: Paulist Press).
Giddens, A. (1991) *Modernity and Self-identity* (Cambridge: Polity Press).
Guitierrez, G. (1988) *A Theology of Liberation* (transl. SCM Press).
Hayek, F.v. (1982) *Law, Legislation and Liberty* (London: Routledge & Kegan Paul).

John Paul II (1987) 'Solicitudo Rei Socialis', Sect 36.

Kerr, F. (1997) *Immortal Longings, Versions of Transcending Humanity* (SPCK).

Kohlberg, L. (1973) *Collected Papers on Moral Development* (Cambridge, Mass.: Harvard University Press).

Maslow, A. (1970) *Motivation and Personality* (New York).

Murray, R. (1959) *Bellarmine Commentary* (*Heythrop*, published by Woodstock).

O'Keefe, M. (1990) *What Are They Saying About Social Sin?* (New York: Paulist Press).

Rilke, R.M. (1995) *Das Stundenbuch* (*Book of Hours*) (Berlin: Insel Verlag).

Part II

Contexts of Inclusion: Areas of Ambivalence and Tension

8
The Consequences of Globalization and Corporate Structures for Projects of Social Inclusion

Jonathan Perraton

Introduction

Although there is a large literature on globalization, debates over the implications for social inclusion have, like debates about globalization generally, become unhelpfully polarized between a few, often extreme, positions.[1] This chapter examines three main views – the hyper-globalization approach, those sceptical that globalization amounts to anything new, and the emerging position on globalization from stakeholding theorists. For the hyper-globalization school economic globalization largely spells the end of possibilities for inclusive social projects at the national level, and many of these authors have little faith in the possibility of operating such projects at the regional or global level. The globalization sceptics regard the supposed trends in the global economy as greatly exaggerated. In their view economic activity largely remains national and from this they conclude, typically without intervening argument, that economic agents can be incorporated into inclusive national projects. The stakeholder view sees particular dangers in the globalization of finance, but often accepts much of the sceptical position on other globalization tendencies.

This chapter sketches an alternative to these limited positions which highlights the impact of recent increases in international economic activity, but also the policy space remaining. Space only permits a sketchy account, and inevitably key topics will be considered in too little detail; the reader is referred to further material. The next section sets out existing positions on globalization, and the section following suggests an alternative approach. The major contemporary transformations in the world economy and how they may affect social inclusion strategies are then outlined, followed by a consideration of the operations of multinational corporations specifically. Some implications from recent studies concerning changes in the workplace are then discussed.

Globalization: current views

The alternative positions are increasingly well-known. The hyper-globalization view posits that approximately perfect global markets have developed so that goods, capital and finance are freely mobile internationally. Governments are effectively rendered powerless to intervene. In the radical version of this view globalization can be expected to lead to a 'race to the bottom' in wages, welfare provision and social and environmental standards through trade competition and multinational corporations (MNCs) relocating to low-cost countries (Gray, 1998; Hines and Lang, 1993). Multinationals' lobbying is believed to have played a crucial role in setting the rules for international markets through international institutions, notably the World Trade Organization and the OECD's attempts to negotiate a Multilateral Agreement on Investment. A contrast is drawn between a 'Club Class' elite, mobile internationally both physically and virtually through new communications technology, and the localized majority (cf. Bauman, 1998). Globalization is predicted to accentuate the inequalities between these two groups.

Further, the mobility of the elites (combined with the end of the Cold War) makes it increasingly difficult to tie them into national inclusive relationships. Finance is predicted to flow against countries who pursue social policies and to limit the extent to which national governments can expand their economies to ensure high employment. Taxes, especially on corporations, are driven to low levels making it increasingly difficult for governments to fund social expenditures.

The neo-liberal version of hyper-globalization is something of an optimistic mirror image of this argument, celebrating the triumph of global markets (see for example Ohmae, 1990). Global competition is conceived as sharpening the difference between the potential gains from appropriate responses and the potential losses from inappropriate ones. Jack Welch Jr, chairman of General Electric, claimed recently to his shareholders that 'ahead of us are Darwinian shakeouts in every major marketplace, with no consolation prizes for the losing companies and nations' (*The Observer*, 10 January 1999, p. 15). Whilst management literature versions of this approach sometimes see globalization as presaging the end of the nation state, a politically influential version of this argument still sees an important role for national states in liberalizing markets, operating 'business-friendly' policies and promoting human capital accumulation amongst its citizens. The radical hyper-globalization approach effectively questions how plausible the potential gains really are, their likely distribution between social groups and countries, and the extent to which these processes can deliver on wider social goods.

These are particular extreme versions. They tend to see recent changes as irreversible, although some variants do allow for possible political action to modify these tendencies (Greider, 1997; Reich, 1991). A particularly influential version accepts that while most of the labour force, unlike capital, is immobile internationally, policies to enhance human capital remain the most effective, if not the only, means of enhancing national prosperity.

Against this is the sceptical view of economic globalization (Hirst and Thompson, 1999), which is fast becoming orthodoxy in some circles. They argue that economic activity remains largely national, notwithstanding recent rises in international economic activity. They deny that international trade has had a significant impact on advanced countries' labour markets. They point out that far from welfare states making open economies uncompetitive, amongst advanced countries there is a positive association between welfare provision and the share of trade in national income (Rodrik, 1997). They believe the limits international finance set on policy autonomy are secondary. Even multinational corporations (MNCs) are seen as having a strong national base and distinctive national culture, they are typically embedded in industrial districts with strong relationships to other local firms. Most foreign direct investment (FDI) is located in other developed countries, so that there is no strong evidence of MNCs systematically relocating production to low-wage economies. As such, MNCs remain amenable to inclusive national projects.

The emerging position from stakeholding theorists is more subtle (Hutton, 1999; see, further, Perraton, 1997). In their view international finance is the key problem, as the most mobile factor. Global private financial markets are seen as Anglo-Saxon finance writ (very) large. The development of global financial markets is expected to increase speculative activity and short-termist pressures

on business which will undermine the basis for long-term relationships of commitment between businesses and other stakeholders.
By contrast, for MNCs exit costs are often considerable and they
therefore typically aim to establish lasting production sites which,
in turn, entails forming relationships with a range of stakeholder
groups. Whilst stakeholder theorists may see some particular dangers in other globalization processes, their emphasis is on controlling
international finance.

Existing responses from proponents of inclusive projects to
globalization have generally followed these positions. For hyper-
globalization theorists there is little alternative to neo-liberal policies
which will render inclusive projects uncompetitive. Many radical
hyper-globalizers have stressed resistance at the local level, but it is
hard to see this as a coherent political strategy. For neo-liberals
inclusive projects impose costs on businesses and thus *laissez-faire*
is the route to general prosperity anyway. New Labour in the UK
and other governments appear to have accepted parts of the neo-
liberal hyper-globalization position. Whilst they may accept that
domestic markets sometimes require regulation and framing, essentially they take global markets as a given and frame economic policy
in a fashion that appeals to these markets (see, further, Held, 1998).
Nevertheless, enhancing human capital is seen not only as enabling
citizens to prosper in the face of new global competition but as
providing the basis for social inclusion.

For the sceptics recent trends in the world economy make only
limited difference. Failure to attempt inclusive projects is attributed
to a failure of political will – perhaps precisely because politicians
have accepted the 'myth of globalization' or used it as an excuse –
or a failure of political coalitions. Social inclusion can enhance
productivity by encouraging the acquisition and application of skills
and encouraging worker commitment. Countries that operate socially
inclusive policies are thus still capable of competing in international
markets, retaining their own multinationals' operations and even
attracting inward FDI.

An emerging position across several perspectives stresses the 'high
road' against the 'low road' for developed economies. All note that
it is lower-skilled jobs that are most at risk from low-wage international competition. The radical hyper-globalization position tends
to see the high skilled group as comprising a minority, sometimes
a small minority, of the workforce. The view propounded by New
Labour and other governments sees education and skill formation

as central to ensuring prosperity by raising productivity. The version of this view propounded by globalization sceptics and stakeholder theorists is wider. For educated and skilled workers to realize their productive potential fully they must be granted autonomy and discretion at work. This results in less hierarchical and more inclusive work organizations. Higher productivity in the economy also permits better quality public services to be funded through reasonable tax levels. In the globalization sceptics' position international economic forces pose no problems for this 'high route' (Garrett, 1998): high productivity allows a country to prosper through trade in the international economy; domestic MNCs will retain advanced operations at home and overseas MNCs may be attracted by the productive workforce; taxes may be higher than elsewhere but this cost will be offset by the more productive workforce and better infrastructure; international financial flows will not penalize an economy with prospects for strong performance and an ability through this to fund its government expenditure. This view takes such policies as unproblematic and involving little potential conflict; as such it is difficult to see why governments would not adopt them.

Globalization: an alternative perspective

This chapter argues that the sanguine view of globalization promoted by the sceptics is untenable, whilst the hyper-globalization view is not merely too simplistic but often actively misleading. In effect they share much of the same framework, conceiving of globalization having a single implied end-point; the stakeholding position is more considered, but its exclusive focus on finance is limiting. Sceptics test the hyper-globalizers' claims and, not surprisingly, find them wanting. In terms of firm strategy both positions tend to conceive of a global firm as a footloose MNC able to relocate production easily to low-cost areas. Nevertheless, in some management literature the emerging best-practice corporate structure is that of Japanese 'lean management'. Although the implications of such structures are debated, they have entailed high rewards at least for the core workforce and long-term relationships with local suppliers.

In general, it seems highly unlikely that social processes have one end-point: historical forms of globalization – both as a general social phenomenon and in their specific forms – have multiple causes and, given the likelihood of multiple equilibria, are unlikely to have a single even implied end-point. End-point analysis obscures the processes at work here. Rather, globalization is more appropriately conceived as an historical process which engenders a shift in the spatial reach of networks and systems of social relations to transcontinental (or interregional) patterns of human organization, activity and the exercise of social power. In the economic spheres this entails economic activity being stretched internationally with economic variables increasingly determined at the global level. Thus, as international trade has grown relative to output, global markets have emerged for a range of goods and, increasingly, services. Growing international financial markets have meant that capital funds flow globally and key macroeconomic variables like interest rates are determined in global markets. Technological knowledge increasingly flows internationally. MNCs have created global competition in a range of products and have increased their ability to produce internationally. These changes have their route in several causes, notably technological advances, market activity and changes in government policies. Although these changes often operate to increase the power of private actors, this does not mean that they are unamenable to regulation or render governments powerless, nor do they imply a single appropriate response from government, firms or other social groups.

Nor do they necessarily lead to a 'race to the bottom'. Arguments that a particular policy would make a country 'uncompetitive' are based on basic misunderstandings of trade theory.[2] More generally, neo-liberal arguments for the ineffectiveness of government intervention have little to do with globalization *per se*. If markets worked in perfect textbook fashion then these policies would be ineffective largely irrespective of how open the national economy was to international flows. Further economic theory indicates that although globalization might increase the gains from openness to international economic activity and potential losses (or benefits foregone) from inappropriate policies this would be some way from any 'Darwinian struggle' or 'race to the bottom'.

This does not preclude sharp effects of increased international integration on particular groups. Higher international trade and capital mobility tends to increase the elasticity of demand for labour (Rodrik, 1997). As such, although increased openness should raise a country's welfare overall, within a country there may be sharp patterns of gainers and losers with particular groups of labour seeing their incomes fall. Increased company mobility would tend to raise its bargaining power relative to organized labour and government regulation.

Contemporary transformations

At first sight the evidence on the relationship between economic openness and national inclusive projects appears to support the sceptics' position. There are clear cases of national social inclusion projects in several European economies characterized by strong openness to trade and whose leading companies are often MNCs. Indeed, the external discipline of world markets has been held to be central to ensuring that national social bargains operate effectively (Katzenstein, 1985). Further, amongst advanced countries overseas FDI by US multinationals appears to be attracted to high-wage, high-productivity countries, although some government regulations do appear to have had a negative impact on this investment (Cooke and Noble, 1998). Nevertheless, one does not have to accept all the hyperbole surrounding the 'crisis' in the German, Swedish and other models, or to attribute all their problems to globalization, to acknowledge that significant problems have emerged with the social bargains in these countries. We can sketch an account here.

Firstly, there has been a shift in the nature of trade. For much of the postwar period developed countries' trade was largely with other developed countries in the form of intra-industry trade, the exchange of similar products (Held *et al.*, 1999, ch. 3; OECD, 1996, ch. 1). There are theoretical grounds for expecting this to benefit all factors of production, and the evidence indicates that intra-industry trade tends to benefit workers generally but that inter-industry trade tends to have a differential impact by worker skill level (Oliveira Martins, 1994). Further, these countries typically enjoyed niches in particular product areas. Their technological specialization was important to their success: not only did this allow the workers in such industries to enjoy high incomes, but through the labour market and taxation for public services others throughout the economy also benefited. As technology has diffused internationally this can have the effect of sharpening the income distribution effects of trade.

The most pronounced effects arise when technology has diffused to developing countries. Rising inter-industry trade with developing countries has reduced demand for low-skilled workers in developed countries, whilst increasing it for high-skilled workers. A country can still be expected to gain overall from more open trade, but with potentially strong income distribution effects, the gainers could fully compensate the losers and still be better off than before; the welfare state may partially operate to effect such transfers. Nevertheless increasing trade with strong income distribution effects can be expected to increase welfare state expenditures. For two reasons here we can largely talk past the recent debate over how far these shifts in labour demand are due to technological shifts and how far they are due to trade with developing economies.[3] Firstly, the generality of this shift suggests that new technology has diffused across most developed countries with varying social bargains. Secondly, this trade-versus-technology dichotomy ignores the impact of management strategies on labour.

Space precludes a detailed analysis of the effects of international finance. Financial liberalization during the 1980s in Sweden and elsewhere was associated with instabilities in asset prices and a major banking crisis. Since the early 1980s Mitterrand experiment, few governments have experimented with macroeconomic policies that are radically different from the rest of the world, making it difficult to assess how far financial markets impinge on macroeconomic autonomy. Markets do tend to assign a risk premium to interest rates in countries pursuing progressive policies; the short-term focus of the markets means they are unlikely to place much weight on the potential long-term gains from social inclusion. Further, the risk premium can be seen as more than market prejudice; it reflects a market judgement on the ability of a government to manage the conflicts that particular policies will entail (Bleaney, 1993; Glyn, 1998).

Striking evidence for the stakeholder position comes from the East Asian currency crisis. Although the nature of social inclusion in these countries differs significantly from Europeans cases, the East Asian newly-industrializing economies were acknowledged to have high levels of social cohesion, combining rapid growth with relatively egalitarian income distribution (see for example World Bank, 1993). Their pre-crisis performance is well-known: they achieved rapid growth with a strong export performance, a sound fiscal stance and low inflation. Some attracted heavy inflows of MNC investment. Whatever the imbalances in these economies in 1997, it is hard to see how the size of the falls in their currencies could be justified by underlying fundamentals and the ensuing crisis has been enormously disruptive to the social and economic arrangements that had previously underwritten prosperity.[4] Speculative capital inflows in the 1990s had led to distortions of asset prices and the real exchange rate and misallocation of investment. Overall it is hard to maintain a sanguine view of the effects of global finance after this episode.

Returning to the position in developed economies, the role of technology may be seen as central. Underpinning the concepts of national inclusive projects in the stakeholder and globalization sceptics' approaches is the view that prosperity can be generated and shared domestically. If MNCs locate their technology generation and advanced production at home, then the fruits of that will be realized there. This will provide the basis for trade performance and higher incomes generally, as suggested above. Nevertheless, technology increasingly spills over internationally through trade, MNCs and other channels (Cantwell, 1995; Coe and Helpman, 1995; Frantzen, 1998). MNCs can transfer technology abroad, so that some of the returns to it are realized outside of their home country, whilst MNCs increasingly invest in R&D ventures abroad and often engage in strategic alliances with other firms to develop technology, around a half of such alliances being with firms in other continents (OECD, 1996). These arrangements are particularly marked in the most technologically dynamic industries. Thus, not only are MNCs able to diffuse technological advantages generated at home to locations overseas, they also tap into foreign innovation networks as increasingly the national base is becoming insufficient to generate their technological advantage. These changes make it harder to tie firms into national economic relations with the state and other stakeholders.

Within European economies characterized by strong social bargains, MNCs have played an important recent role in undermining these bargains (Crotty *et al.*, 1998). Their wage bargaining has increasingly broken away from previous arrangements, and their location of technologically advanced production abroad in response to wage and social costs at home has undermined the postwar basis for social prosperity outlined above. Thus, MNC investment in other developed countries, as well as in low-wage developing economies, can be important in undermining national social bargains. Further, MNCs have often played an important political role in lobbying for a shift away from socially inclusive policies towards more neoliberal ones (McCann, 1995). None of this means that domestic factors were unimportant, nor that such bargains are finished. But it does illustrate the problems such bargains have encountered. Wider diffusion of technology will, as we noted above, tend to raise the incomes of particular skilled workers but may adversely affect the incomes of the less skilled. This would still lead to higher incomes in advanced economies, but may disrupt the distributional coalitions on which socially inclusive projects are built. In the next section we examine the operations of MNCs generally.

The operations of multinational corporations

Crude estimates indicate that MNCs account for at least a quarter of the GDP of market economies and the majority of their trade (Held *et al.*, 1999, ch. 5). Their employment shares will be less than this. Most people do not work for MNCs, although increasingly small and medium-sized enterprises are being incorporated into international networks of production too. Nevertheless, MNCs – domestic and overseas – typically account for a majority of a country's exports and are central to technology generation.

The sceptics' view that MNCs remain essentially national companies is becoming increasingly dated. We have seen above that MNCs both diffuse technology internationally and increasingly tap into foreign sources of technology through locating research establishments abroad and through strategic alliances with foreign companies. The view that foreign operations of MNCs are secondary to their core business is increasingly difficult to maintain. For the leading 100 MNCs, over half of their sales and more than 40 per cent of their assets and employment are overseas (*ibid.*, p. 271). Major MNCs have global strategies for production and sales and overseas activity is not secondary, let alone marginal, to their operations.

The second sanguine view, adopted by some stakeholder theorists, is that countries with socially inclusive projects can still attract overseas investment and retain significant operations of their own MNCs. There is more evidence for this viewpoint. Although MNCs may put downward pressure on corporate taxation and manipulate their tax bills through transfer pricing, this is probably secondary and still leaves considerable autonomy for national tax policy (Chennells and Griffith, 1997). MNCs themselves often do have relatively high wages and good conditions, although how far this holds once other factors are controlled for is unclear (Caves, 1996, ch. 5).

MNCs have, together with world trade in which they are heavily involved, both created and are subject to global competition. It should be noted that this does bring important benefits for consumers. Nevertheless, its impact on profits combined with the increased mobility of MNCs may diminish their willingness and ability to operate in socially inclusive projects. Measured at economic, not accounting, rates of return multinationals' profits are not high (Kapler, 1997). Excess capacity and increased competition has driven profit rates to low levels (Brenner, 1998).

One difficulty in discussing MNCs and globalization is the common view that only one corporate strategy constitutes globalization. Ruigrok and van Tulder (1995) offer a useful typology of corporate strategies. They note that MNCs enter into bargaining relationships with groups inside their value chain (workers, suppliers, distributors, etc.) and outside it (financiers, governments, etc.). The relative power positions between MNCs and these actors can vary considerably and a diversity of arrangements is observed. Responses to global competition and greater potential for international production similarly vary (*ibid.*, ch. 8), although, unhelpfully in their taxonomy, only one strategy is labeled 'globalization'.[5] There are also important variations by firm and by industry. Broadly strategies can be distinguished by the degree of geographical dispersion or concentration, and the degree of central control from the home country headquarters over international operations. The most obvious globalization strategy is geographical dispersion under strong central control, where different stages of the chain of production are located internationally. This is usually expected to have the most radical effects in terms of increasing the bargaining power of MNCs relative to domestic actors. US and UK MNCs have often been most advanced down this route; other European MNCs have often had more limited regional divisions of labour. Over time, for MNCs generally the extensity of their international operations has tended to grow with improvements in communications technology and management techniques for international production. Some overseas investment by these MNCs is 'multidomestic' production to serve particular markets. As such it is not integrated into an international value chain and such overseas affiliates may be more amenable to pressure in their host countries.

For much of the postwar period Japanese companies operated different strategies. Production was heavily concentrated at home, and early overseas production was largely confined to low-wage operations in developing countries with core operations retained at home. The need to serve the large European and North American markets led to larger investment overseas in the 1980s of major production operations. The production and management techniques of Japanese MNCs often required close proximity to suppliers, so that rather than an international chain of production, Japanese overseas operations were embedded into local networks partly of existing producers in the host country and partly through multi-national production by components producers. Overall we cannot say that MNCs are converging on the model of a global value chain, but we can observe secular rises in international production and intra-firm trade; over time, even Japanese firms are finding it easier and more profitable to disperse parts of the value chain. Further, some MNCs have responded to global competition by restructuring and concentrating their operations, making much greater use of sub-contracting arrangements with smaller, independent firms often outside the MNC's home country. The implications for the workforce are sketched in the next section.

Globalization and the workforce

Changes in the workplace is a huge subject and this section is necessarily brief and suggestive. The conception of a 'high' road for advanced countries entails a well-educated workforce which employers trust and value sufficiently to train further and allow autonomy and discretion at work so that they can operate most productively. Core firms in such nations will typically have exten-sive long-term relationships with a network of smaller firms in their surrounding industrial region. The high incomes generated by these operations would be expected to have the wider benefits outlined above. Under the 'low' road, by comparison, employers remain largely distrustful of their employees; they provide little training and limit employees' discretion (see for example Gordon, 1996). As such, productivity and wages are likely to be low. This leaves such work-ers more vulnerable to MNC relocation to low-wage countries and/ or trade competition from there. This also raises the key point that education strategies still require social bargains to be effective, not just public provision and incentives for the workforce, but also investment and appropriate work organization by business.[6]

Recent evidence suggests that the picture of the 'high' road may be too sanguine. Where foreign MNCs have transferred new work practices to the UK they do not appear to have fostered noticeable commitment or inclusion amongst the workforce (Delbridge, 1998).

In Britain, the introduction of new work practices and technologies has been associated with an intensification of surveillance and does not appear to lead to greater autonomy for workers (Gallie *et al.*, 1998, ch. 3). Although continental European MNCs have usually adopted the work councils detailed in the Social Chapter of the Maastricht Treaty, in Britain such councils are seen as making little difference to decisions or worker motivation (*ibid.*, ch. 4).

A key aspect of social inclusion is working hours. Long working hours are well-known to strain family life, and demand for leisure is typically income-elastic. Nevertheless, the century-long trend for the working day to shorten has virtually come to a halt, and there is evidence of a reversal for full-time male employees in the US and UK (OECD, 1998, ch. 5). Part of this can be attributed to slowdowns in productivity growth. Partly it may reflect employees' preferences, but it is difficult to see this as the desired work–leisure trade-off. Some employees may be working long hours simply to compensate for low wage rates. It may be difficult for employees individually to choose shorter hours without radical 'downshifting' (Schor, 1995). Rather, shorter hours seem largely to be achieved through collective action by trade unions and governments. New technology and working practices are associated with an intensification of work, including outside formal hours (Gallie *et al.*, 1998, ch. 2); thus, even where productivity is raised this does not necessarily lead to shorter working hours. Overall it is hard to explain these without reference to greater employer power.

Finally there is the position of the lowest skilled workers. Only the most naive advocate of the 'high road' would believe that the whole workforce can be transformed into high-skilled workers. Partly as a result of globalization, the great majority of the low paid in Britain are in the non-tradable sector and do not face international competition; as such, minimum wages and similar measures would not have a direct impact on competitiveness. How far corporations have squeezed these workers (Gordon, 1996) could be investigated further. Under competitive labour markets this notion would make little sense. However, recent studies have indicated that the labour markets for low-skilled workers in advanced countries may be some way from perfect with employers possessing considerable power (Card and Krueger, 1995).

Conclusions

This chapter has reviewed three main positions on the implications of globalization for social inclusion. The conception of globalization as having a single end-point bedevils this analysis. Thus, the hyper-globalization position sees the prospects for social inclusion as being swept away, ignoring the way in which shifts in power in the world economy are relative rather than absolute. Some of its specific claims are simply unsustainable. But this position allows the globalization sceptics to claim that relatively little has really changed. Although governments like New Labour in the UK have sometimes seemed in thrall to a hyper-globalization position, with increasing human capital about the only tool to ensure prosperity left, latterly governments have shown a greater interest in regulating the global economy.

The globalization sceptics and stakeholder theorists share the view that social inclusion can generate economic prosperity and strong trade performance and thus are not in conflict with international markets. Stakeholder theorists do, however, see potential conflict with the short-term focus of financial markets, as illustrated by the recent East Asian crisis. A key problem with these approaches is their view that the 'high road' is essentially unproblematic and does not involve potential social conflict.

Recent trends that can be labelled globalization illustrate this. International diffusion of technology acts to undermine the relationships that operated in earlier periods where the benefits of technological advantage were realized and widely shared within the country in which they were generated. Greater international diffusion of technology, and the rise in trade with developing countries, tends to increase differentials between workers of different skill levels. Increased trade and capital mobility tends to increase the elasticity of demand for labour. This is, thus, a relative rather than absolute shift in power. Nevertheless, MNCs have seen an increase in structural power – this or that measure will not make a country 'uncompetitive' or lead to a large capital outflow. But at the margin MNC activity and trade competition will act to limit worker power and the ability of governments to regulate for social and environmental objectives. Shifts in working conditions appear to bear this out. Further, MNCs have important political power and have used this to push for favourable policies. Governments have been drawn into a 'beauty contest' of offering inducements to attract inward investment, the subsidies sometimes amounting to tens of thousands of pounds per job.[7]

Inclusive social arrangements do offer the possibility of widespread prosperity, including properly funded and high-quality public services. In delivering this it is not a case of simple antagonism between workers and governments against international business and finance. But nor are their interests simply aligned either. Potential conflict needs to be recognized. Business, even MNCs, has to produce somewhere and it is possible to ensure that the *quid pro quo* of a productive workforce is wider benefits for society from business. Devising policies to do this is not easy. Little is gained from ignoring potential conflicts or underplaying the challenges that globalization brings to this.

Notes

1 On these debates generally see Perraton *et al.* (1997) and Held *et al.* (1999).
2 A common feature of hyper-globalization texts is their sloppy dismissal of trade theory, see, e.g., Paul Krugman's review of Gray (1998), *New Statesman* (8 May 1998).
3 See the symposia in *Journal of Economic Perspectives*, vol. 9 (3) (Summer 1995) and *Economic Journal* (September 1998).
4 See, further, Radelet and Sachs (1998) and the special issue of the *Cambridge Journal of Economics*, vol. 22 (6) (November 1998).
5 The following also draws heavily on OECD (1996).
6 See the symposium on 'Education and Growth' in *New Political Economy*, vol. 3 (1) (March 1998) and the references therein.
7 See editorial, 'Silly subsidies', *Financial Times* (7 September 1998).

References

Bauman, Z. (1998) *Globalization: The Human Consequences* (Cambridge: Polity Press).

Bleaney, M. (1993) 'Politics and the Exchange Rate', *Economic Notes*, vol. 22, pp. 420–9.

Brenner, R. (1998) 'The Economics of Global Turbulence: A Special Report on the World Economy, 1950–98', *New Left Review*, vol. 229.

Cantwell, J. (1995) 'The Globalization of Technology: What Remains of the Product Cycle?', *Cambridge Journal of Economics*, vol. 19, pp. 155–74.

Card, D. and Krueger, A. (1995) *Myth and Measurement: The New Economics of the Minimum Wage* (Princeton: Princeton University Press).

Caves, M. (1996) *Multinational Enterprise and Economic Analysis* (Cambridge: Cambridge University Press).

Chennells, L. and Griffith, R. (1997) *Taxing Profits in a Changing World* (London: Institute for Fiscal Studies).

Coe, D. and Helpman, E. (1995) 'International R&D Spillovers', *European Economic Review*, vol. 39, pp. 859–87.

Cooke, W. and Noble, D. (1998) 'Industrial Relations Systems and US Foreign Direct Investment Abroad', *British Journal of Industrial Relations*, vol. 36, pp. 581–609.

Crotty, J. Epstein, G. and Kelly, P. (1998) 'Multinational Corporations in the Neo-Liberal Regime', in D. Baker, G. Epstein and R. Pollin (eds), *Globalization and Progressive Economic Policy* (Cambridge: Cambridge University Press).

Delbridge, R. (1998) *Life on the Line in Contemporary Manufacturing: The Workplace Experience of Lean Production and the 'Japanese' Model* (Oxford: Oxford University Press).

Frantzen, D. (1998) 'R&D, International Technology Diffusion and Total Factor Productivity', *Kyklos*, vol. 51, pp. 489–508.

Gallie, D., White, M., Cheng, Y. and Tomlinson, M. (1998) *Restructuring the Employment Relationship* (Oxford: Oxford University Press).

Garrett, G. (1998) 'Global Markets and National Politics', *International Organization*, vol. 52, pp. 787–824.

Glyn, A. (1998) 'Internal and External Constraints on Egalitarian Policies', in D. Baker, G. Epstein and R. Pollin (eds), *Globalization and Progressive Economic Policy* (Cambridge: Cambridge University Press).

Gordon, D. (1996) *Fat and Mean: The Corporate Squeeze of Working Americans and the Myth of Managerial 'Downsizing'* (New York: Free Press).

Gray, J. (1998) *False Dawn* (London: Granta Books).

Greider, W. (1997) *One World, Ready or Not* (London: Penguin).

Held, D. (1998) 'Globalization: The Timid Tendency', *Marxism Today*, special issue, (November/December).

Held, D. McGrew, A. Goldblatt, D. and Perraton, J. (1999) *Global Transformations: Politics, Economics and Culture* (Cambridge: Polity Press).

Hines, C. and Lang, T. (1993) *The New Protectionism* (London: Earthscan).

Hirst, P. and Thompson, G. (1999) *Globalization in Question: The International Economy and Possibilities of Governance*, 2nd edn (Cambridge: Polity Press).

Hutton, W. (1999) *The Stakeholding Society* (Cambridge: Polity Press).

Kapler, J. (1997) 'The Theory of Transnational Firms: An Empirical Reassessment', *International Review of Applied Economics*, vol. 11, pp. 195–211.

Katzenstein, P. (1985) *Small States in World Markets* (Ithaca: Cornell University Press).

McCann, D. (1995) *Small States, Open Markets and the Organization of Business Interests* (Aldershot: Dartmouth Press).

OECD (1996) *Globalization of Industry* (Paris: Organization for Economic Cooperation and Development).

OECD (1998) *Employment Outlook* (Paris: Organization for Economic Cooperation and Development).

Ohmae, K. (1990) *The Borderless World* (London: Collins).

Oliveira Martins, J. (1994) 'Market Structure, Trade and Industry Wages', *OECD Economic Studies*, vol. 22, pp. 131–54.

Perraton, J. (1997) 'The Global Economy', in G. Kelly, D. Kelly and A. Gamble (eds), *Stakeholder Capitalism* (Basingstoke: Macmillan).

Perraton, J., Goldblatt, D., Held, D. and McGrew, A. (1997) 'The Globalization of Economic Activity', *New Political Economy*, vol. 2, pp. 257–77.

Radelet, S. and Sachs, J. (1998) 'The East Asian Financial Crisis', *Brookings Papers on Economic Activity*, No. I.

Reich, R. (1991) *The Work of Nations* (London: Simon & Schuster).

Rodrik, D. (1997) *Has Globalization Gone Too Far?* (Washington DC: Institute for International Economics).

Ruigrok, W. and van Tulder, R. (1995) *The Logic of International Restructuring* (London: Routledge).

Schor, J. (1995) 'Can the North Stop Consumption Growth? Escaping the Cycle of Work and Spend', in V. Bhaskar and A. Glyn (eds), *The North, the South and the Environment: Ecological Constraints and the Global Economy* (London: Earthscan).

World Bank (1993) *The East Asian Miracle: Economic Growth and Public Policy* (Oxford: Oxford: University Press).

9
Unpredictability and Exclusion in the Weightless Economy

Diana Coyle

For a while, during the summer of 1998, the world's bankers began to speak of the unspeakable. It seemed, following the collapse of a speculative investment fund, Long-Term Capital Management, and the Russian government's default on its debt, that the financial markets were about to disintegrate. The entire global banking and financial system was as close as it has ever been to collapse. As Michael Mussa, the economics director of the International Monetary Fund put it: 'We had a millennial event. That is, something which the probabilistic model said would happen once in a thousand years happened in August.'

As with all financial crises, the turmoil eventually passed leaving a landscape that was still recognizable. Nevertheless, the events marked a watershed in perceptions of the financial markets. Ultra-free market rhetoric went promptly out of fashion – and left an intellectual vacuum – since a return to the interventionist approach of the 1970s is impossible, much as many commentators clearly yearn for it. In reality we live with a 'new economy', a phrase much in vogue in the months ahead of the 1998 crisis. But it is not the *shangri-la* of universal growth, plenty and prosperity that some of its ideologues would have us believe. It is a world of large-scale industrial restructuring across national boundaries, of huge swings in investment and employment, a real hurricane of Schumpeterian creative destruction. New certainly, but better for the majority of the population only if the energy of change can be harnessed by the political process.

This chapter looks at the deep, underlying technological transformation of the advanced economies that has barred the way back to traditional government interventions, particularly in welfare, while at the same time increasing inequality and social exclusion. It goes on to suggest an alternative policy approach to both the *laissez-faire* and the earlier top-down interventionism. This approach must equip citizens for economies based on flows of information, economies of signs and space, where change is pervasive and human creativity the key productive resource.

The unpredictability of the weightless economy

Modern economies have been given many names, such as the 'knowledge economy', even though economies have always been based on knowledge. I prefer to describe what is distinctive about current economic change as weightlessness. This refers to the fact that economic value – what people want and are willing to pay for – is increasingly intangible or literally weightless. The gross domestic product of the advanced economies has increased 20-fold this century, but it weighs about the same as it did a hundred years ago. Not only have services steadily expanded as a share of output; but even within manufacturing what is valuable is less and less the material content, more and more the intellectual or creative content. The cost of materials represents only a fraction of the total cost of any product. So, even though we continue to acquire things, the economic process of which they are the end product has become steadily more weightless.

These developments have resulted from the spread throughout the economy of new information and communications technologies. Some three or four decades after the key advances in computer science, these innovations have finally worked their way to the furthest reaches of the economy, transforming production and consumption. So, to take a striking example, the microchip in a musical greetings card has as much computer power as existed on earth in 1945.

Predictably, the wide spread of new technologies is changing the industrial structure of the advanced economies. Broadly speaking, low-value-added production has moved from north to south. Thus basic consumer electronics assembly, clothing and footwear manufacture and other traditional manufacturing industries are migrating. Some of the biggest corporations no longer make the products with which they are associated in the public's mind. Nike makes no shoes and Dell no computers. Both have contracted out the manufacture of the items which they design, brand and market. Most of the profit is in the intangible parts of the production and sales process.

So the unpredictability of modern economies lies in more than the fact that production can relocate across national borders. It is not always easy to figure out where the economic value is added in the production process; and it is hard to get a grasp of exactly what the value is or where it is produced. The accounting concepts are ill-defined, the statistics unavailable and the pace of change extraordinary. Companies trying to cope with this are experimenting with new forms of organization and patterns of employment. At the same time, technology is making possible alternative ways of working, tending to delink people from a clearly defined job.

Unpredictability is pervasive. It is exacerbated by the importance of economies of scale and network effects in modern industries, making business success more tenuous. Huge factories can be opened one year to close the next. Unpredictability is manifested in the self-fulfilling stockmarket bubbles. The traditional mechanistic analysis of economies is truly consigned to history. It is therefore easy to see why the restructuring of industry that has taken place in recent years has prompted fears of the 'end of work' and encouraged populist politicians to claim that developing countries are taking 'our' jobs. As ever, some authors have fallen for the 'lump of labour' fallacy that holds there is only a certain amount of work to go around. It flies in the face not only of economic theory, but also of historical experience. The stock of available jobs has never stood still, but has grown more or less in line with the labour supply over long periods, and has shifted to an incredible degree. So, while manufacturing employment in the UK fell from 10.5 million in 1979 to 6.5 million in 1995, employment in services expanded by nearly 5 million to 18.4 million. Within services, there has been extraordinary growth in financial services on the one hand, and 'community, social and personal' services, which includes jobs like caring, counselling and teaching as well as work in the voluntary sector, on the other. Whole professions come and go within a generation. This broad pattern holds for all the industrialized countries. A decade ago nobody could have foreseen the demand for traders in the financial markets, yet in another decade the number might well have shrunk equally dramatically.

But, of course, it is not a complete answer to the fears triggered by globalization to argue that there are still plenty of jobs around. There are two additional considerations. One is the uncertainty and insecurity generated by industrial restructuring. No young person can enter the job market sure that they are embarking on a lifelong career path. While the great majority of employees stay in a given job as long as they ever did, there have been enough redundancies and enough of a spread of insecure forms of employment so that almost nobody can count on their luck holding. Paradoxically, the creation of new jobs has not, in contrast to the 1950s and 1960s, resulted in greater optimism and stability.

The second factor is the greater inequality of the weightless economy. In continental European countries unemployment remains untenably high, while in the Anglo-Saxon economies real incomes have either fallen or stagnated for the bulk of those who have work. Alongside the destruction of millions of traditional jobs has come inequality and exclusion – either inequality in the distribution of work or in the distribution of earnings. This has, too, a malign geographic footprint. The resulting deprivation and social exclusion is increasingly concentrated in particular areas, either a whole region that used to depend on traditional manufacturing, or certain urban ghettos within our busiest cities; so that the extremes of poverty and wealth, of unemployment and workaholism, of exclusion and power, rub shoulders blatantly and uncomfortably every day.

Economic factors behind social exclusion

The raw material of the weightless economy is not so much information as intelligence. New technologies are not substitutes for all human skills, but instead complement some of them. The most immediate impact of industrial change has been a collapse in demand for mechanical skill and increase in demand for intellectual and creative ability.

No country has escaped the consequences of this switch. In the socially cohesive democracies of continental Europe, politicians have tended to safeguard existing employment patterns and social conditions. There has been a deliberate rigidity in the management of the labour market and provision of welfare. The cost of this act of preservation has been long-lasting high unemployment, particularly for young people and members of ethnic minorities, those on the margins of the labour market. While trying to safeguard social cohesion, these policies have simply given exclusion one particular shape. It is a mistake made by privileged white males to congratulate the governments concerned for their defence of traditional social safeguards when these have profoundly marginalized immigrant groups, women or teenagers. There may be greater social certainty, but for some groups it is simply the certainty of poverty.

In the UK, US and other Anglo-Saxon economies, the social cost of technology-driven change has instead taken the form of a rapid increase in income inequality. Notoriously, in the UK male earnings in industry have become more unequal than at any time since the last century. By no means all, but certainly some, of the jobs growth in these countries has consisted of low-paying 'McJobs', while incomes for those in the bottom fifth or so of the distribution have barely risen. The fall in real incomes for some categories of worker in the US have been described as catastrophic, and more and more Americans have had to take more than one job to make ends meet.

Many authors have noted both the extent of inequality in the weightless economy and its pernicious social effects. Western economies are in effect experiencing a social Balkanisation, with both the new rich and the new poor. The latter are the victims of the fact that demand is shifting dramatically, while the former the beneficiaries of the fact that it is shifting towards weightless activities. For certain features of the advanced economies make them inherently more prone to startling inequality. In his recent book on globalization, Zygmunt Bauman wrote:

> New fortunes are born, sprout and flourish in the virtual reality, tightly isolated from the old-fashioned, rough and ready realities of the poor. The creation of wealth is on its way to finally emancipating itself from its perennial – constraining and vexing – connections with making things, processing materials, creating jobs and managing people. (1998: 72)

Robert Reich, the former US Labor Secretary, was one of the first to put the spotlight on the emergence of a global class of the super-rich, the beneficiaries of the new type of economic activity, labelling them 'symbolic analysts'. More recently, Manuel Castells has characterized them as informational producers, as distinct from 'generic labour'.

One way of understanding the phenomenon at the top end of the income scale is to appreciate that 'winner takes all', or 'superstar' rewards, are spreading throughout the economy. Acting is one field where the range of incomes is extreme, from the movie star down to the hopefuls scraping by on occasional small parts and a waitressing job. In the days of theatre and music hall, actors' earnings came within a much narrower band. But film and television technology made it possible for the stars to capture a much bigger share of a much bigger audience. They could replicate their output – their performance – for almost no extra effort and reach a mass market at zero marginal cost. For their part, audiences quickly came to prefer the known faces, just as cheap to see on screen as an unknown one.

The new technologies have spread the superstar phenomenon to a much wider range of professions than the performing arts and sports. There are stars in medicine, law, finance, academia. A minority of individuals is able to lever up the demand for their own output and supply that demand.

The technological explanation can be supplemented by another: the greater willingness on the part of both politicians and public to tolerate high incomes. Increases of tax rates are shunned on the grounds that they penalize effort without raising much by way of government revenue. In the US and increasingly the UK, policymakers are also keen to keep the tax burden for enterprise as low as possible in the light of the prospect of generating great wealth. Surprisingly, there appears to have been no increase in resentment concerning the increase in the numbers of super-rich. The notion of the deserving rich appears to have growing currency. Few these days begrudge hard-working entrepreneurs their money; on the contrary, they are much admired. Few even appear to mind the millions that successful footballers or singers can earn – perhaps because we can believe that any of us could in principle become the next one. Barriers to entering these wealth stakes are low. If any superstar earners are widely despised it is the executives, lawyers and financiers, but they were never top of the popularity stakes in the first place.

However, divergences between individuals are not the only aspect of increasing inequality. It also has a pronounced geographical dimension. As Manuel Castells writes in *The Rise of the Network Society*, volume I of this great trilogy: 'Elites are cosmopolitan, people are local.' The great world cities are thriving economically as nodes of activity in the weightless world, benefiting from the paradoxical clustering that is the result of the fact that much valuable economic activity can take place anywhere thanks to new technology. Clustering is a marked characteristic of current economic change, a long-standing phenomenon encouraged by better and cheaper communications technologies on the one hand, and the much-increased value of human interactions in many industries on the other.

Meanwhile, poverty and deprivation are at the same time increasingly concentrated in bounded areas of those same cities, subject to their own clustering. They suffer a vicious circle of decline while neighbouring areas enter a virtuous circle of success. Thus Hackney and Tower Hamlets, two of the UK's poorest boroughs, lie alongside the City of London and Canary Wharf, key locations in the global financial marketplace. Yet rich and poor are not walking the same streets, never mind learning and being cared for together. The question is whether it is essential to tackle both extremes of the phenomenon for the purposes of social inclusion – and what measures are practicable.

The breakdown of conventional policy

This is a question that arises because existing policies for reducing exclusion and limiting poverty appear to have broken down, although in ways that vary enormously across countries. In high unemployment countries the principal manifestation is pressure on government budgets through the benefit bill, not quite matched by willingness on the part of other citizens to pay higher taxes and therefore leading to – arguably unsustainable – deficit finance.

At the other extreme in the US most of what Europeans would recognize as a welfare state has been dismantled; the government has partially withdrawn from the provision of economic security to its citizens. This recognizes the greater unpredictability of the modern economy, admitting that policy-makers are no better than anybody else at anticipating and reducing uncertainty. It also marks great dissatisfaction with how welfare has worked in practice – at the right-wing extreme, the provision of welfare has been blamed for cementing the existence of ghettos. This discontent has been echoed in Britain, where the achievements of fifty years of the Beveridge welfare state look very patchy, to as many on the left and centre as well as the right.

The underlying problem of the welfare state is not one of affordability. The advanced economies display a range of size of government in terms of the ratio of public expenditure to GDP. While it is true that in most cases tax revenues have not kept pace with the rise in spending, resulting in the biggest ever peacetime budget deficits during the 1980s, and exposing governments to the pressure of the financial markets from which they had to borrow the difference, there has been nothing in theory to prevent governments from taxing more to spend more. However, tax increases have become so unpopular that politicians are reluctant to put their electability at risk by proposing them. The crisis is one of legitimacy. Voters, observing poverty, unemployment and inner city blight, no longer trust politicians to spend their money well.

Why, then, has the spending of hundreds of billions of pounds each year across the industrialized world resulted in a social safety net with such gaping holes? The critique of the incentives set up by most social security systems – most notably made by Frank Field in the UK – is a powerful one. The means-testing of benefits has created the poverty trap. After just one generation, families living on sink estates without the prospect of well-paying work settle into a life of pitting their wits against the benefit authorities in an attempt to maximize their income from the state. The incentives for them to do anything else are non-existent. The most fundamental form of social security, an adequate old age pension, is no longer provided by the state. State pensions have been shrunk to inadequate levels in order to protect government budgets from the pressure of an ageing population. The better-off therefore make private provision, while those who are poor in work must stay poor in retirement. The Labour government's planned compromise of a minimum pension guarantee for low earners will, however, discourage saving because of its rigorous means-testing.

More fundamentally, however, any rigid structure of welfare provision will work less well at a time when the world is changing rapidly. Already there is no typical pattern, as young professionals put in 60-hour weeks during their peak career years while mothers opt for part-time, term-time hours for a decade of their working life. The new economy not only accommodates such variations; it positively demands the flexibility. People will need to become very much more adaptable than they have been in the half-century after 1945 – and are indeed becoming so.

But not the state. No aspect of the public sector has matched this increase in adaptability, and the state is fundamentally failing its citizens. Where these are urged to be flexible and entrepreneurial, they find no matching flexibility on the part of the public authorities. The failure is even worse where the government pretends that adaptability is unnecessary.

Neither education, social security nor macroeconomic policies –

none has adjusted to the inherent uncertainty of the modern economy. Most governments still believe they can fine-tune the macroeconomy – and this belief has actually revived in continental Europe with the election of new social democratic administrations in several countries. Most still specify in extraordinary and centralized detail what pupils must learn at school, and disregard the fact that more than ever it is not what you know but who you know that equips people to prosper. Equally, tax and social security structures are arranged for only one pattern of life, and there is simply no move to introduce the flexibility that will make easier a multiplicity of patterns. So, for example, pensions are not portable, benefit payments are withdrawn for people in irregular work, moving into and out of work is an administrative nightmare, retraining is out of the question for most adults as the state only offers financial support for education for young people – the list is daunting.

The failure is certainly not one of intent, however. At present there is a remarkable consistency of political opinion across most of the developed world. Governments of the centre-left all put social inclusion at the top of their agenda. There is in addition an explicit recognition of the need for a new approach. Yet many apparently find it impossible to concede that command and control is an inappropriate model for economic policy at present. Anthony Giddens, in his recent book on the Third Way, exemplifies this, despite his crystal clear understanding in other work that the economy has become inherently unpredictable. In his economic policy prescriptions he envisages more extensive government decision-making.

Equally, the typical response to the latest financial crisis is to argue that the capital markets need firmer direct controls. While the aim of such controls, greater stability, is highly desirable, there is little understanding of the practical impossibility of conventional direct control over the ultimate weightless market. They were easily evaded in the 1970s – fans of capital controls forget there were good reasons for dismantling them in the first place – and could be even more lightly avoided now. A subtler approach is necessary. Economic management is simply not as easy as it used to be in a more certain world.

Taxation and management of inclusion

Is increased inequality inescapable? I believe that the nature of new technologies means that it is. One response would be to reintroduce penal rates of income taxation for high earners; but discussion about taxation tends to conflate two aims: raising revenue, and equalizing incomes. The former aim certainly has its merits. It is hard to disagree that a somewhat higher top rate of income tax would put government taxes on a sounder footing and allow more spending on popular programmes like health and education. However, it would hardly affect the redistribution of incomes. To bring top earners' net income down closer to that of the middle range would require a substantial tax increase at the top. There is no doubt that this would trigger evasive efforts and yet not raise revenue substantially. According to calculations by the Institute Of Fiscal Studies, an increase of the present higher rate of tax on incomes above £50 000 to 50 per cent would produce only about the same amount of money as a penny rise in the basic rate. And the very highest earners are now so footloose that such an increase would not scratch them at all.

Besides, there is no big public appetite for penalizing the rich. Whilst this seems to be the ambition of one segment of centre-left intellectuals, many others would rather have a go themselves at making a lot of money, whether by setting up business or by lottery tickets. The politics of envy have not vanished. Pressure on the rich is taking, rather, the form of heightened expectations that they will acknowledge social obligations: for example, through increased charitable sharing.

Income inequality can be compensated for by the outcome of greater social and economic mobility. For example, in order to stay deserving in public opinion, the new rich will have to demonstrate a greater sense of their social responsibility. Public attitudes will not remain so benign if they, as their new peers, shut themselves off in gated estates or withdraw wholesale from state schools. They cannot become too different from their fellow citizens – the backlash in terms of clamour for redistributive tax measures will become irresistible; though, as usual, counterproductive.

Here is one avenue which governments can follow in pursuit of social inclusiveness. Tax and regulatory systems, planning laws and transport can be directed to make it harder to withdraw from society. The well-off should become subjected to a variety of pressures which make it attractive to use state schools and public transport, for instance, and in turn remain willing to fund these. Though income tax has become far less progressive, tax and public spending structures remain highly redistributive. Public expenditure on a common standard helps the well-off more than the wealthy.

Political economy in the service of inclusion

In the UK the path to privilege through a separate and better education is one of the main channels of exclusion: it isolates children
from understanding how others live and guarantees them, and their
children in turn, far better life chances than their contemporaries
in the state sector. The implications of widespread private education are malign. Children in different schools learn different forms
of the English language. They are far less likely to know and play
with different groups of children, whether the difference is of ethnic origin, religion or social class. Private schools even contribute
significantly to air pollution, because so many of those attending
them travel further from their homes in a private car. Thousands
of schoolchildren have never taken a bus. Taken together, these
factors cement the division between included and excluded through
successive generations. Yet mainstream politicians, no matter how
pious they sound about inclusiveness, will not grasp this thorn.
There is the shibboleth of choice.

There remains the genuine issue of how to generate and sustain
academic excellence in state schools. Many of the failing state schools
need a lot more money. In schooling as in transport, people who
have opted for private provisions should not be forced back into
public ones, unless these are made the more attractive option for
them. Even so, a few twitches of the tax system can be effective in
making social withdrawal into private education unappealing for
all except the super-rich.

Equipping citizens to fit into a weightless and uncertain world

This analysis does not point to the depressing conclusion that
social inclusiveness is unachievable in the weightless economy.
On the contrary, some might find the fact that it is beyond the
capability of the entrenched technocracy to deliver their own
vision of an acceptable society rather cheering. For the key les-
son from the unpredictability of the weightless world is the
necessity of devolving policy decisions and empowering people
to take responsibility for their own well-being. Big brother is
powerless – not because he has no power, but because he does not
know what is happening. The exercise of traditional economic powers
is likely to lead to perverse results, because of the profoundly greater

uncertainty about every aspect of our world than we were used to.

In order to equip citizens to prosper, governments must transform themselves from decision-makers into facilitators. In the UK this will require abandoning decades of centralization and bureaucratic outlooks. The devolution of power to the regions has begun, but right away the new regional governments are at risk of turning into mini-Whitehalls. Better – indeed, ideal – units of government are economies of clusters, namely the cities, where the administration can be aware of local conditions and more immediately responsive to local voters.

In addition, government must match the flexibility now required of individuals. If people must switch jobs, retrain and move house, then the onus is on government to make it easier for them, rather than setting obstacles in their way. This should be the objective of detailed reform of tax law, benefits and pensions, rather than policy statements. The history of economic policy is littered with failed attempts to alter the underlying structures of the economy and with accidental damage to economic potential. There is never a widespread desire to embrace uncertainty and flexibility; most people would be happier with something more predictable and are therefore reluctant to consider the structural policy changes even though they are needed.

Inclusiveness in the modern economy will not depend on delivering a specific set of measures but on generating a sense of hope and possibility. At the same time, the inclusive society will have to be fluid, reflecting the uncertainty of the economy. If the state has to return to individuals the responsibility for their own well-being, it must equip them to cope. In the United Kingdom, under a government that seems to broadly reflect the desires of a resounding majority of the citizenry, and in unison with other centre-left administrations in Europe, the construction of this vision is more possible than it has been at any other time for fifty years.

References

Bauman, Z. (1998) *Globalization* (Cambridge: Polity Press).
Casteles, M. (1996–98) *The Information Age*, Vols I–III (Oxford: Blackwell).
Coyle, D. (1997) *The Weightless Economy* (London: Capstone).
Coyle, D. (1998) *Britain's Urban Boom: The New Economics of Cities* (Comedia in association with Demos).
Giddens, A. (1998) *The Third Way* (Cambridge: Polity Press).
Giddens, A. (1994) *Between Left and Right* (Cambridge: Polity Press).
Goldfinger, C. (1998) *Travail et Hors Travail: vers une societie fluide* (Paris: Editions Odile Jacob).

Institute for Fiscal Studies (1997) *Green Budget.*

Krugman, P. (1993) *Geography and Trade* (Camridge, Mass.: MIT Press).

Lash, S. and Urry, J (1994) *Economies of Signs and Space* (London: Sage).

Mandel, M. (1996) *The High-Risk Society* (New York: Random House).

OECD, *Employment Outlook*, annually.

Quah, D. (1998) *Superstar Knowledge Products in a Model of Growth*, working paper, London School of Economics, March.

Reich, R. (1991) *The Work of Nations* (New York: Simon & Schuster).

Rosen, S. (1981) 'The Economics of Superstars', *American Economic Review*, vol. 71(5), pp. 845–58.

Schumpeter, J. (1942) *Capitalism, Socialism and Democracy*, (London: Allen & Unwin).

10
Employment and Social Inclusion
Peter Robinson

'In economic policy, the big debate is not about macro-economics: we are all globalists now.'

Tony Blair, *The Independent*, 7 April 1998

There appears to be a new consensus. Technological change and 'globalization' are apparently having a fundamental impact on the labour market and on society. Inequality is increasing and we may even face the threat of the 'end of work'. Countries are locked in a life and death competitive struggle with each other and global forces have made redundant both some of the traditional objectives of governments and many of their traditional policy instruments. In these circumstances the objective of greater social inclusion seems to be under mortal threat.

If there was one thing which lay at the heart of the postwar consensus in the industrialized nations, it was the commitment to full employment. In Britain the success of the Beveridge plans for social insurance was from the start predicated on the belief that wise management of the economy would deliver full employment. If any one factor has put the greatest strain on the prospects for a more inclusive society it is the failures of economic management after 1973. This last sentence makes the theme of this chapter clear. High unemployment is not primarily the result of technological change or the impact of globalization. It is not primarily a result of the lack of 'employability' of those out of work. It is the result of structural problems in the product and labour markets of some countries, allied to macroeconomic mismanagement in many countries. It can be solved by Governments pursuing well thought through economic and social policies. There is no threat of a 'fundamental insufficiency of work'.

This chapter will argue that while low levels of unemployment are desirable to promote social inclusion, high levels of employment are a necessary but not a sufficient condition for a more inclusive society. Other policies, including a redistributive tax and benefits system, are also important. One of the main blocks on higher levels of employment is the current economic orthodoxy which suggests that macroeconomic policy can play no role in reducing unemployment. Any possible blocks on a more redistributive welfare state are primarily political and not economic.

The chapter takes a decidedly empirical line. However, it is necessary to start off with some working definition of what is meant by social inclusion. Loosely it might be defined as a situation where everyone is able to participate fully in society and no-one is blocked from doing so by lack of political and civil rights, by lack of employment or income, by ill-health or lack of education. In terms of things which are objectively measurable, an inclusive society would seem incompatible with high levels of income poverty and inequality and with high levels of unemployment.

The chapter challenges two main theses which seem to paralyse policy-makers, especially in Western Europe. The first is the notion that there is something out there called 'globalization', which is simultaneously increasing social exclusion through its impact on employment and the income distribution, while also robbing the nation state of the ability to respond by constraining the use of traditional instruments of economic and social policy. This is the thesis set forth by such authors as John Gray (1996) and Anthony Giddens (1998). The second is the natural rate of unemployment hypothesis, which says that macroeconomic policy can play little or no role in reducing unemployment. This thesis was at the heart of the Delors White Paper which aimed to set out the framework for economic policy in Europe (Commission of the European Communities, 1993) and was given further legitimacy by the influential OECD *Jobs Study* (1994).

Both of these hypotheses are overblown and misleading, and overthrowing them is the first step towards designing policies to promote greater social inclusion.

A fundamental insufficiency of work?

The 'end of work' has been forecast for many decades. One can always find someone prepared to describe a world in which a lucky few have work and wealth while the majority experience drudgery and poverty. Technological change has usually been seen as the culprit, allied more recently with the impact of 'globalization'.

The notion that technology must cause unemployment is as old as machines. Technological change usually means that **any given level of output** can be produced by fewer workers. More recently this observation has been allied to scare stories of how goods and services once produced in the West can now be produced more cheaply in newly industrializing and developing economies. These twin forces are alleged to be inevitably grinding down overall levels of employment and/or wages in the industrialized countries.

The analytical flaw in this argument is a simple one and stems from the phrase for 'any given level of output'. Only if world output is somehow fixed is there a justification for seeing international economic relations as a competitive, zero-sum, global struggle to share out the work available. The increased productivity made possible by technological innovation, or the extra output made available as more countries industrialize, will not increase unemployment if the demand for goods and services is rising, as of course it does year by year. The mechanisms which generate a higher level of demand may not be automatic and may need to be managed by governments, but it is clearly wrong to believe that the level of world output is somehow fixed. Even if we thought that affluent westerners did not want to consume more (and there is plenty of evidence that affluent westerners do want to consume more), there are billions of consumers in the third world who would like to raise their standard of living. World output cannot be constrained because people do not want to consume more goods and services.

It is relatively simple to check on the hypothesis that technology and 'globalization' are remorselessly grinding down employment in the industrialized West. Table 10.1 shows the proportion of the adult population in work in the OECD economies in 1996, and in 1974 at the peak of the postwar boom. Bearing in mind the problems of comparability of data across a long time span, it is clear that overall employment levels in the mid-1990s were similar to those in 1974, with about two-thirds of the adult population in work in the OECD economies. So in a period which witnessed severe

Table 10.1 Employment–population ratios in the OECD economies, 1974–96

| | % of the population aged 15–64 in work | | |
	1996	1983	1974
Norway	76.8	77.3	67.6
Switzerland	76.1	73.8	77.4
United States	75.0	68.0	64.8
Denmark	74.7	71.8	73.9
Japan	74.6	71.0	69.9
Sweden	72.7	80.2	75.3
New Zealand	72.2	61.6	65.3
United Kingdom	71.0	67.0	71.5
Canada	68.5	64.8	64.0
Australia	68.3	62.1	68.4
Austria	68.1	62.9	68.0
Portugal	67.2	69.7	70.9
Netherlands	66.0	52.0	55.6
Germany	64.0	62.2	67.7
Finland	62.2	73.2	71.6
France	59.6	62.0	66.0
Belgium	56.6	53.5	61.2
Ireland	56.2	54.0	59.7
Italy	51.3	55.0	55.7
Spain	48.1	49.5	59.6
Total OECD	66.5	64.8	65.8

Source: OECD.

Note: Breaks in series for most countries between these dates.

economic shocks as well as the ongoing trends of technological change and 'globalization', there was no overall decline in employment. Indeed since 1983, after the most damaging adverse shocks to the industrialized economies had occurred, overall levels of employment in the West have clearly risen.

However, the most interesting feature of Table 10.1 is the divergence of experience across countries. Some countries, and especially the United States, have been successful in maintaining or even increasing overall levels of employment. Other countries, including Spain and France, have seen sharp falls in employment. One might anticipate that technological change and 'globalization' would have a more or less even impact across countries. The fact that some countries have been successful in maintaining or improving levels of employment and others have not, suggests that it is the structural features of some economies and the economic policies pursued by governments which are of greatest importance in explaining comparative trends in employment.

'Globalization' is one of the most widely used terms in modern political discourse, and is also one of the most ill-defined. It refers in part to the greater openness of the world economy to trade, investment and financial flows. There is no doubt that such a process of 'internationalization' has occurred in the postwar period, though it has also been observed that the world economy was in many ways just as open before the First World War (Krugman, 1995). International trade as a share of world GDP has increased but the vast bulk of this trade is between countries with similar standards of living. For example, the UK now trades more largely with other EU member states. Exports of manufactured goods from the newly-industrializing economies accounted for only 1.6 per cent of the GDP of the industrialized countries in 1990, up from 0.24 per cent in 1970 (*ibid.*). This increase in trade between the OECD and developing countries is simply too small to produce any significant grinding down of overall levels of employment or wages in the West, even if they have impacted more on certain industries such as textiles, clothing and footwear, and on certain parts of the labour force. It is one of the simplest insights of economics that international trade is mutually enriching and not a zero-sum game. If a country concentrates on producing the goods and services that it is most efficient at producing (in which it has a comparative advantage) and trades them for goods and services it is relatively less efficient at producing, then the country's overall welfare will be increased. Countries are not locked in a life and death competitive struggle for markets. If this were true then the problems faced by several Asian economies in the late 1990s would be a cause for celebration in the West. Instead, the potential reduction in demand for western exports and in direct investment flows has produced the fear of job losses. This describes a world in which countries are interdependent, not engaged in zero-sum competition.

Indeed most economic analysis of the impact of technological change and 'globalization' is much more subtle. It is widely agreed that technology and trade have altered the **balance** of jobs on offer in the labour markets of western countries. They help explain the ongoing shift away from primary and manufacturing employment towards the 'service sector', and the shift from skilled and unskilled blue-collar manual jobs largely towards white-collar managerial, professional and technical jobs.

Table 10.2 Changes in the occupational structure of employment,
1948–98

Occupation	% of total employment			
	1984	1990	1993	1998
1. Managers/administrators	12.5	13.8	15.8	16.1
2. Professional	8.9	9.2	10.1	10.5
3. Associate prof. & technical	7.7	8.8	9.3	10.0
Total: managerial/professional/ technical	**29.1**	**31.8**	**35.2**	**36.6**
4. Clerical/secretarial	16.1	17.0	15.5	15.0
5. Craft and related	17.7	16.0	13.3	12.2
Total: intermediate	**33.8**	**33.0**	**28.8**	**27.2**
6. Personal/protective services	7.3	7.5	10.0	10.9
7. Sales	7.0	7.5	7.9	7.9
8. Plant and machine operatives	11.6	10.7	9.5	9.4
9. Other occupations	11.3	9.6	8.7	8.0
Total: less-skilled	**37.2**	**35.3**	**36.1**	**36.2**

Source: Labour Force Survey, Spring.

This is illustrated for the UK in Table 10.2 which shows changes
in the share of employment by occupation over the period 1984–
98. The share of employment in the managerial, professional and
technical occupations has risen, largely at the expense of employment in the 'intermediate' occupations and, especially, skilled manual
or craft jobs. The declining share of less-skilled manual employment has been largely offset by the increased share of the
personal-service occupations covering such jobs as care assistants
and providers of child care.

Sharp changes in the structure of employment in the UK have
been associated with recessionary shocks. Between 1979 and 1984
there was an unprecedented and precipitous decline in the share of
manufacturing employment. However, this is the only example of
a significant acceleration in the pace of change in the structure
of employment by industry. In the 1990s, the decline in the share
of manufacturing employment slowed down markedly. Within the
'service' sector it is the business and financial services and the public
and social services which have increased their shares of total
employment. Importantly, a large share of employment in the UK
is now in the service industries which are more or less sheltered
from international competition and largely immune from technol-

ogical change. Machines and third world workers can more efficiently manufacture T-shirts, but they cannot care for children or the elderly or provide the whole range of professional and personal services where most net employment generation has been taking place.

These shifts in the structure of employment, with the move away from the manual occupations primarily to the managerial, professional and technical occupations unambiguously imply an increase in the demand for skills, for which in most occupations education qualifications provide the necessary formal basis. Of course in Britain, as in all other OECD countries, average levels of educational attainment have also been rising steadily, primarily as less well-qualified older cohorts of adults are replaced by better qualified younger cohorts. Much research has tried to establish whether it is the increase in supply of better qualified labour or the decline in demand for less well qualified labour which has been the faster trend. This research shares the concern that low educational attainment could be associated with social exclusion, primarily because it reduces individuals' chances of participating in the labour market at good wages.

This research is part of the ongoing debate over some of the causes of rising unemployment in some countries and rising wage inequality in others. Over the period between the late 1970s and the mid-1990s there was a significant increase in wage inequality in the UK, which was out of line with both historical experience and the experience of other European countries, though not the United States. This growth in wage inequality in the UK (and the US) has produced a large literature (reviewed by Atkinson, 1997). Two main hypotheses have been put forward, one focusing on changes in the demand for labour biased against unskilled workers, and the other on changes to the institutions which determine pay and the attitudes which underlie that institutional framework. In the 1980s there was a modest increase in the pay premium attached to holding higher qualifications in Britain, but for men increased returns to education and experience accounted for only one-third of the overall increase in wage inequality after 1979 (Schmitt, 1996). There is little doubt that institutional changes have also contributed to the increase in wage inequality. The decline in unionization, the reduction in and eventual abolition of minimum wage rates, the abandonment of incomes policies for the private sector after 1979, and the increased decentralization of pay bargaining, all played a role in the 1980s and early 1990s.

One of the most difficult features of the growth in wage inequality to explain is that the greater part of that growth has occurred *within* occupational or educational groups. There has been a process of 'marketization' of reward for work (Vandenbroucke, 1998), illustrated most spectacularly by the huge pay increases for senior managers, and for film actors and sports stars.

These changes have been more apparent in the Anglo-Saxon countries than elsewhere. Some smaller European countries have managed to maintain high levels of employment and have tempered any growth in inequality. It is the experience of these countries which might lead one to decisively reject the second part of the 'globalization' hypothesis, that nation states are powerless to resist those forces which also render traditional economic and social policies ineffectual. One would think that it would be precisely small economies like Norway, Austria or Denmark which would suffer most in the newly 'globalized' world. But it is precisely their relative success that should lead one to question the hypothesis. Closer to home, the successful economic recovery in Britain between 1992 and 1997 owed a great deal to astute macroeconomic management, and showed that a medium-sized economy could pursue its own successful independent economic policies, which are certainly constrained by international economic integration but are not rendered ineffectual. And if by the time this book is read unemployment in Britain has been rising again, that will be the result of macroeconomic mismanagement since 1997, not the result of international forces.

The causes of unemployment

The dominant theory of unemployment in the industrialized economies is based on the notion that there exists a 'natural' rate of unemployment, determined solely by supply-side factors, below which inflation will accelerate. Macroeconomic policy can play little role in reducing unemployment. The dominance of this theory over the monetary authorities in Western Europe, though ironically not in the country of origin, the United States, is a much better explanation for the higher unemployment in parts of Western Europe when compared with the US, than 'globalization'.

The fear that a fall in unemployment below the natural rate will generate an immediate acceleration in inflation has conditioned many European Governments and central banks, and the new European Central Bank, to be inherently cautious in their conduct of monetary policy. Any sign of incipient inflation is taken as the signal to slow the economy down and prevent any further falls in unemployment. By contrast, the US monetary authorities have behaved with the utmost pragmatism in pushing growth and employment as far as they will go. Academics in the US are divided between those who regard the natural rate hypothesis as a useful way of ordering one's thoughts while not using any estimates of the natural rate too seriously as a guide to policy, and those who regard the theory as complete bunk (*Journal of Economic Perspectives*, Winter 1997). It is this theory as much as the perceived constraints of 'globalization' which paralyses Western European policy-makers.

The Labour government in Britain believes fully in the conventional wisdom embodied in the natural rate hypothesis, while identifying a slightly different set of supply-side factors which are held to explain high levels of 'structural' unemployment, leading to a set of supply-side policies with a somewhat different emphasis. At the heart of this analysis lies another of the great buzzwords of the late 1990s – 'employability'. This appears to be defined narrowly as equipping individuals with the skills, experience and attitudes which will make them better able to take up a wider range of jobs in an ever-changing labour market. This would embrace policies such as education and training to improve skills, job subsidies and work placements to help promote labour market experience, and other polices designed to work on attitudes.

A major feature of this approach is its reliance on alleged dramatic changes in the labour market which have altered the meaning of full employment as well as making redundant some traditional policy instruments. Apparently, full employment no longer means having a 'job for life'. Then again, of course, it never did. The cohort of older workers nearing retirement in the mid-1990s in Britain, who would have entered the labour market around 1950, have on average had six jobs (McKay, 1998). Lifetime employment was always a myth except for a minority. Old-fashioned full employment apparently meant full-time employment for men. In 1973, 37 per cent of the employed workforce was female and about 16 per cent of the workforce was part-time. By 1998, a quarter of a century later, 45 per cent of the employed workforce was female and 24 per cent worked part-time. These figures illustrate a labour market *evolving* over time, not one in the midst of a permanent revolution which in some undisclosed way renders both old definitions of full employment redundant and apparently also the policies which delivered full employment.

Worryingly, the focus of the 'employability' agenda seems to be on individual deficiencies as the main barrier to reducing aggregate unemployment. Unemployment is not a function of governments messing up the running of the economy. The implication is if only the skills and attitudinal deficiencies of individuals were tackled then everything would come right.

As an explanation of cross-country differences in unemployment this approach seems to offer little. It is hard to see why individuals in France or Germany should be far less employable than individuals in Britain and the United States. Comparative measures of education and skills attainment seem very poorly correlated with unemployment across countries. Moreover, the experience with 'welfare to work' or active labour market policies in industrialized countries is that they are easily swamped by recessionary forces which are the product of mistaken macroeconomic policies, with the experience of Sweden in the early 1990s as a prime example (Robinson, 1995).

It is probably the case that the structural features of product and labour markets in different countries have an impact on employment. The very heavy regulation of product and labour markets in some southern European countries may depress employment rates, especially for women and young people. On the other hand 'intermediate' models of labour market regulation in some northern and central European countries seem perfectly compatible with reasonable employment records. In Britain after 1979, individual employment rights were in many cases enhanced as the result of EU Directives and Court interpretations of the Treaty of Rome, so that any relative improvement in the UK's employment record occurred alongside some additional labour market regulation.

However, this focus on product and labour market regulation puts the ball firmly back in the hands of governments. It is their management of the macroeconomy and their ability to foster structural change in product and labour markets which is the key to tackling unemployment, not making individuals more 'employable'.

It is right to be concerned about parts of the labour force who seem most vulnerable to changes in the structure of employment. Two groups stand out: the residual number of young people who continue to leave full-time education with no or few skills and qualifications, and older unqualified workers displaced from manual jobs. For the former group early intervention and getting the incentives right within the education system so that they receive more attention, are priorities. For the latter group, more flexibility in the form of being able to mix part-time employment opportunities with continued receipt of some benefit might be an option. But needless to say, any measures aimed at helping specific groups presuppose the existence of a macroeconomic environment which is creating jobs.

Employment and social inclusion: an imperfect link

In the introduction social exclusion was linked to the extent of income poverty and inequality. It was suggested that one way of measuring the social inclusiveness of society would be to look at poverty rates and measures of income inequality. But to do so across countries would reveal a weaker than expected link with aggregate levels of employment. Other things being equal, higher levels of employment should result in less poverty and a more inclusive society. However, the United States stands out not only in having high levels of employment, but also in having relatively high poverty rates and levels of income inequality.

Why employment levels and income poverty are imperfectly correlated can be seen by looking across countries in Europe. Several European countries experienced increases in unemployment from the late 1970s to the early 1990s which were as severe as in the UK, but without the same dramatic increase in relative poverty seen in this country.

Figure 10.1 shows relative poverty rates in the early 1990s for nine EU countries before and after taking into account the impact of direct taxes and benefits. The Figure uses the 'standard' measure of relative poverty, defined as the proportion of households with incomes below 50 per cent of average household income, adjusted for household size. It shows that the primary distribution of income, that is before taxes and benefits, is as unequal in countries such as Belgium, Sweden and Denmark as it is in the UK. It is only after the impact of taxes and benefits that relative poverty rates in other western European countries improve dramatically compared to the UK. These countries have a far more redistributive tax and benefits system and it is this which largely accounts for their more inclusive societies, defined in this way. The comparative lack of such redistributive mechanisms in the US and the UK helps to explain their much higher relative poverty and inequality despite apparently good employment records.

Further clues as to why the overlap between employment and poverty is weaker than might be expected can be gleaned by looking

Figure 10.1   Relative poverty rates in nine EU countries (households below 50% of average income)

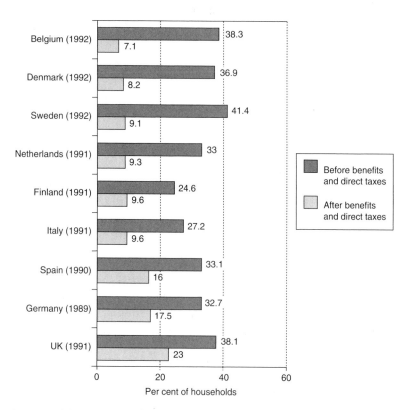

Source: Bradshaw and Chen (1997).

at the household types which in Britain have a much higher poverty rate when compared with other European countries. Two household types stand out: retired households and lone-parent households. The elderly of course are not expected to have any current attachment to the labour market; for them 'welfare to work' is irrelevant. Their higher poverty rates reflect the relative lack of generosity of state pensions in the UK for those on low lifetime earnings who cannot be expected to save enough to look after themselves in retirement. Lone parents can participate in the labour market, but often prefer to work for limited hours. This means that their income from work is rarely sufficient to support the household without being supplemented by in-work benefits.

Other things equal, lower levels of labour market exclusion would make a significant contribution to tackling poverty. Moreover, improving people's employment rates is also rightly seen in its own right as a vital means of promoting inclusion. High levels of unemployment are associated not only with poverty, but also with physical and mental ill-health and social isolation. The non-material benefits of work are very important. However, it is a legitimate question to ask at what level of labour market participation these non-pecuniary benefits of work click-in? It is probable, for example, that social isolation is broken down even for individuals engaged in eight or 16 hours of paid work, or engaged in voluntary work only, and not just for those working close to 'normal' hours. For groups such as lone parents, this level of limited labour market participation might be a legitimate policy goal.

If the lower poverty rates of other European countries are to a large extent the result of a more redistributive tax and benefits systems, what stops the UK from following this route? It is at this point that the last of the assertions of the 'globalists' pops into place. It is alleged that international tax competition is limiting the ability of western countries to maintain the funding of their generous welfare states. Again it needs to be stressed that the weight of empirical evidence is against this proposition.

Perhaps the most revealing evidence is provided by a study of trends in the taxation of corporate profits (Chennells and Griffith, 1997). If globalization was forcing countries into a race to the bottom in terms of lowering corporate taxes in order to attract investment and jobs, one would expect to see it show up starkly in the data. Over the period 1979–94 there was a trend towards a lowering of corporate tax rates, but accompanied by a reduction in the value of allowances given for investment. The amount of tax revenue collected from corporate income taxes as a proportion of GDP remained relatively constant across the OECD. None of the evidence to date suggests that tax competition is driving down corporate tax rates or revenues.

Since 1997 the Labour government in Britain has in fact raised significant extra revenue from corporate taxation. Labour's whole 'welfare to work' strategy is funded by a windfall tax on part of the corporate sector. The government has also raised taxes on the personal sector, by phasing out such tax expenditures as mortgage interest tax relief and the married couples allowance, using the revenue to fund a package of tax and benefit reforms aimed mainly at families with children.

There seems to be little evidence that there are any overwhelming economic forces which stop a country from having quite high levels of public expenditure and taxation if that is what the electorate chooses. Any potential constraints on a more redistributive tax and benefits system are political rather than economic. The somewhat hesitant moves towards more redistribution by the current Labour government reveals an administration testing the waters for the political reaction from middle England, rather than worrying about the pressures of 'globalization'.

The features of an inclusive society

There will always be individuals putting forward dramatic new paradigms which purport to offer an original way of understanding the evolution of society. Those involved in the political process are always searching for new ways of presenting their distinctiveness to the electorate. Often the latter feed off the former, but most new ways or third ways are either intellectually hollow or are merely a re-packaging of what has gone before.

The challenge for all industrialized economies at the end of the twentieth century remains as it always was: to combine an efficient economy and a labour market which generates jobs, with an inclusive society which prevents poverty and limits inequality. There are some countries which have a generally enviable economic record, but divided and unequal societies. The United States stands out here, but if the United Kingdom after 18 years of Conservative government had shown some signs of improvement in its relative economic performance, it paid a heavy price in terms of the growth of poverty and inequality. Most European countries have poorer employment records when compared with the Anglo-Saxon world, but these same countries often have lower poverty rates and less inequality too.

A handful of small north-western European countries combine relatively high levels of employment with low levels of poverty and inequality. These countries – such as Norway and Denmark, and perhaps the Netherlands and Austria – might also score highly on some other 'softer' indicators of inclusion, such as the quality of political and civil discourse and their attitudes to minorities. In terms of economic and social policy are there related features in this small band of countries which give us clues about how to move towards a more inclusive society?

These countries have more or less maintained their political commitment to full employment intact through the post-1973 economic shocks, matched by a generous welfare state. Their approach to macroeconomic policy has more features of old-fashioned Keynesianism than of the natural rate consensus, as of course does policy in the United States. And when some models have turned sour – as with Sweden in the early 1990s – this has reflected mistakes in macroeconomic policy as much as anything else. These countries tend to have more co-ordinated systems of pay determination which may explain their relative success in coping with inflationary shocks without being obliged to push unemployment sharply up as the only weapon against inflation. These pay-bargaining institutions have also limited wage inequality.

They may have achieved the right balance in terms of labour market regulation between the US and southern European models, while generally they are committed to open and competitive product markets. They do tend to have higher than average spending on education and active labour market policies, but objective measures of human capital would not put them in a necessarily more advantageous position relative to other industrialized countries, except perhaps and importantly in terms of equality of outcomes. Above all they have very redistributive tax and benefit systems and it is primarily this feature which buys them less poverty and inequality.

Of course there must be some features of these societies which generate the necessary **political** backing for this combination of policy objectives and policy instruments. However, the most important point is that if some relatively small European economies can achieve these outcomes then so can other countries. There cannot be any overriding technological or external forces which render the objective of greater social inclusion impossible to attain. The constraints are internal and must be social and political.

References

Atkinson, A.B. (1997) 'Bringing Income Distribution in from the Cold', *Economic Journal*, vol. 107 (441), pp. 297–305.

Bradshaw, J. and Chen, J. (1997) 'Poverty in the UK: A Comparison with Nineteen other Countries', *Benefits*, vol. 18.

Chennells, L. and Griffith, R. (1997) *Taxing Profits in a Changing World* (London: Institute for Fiscal Studies).

Commission of the European Communities (1993) *Growth, Competitiveness, Employment: The Challenges and Ways Forward into the 21st Century* (Brussels: European Commission).

Giddens, A. (1998) *'The Third Way': The Renewal of Social Democracy* (Cambridge: Polity Press).

Gray, J. (1996) *After Social Democracy: Politics, Capitalism and the Common Life* (London: Demos).

Journal of Economic Perspectives (1997) Symposium on 'The Natural Rate of Unemployment', vol. 11 (1), pp. 3–108.

Krugman, P. (1995) 'Growing World Trade: Causes and Consequences', *Brookings Papers on Economic Activity*, vol. 1, pp. 327–77.

McKay, S. (1998) 'Older Workers in the Labour Market', *Labour Market Trends*, vol. 106 (7), pp. 365–70.

OECD (1994) *The OECD Jobs Study* (Paris: OECD).

Robinson, P. (1995) 'The Decline of the Swedish Model and the Limits to Active Labour Market Policy', Discussion Paper No. 259 (London: Centre for Economic Performance, London School of Economics).

Schmitt, J. (1996) 'Education Isn't Everything', *New Economy*, vol. 3 (4), pp. 204–8.

Vandenbroucke, F. (1998) *Globalisation, Inequality and Social Democracy* (London: Institute for Public Policy Research).

11
Is the Assertion of Minority Identity Compatible with the Idea of a Socially Inclusive Society?

Peter Ratcliffe

Arguably the single dominant issue on the current political agenda in contemporary Europe is the notion of social exclusion. Social marginalization and poverty have become subsumed within this new overarching paradigm. European Union (EU) policy is imbued with its rhetoric, and in 1997 the newly-elected Labour government in the UK wasted no time in establishing a 'Social Exclusion Unit' staffed by civil servants from various departments of state and representatives of the voluntary sector.

Not to be left out of these developments, the term was embraced wholeheartedly by academic social scientists. In respect of minority communities the Economic and Social Research Council (ESRC) convened a workshop on 'Social Integration and Exclusion' (CRER, 1996). With a much more general remit in mind it funded (from October 1997) a major new research centre at the London School of Economics; the Centre for Analysis of Social Exclusion (CASE). What has been lacking in this process is a failure to undertake a serious critique of the central concept: accordingly it has resulted, I would argue, in a form of 'soundbite sociology'. A consensus of content/meaning is simply assumed. Thus, none of the eminent speakers at the CRER workshop even felt it necessary to define what was effectively the object of her/his analysis.

Social exclusion and the polyethnic society

In order to comprehend the notion of inclusivity in relation to polyethnic societies, such a critique is vital. The key point is that there is a multiplicity of meanings within political, policy and academic discourses. To summarize the essential points of the argument (developed in more detail elsewhere, Ratcliffe 1999), these are threefold:

- First, exclusion tends to be interpreted in either a universalistic or a particularistic sense. In the former case, an ethnic collectivity is seen as relegated to a position outside 'mainstream' society, usually as an 'underclass' (Wilson, 1978, 1987; Morris 1994) sometimes spatially segregated in an 'outcast ghetto' (Marcuse, 1997). Cultural geographers (Sibley, 1995) and town planners (R. Gilroy, 1996) have entered the debate; associating space and neighbourhood with states/processes of exclusion. The latter interpretation involves the denial of access to particular institutional spheres, notably education, housing, employment, health services or social welfare (either singly or in combination).

- Secondly, exclusion is invariably seen as essentially dichotomous in form. Thus, unemployment represents exclusion from the labour market (Levitas, 1996), school suspensions or expulsions exclusion from education (Gillborn and Gipps, 1996), homelessness exclusion from the housing market (Power, 1998: 16), and so on. But, this is clearly a dramatic oversimplification, in that labour market segmentation, the denial of equality of educational opportunity, and confinement to poor quality, overcrowded dwellings could also be argued to represent important forms of 'exclusion'. Dichotomization simply results in the concealment of important types of individualized and/or institutionalized discriminatory practice.

- Thirdly, it constitutes a form of discourse which disempowers. External structural forces are emphasized as the sole, or dominant, material factors and, in the process, the efficacy of agency on the part of minorities is denied. The concomitant danger is that 'the excluded' may appear to be responsible for, or at least to collude in, their own state of exclusion.

The multiple meanings and analytical confusions appear to stem from the failure of many social scientists to ask one very simple question: Who is 'excluded', from what, and how (that is, by what process[es] or mechanism[s])? This should in the process lead to an avoidance of the final major problem area; namely the implication that all minorities, or at least all of certain minorities (as 'collectivities' or 'groups') suffer 'exclusion' (see, for example, CRER, 1995: 20). This resort to crude ethnic essentialisms and the implicit denial of class and gender differentiation compound the errors spelled out earlier; as is evidenced by many writers, notably Peach and Byron (1993), Karn (1997), and Modood *et al.* (1997). Whilst the opposite tack, namely a resort to the total dissolution of groups in favour of a paradigm of 'difference' (an approach much favoured by postmodernist accounts of 'race'/ethnicity), is problematic on the grounds that it denies the salience of grand narratives based on modes of 'racial' discrimination/antipathy, there is a need to take the underlying concerns on board.

Integration versus inclusion

Debates about the inclusive society have at times displayed some of the analytical confusions inherent within the exclusion paradigm. Most notably there is a tendency towards the elision of inclusion and integration (Levitas, 1996). In the case of polyethnic societies such as Britain it is particularly important to retain a clear distinction between these two concepts.

To focus on the integration of minorities is to suggest a return to the conservative framework of the 'race relations cycle' first introduced by Robert Park in the Chicago School of the 1920s (Park, 1950). Here integration is the penultimate step en route to assimilation. The 'system' thus finds space within its existing social, economic and cultural configuration for an outsider group which has endured, and survived, earlier phases of ethnic conflict, hostility and accommodationism. Integration is something which is imposed/facilitated from without, rather than emanating from within; for example via a process linked to the efficacy of individual and collective agency on the part of minority communities. From a systemic/state perspective, social control is the key issue. A lack of integration threatens social stability.

If the obverse of exclusion is non-exclusion or inclusion, however, quite different conclusions follow. In the former case, the state plays an essentially permissive role, except for attempting to ensure the removal of actually, or potentially, 'exclusionary' practices. Britain was both slow to respond to the need for anti-discrimination legislation (the first Race Relations Act being passed in 1965), and loathe to take the steps needed to make that and any subsequent legislation truly effective (Sivanandan, 1982; Layton-Henry, 1992; Solomos, 1993). Successive governments since the mid-1970s have refused to take seriously calls from minority communities, and indeed from the Commission for Racial Equality (CRE) itself, to strengthen the current Race Relations Act which entered the Statute Book in 1976.

Perhaps more significantly, Britain never accepted the case for more explicitly 'inclusive' policies such as those in force in the United States. There, 'affirmative action' or 'positive discrimination' legislation actively sought to provide education, housing and employment opportunities previously denied to those from African-American and other minority groups (Allen, 1994; Oliver and Shapiro, 1997). A similar philosophy underlay the 'Sanskritization' policies adopted in India.

The distinction made here between non-exclusion and inclusion, then, is essentially between the permissive/preventative and the proactive in policy terms. Issues of policy are only one aspect of the inclusive society debate, however. Before returning to these issues in more detail two key issues will be addressed. Both are central to the concept of social inclusion. The first relates to spatial patterns and the marshalling of territorial boundaries. The second is concerned with the maintenance and development of ethnic identity, this to include matters of religion, culture and the retention of difference, whether this be in the context of 'tradition' or change/hybridity.

Social inclusion and spatial patterns: the negation of territoriality

One aspect of the truly inclusive society is arguably that it opens its borders to migrants on a non-discriminatory basis. This means that, even within a context of controls, entry operates equitably in respect of 'race', ethnicity and cultural heritage. In practice, of course, this rarely (if ever) happens: both legislative and administrative processes tend to discriminate against (or formally 'exclude') those who are perceived as 'the others' (Cohen, 1994). It is then important to recognize the error of attempting to separate analytically such 'exclusion' on 'racial'/ethnic grounds from forms of social relations within the society which operate in this way. To make the point more explicit: if a state effectively defines certain groups as unacceptable as migrants and/or potential settlers, this sends very clear signals both to extant minority communities and to those from majority communities who seek to bolster their hegemonic social, cultural and political identity. It therefore undermines any claims on the part of the state that it espouses 'non-exclusion' (in the form, say, of anti-discrimination policies).

Thus, in the UK, the only way to reconcile the two parallel streams of legislation (on immigration control and the combating of 'racial' discrimination) was to claim, as successive governments did, that a firm control on numbers entering the country would aid internal 'race relations', in the process making it easier to 'sell' to the majority the idea of equity (Bourne with Sivanandan, 1980; Layton-Henry, 1992). In one sense, it can be interpreted as a social control strategy in that it effectively claimed that white residents would be less likely to be hostile to minorities if they were convinced about the state's commitment to repel migrants at its borders. Britain's commitment to retain border controls, in contravention of both the letter and spirit of European Union law, constitutes at one level a clear rejection of the notion of inclusivity.

It is suggested here that, because of this explicitly hostile stance towards migrants, refugees and asylum seekers, the building of an inclusive society becomes all the more difficult. The question is whether it is possible, and in particular whether it is possible in a context where minority groups maintain their right to be different (both from majority society and from one another). We defer the second part of the question to the next section, and deal here with the more general issues in the context of territoriality.

Some would argue that levels of spatial segregation between communities provide not only a measure of social integration but also a measure of inclusivity. At one pole is 'ethnic cleansing', witnessed in Rwanda and the Balkans in the 1990s. This 'policy', more accurately characterized as genocide, represents spatial exclusion at its most extreme. Similar strategies were adopted by the Nazis in the 1930s. In the nineteenth century, Jim Crow policies were introduced in the United States to prevent equal status contact between whites and the formerly enslaved African population. Whereas *de jure* segregation is always indicative (by definition) of exclusionary policies (in common-sense terms), it is possible to argue that *de facto* segregation may not be.

At the risk of oversimplifying extremely complex issues, the crux of the matter is whether (high) segregation levels are the result of external constraints of various kinds or are the result of conscious decisions on the part of minority households. In the former case, 'racial steering' in both the owner occupier and rental markets compounded by the denial of (mainstream) loan finance probably constitute the most important issues (Smith, 1989; Oliver and Shapiro, 1997; Ratcliffe, 1997). Those who make the case for 'ethnic choice' as a determinant of spatial concentration usually argue that minorities wish to build 'enclaves' as a conscious strategy for maintaining 'traditional' culture and social networks (Dahya, 1974), even though 'racial discrimination' is a factor the effects of which, they admit, cannot be denied (Ballard and Ballard, 1977).

Crucial also, however, are constraints which masquerade as choices. The 'choice' of property in an area containing significant concentrations of households from one's own ethnic heritage may be a reflection not of a desire to live alongside 'co-ethnics' but rather of a concern about safety from 'racial' attacks and harassment. This form of territorial 'exclusion' remains very much in evidence in most Western European countries (Skellington, 1996; Witte, 1996) and in the US (Oliver and Shapiro, 1997).

It is important to recognize that levels of spatial segregation, although extremely high in the US among African-Americans (even the middle-class fractions thereof), are very much lower in the UK; for all the principal minority groups. Only in the case of a very few urban locations, and then only among certain Muslim groups, do rates approach those found almost universally for blacks in US cities (Peach and Rossiter, 1996). The conventional consensus amongst writers on the UK scene is that the existing spatial patterns involving heavy concentrations in poor (largely pre-1919) terraced housing on the part of Pakistani, and more especially Bangladeshi, households is the combined result of poverty, unemployment and negative housing market effects. These factors, combined with the development of an ethnicized social, economic and religious infrastructure serve to reinforce existing spatial patterns.

The crux of the matter, then, is that insofar as minority communities are visibly identifiable and continue to be seen by whites as outsiders/auslander, as 'dark strangers' (Patterson, 1965) or as culturally different/distant, their access to full social citizenship rights will be compromised. Thus, external 'exclusionary' forces target 'visible' minorities and these forces act to a large extent independently of social class: 'racial' antipathy means that affluent, professional households also commonly face hostility if they decide to move into white middle-class neighbourhoods (Basu, 1997). Crucially for the current argument, these events are quite independent of a desire on the part of those concerned to assert a distinct 'minority identity', a point to be explored further in the next section.

The question of 'minority identity'

The assumption in much of the academic literature on Britain in the 1950s and much of the 1960s was that future generations of minority origin would follow the assimilationist route: it was even believed that acculturation was a realistic expectation, or, if not, should be the aim of society. Education policy accordingly sought to solve the 'problems' of minority children by providing remedial language teaching: the aim being to integrate them into the existing educational system (Carby, 1982). There was not felt at that time to be a pressing argument for modifying the basic educational experience, the ethos of schools or their curricula.

Political developments in the US, principally those associated with the Civil Rights movement and the rise of Black Power, allied to the gradual demise of Britain's Empire and more immediate debates about immigration policy, led to a realization that migrants would not simply jettison their 'cultural baggage'. The solution espoused by the state in the late-1960s – multiculturalism – received official endorsement by the then British Home Secretary, Roy Jenkins when he envisioned a society based on ' ... cultural diversity, coupled with opportunity in an atmosphere of mutual tolerance' (Jenkins, 1967: 267). For thirty years, then, there has been a realization that minorities would wish, for the most part, to maintain a separate and distinct identity.

Public debate suggested that policies based on a form of cultural pluralism would best address the identity issue. The questions for the state then centred around the issues of what form these identities would take, and what the implications were for the wider society. More fundamental, and undoubtedly more intractable, problems generated by the unwillingness of whites to accept 'racial'/cultural difference were acknowledged but rarely tackled by the state. These latter problems were in many ways exacerbated following the end of the 'Cold War' with the rise of Islamophobia (Modood *et al.*, 1997: 277; Runnymede Trust, 1997). British Muslims became the new 'enemy within' or ' ... a dangerous fifth column, subversive of Western freedoms: a trojan horse in the heart of Europe with a deadly cargo of "fundamentalist" religiosity' (Lewis, 1994: 1).

The next section of the chapter will address the specific social policy 'solutions' intrinsic to the notion of inclusivity; namely, those ostensibly aimed at redressing the material inequalities stemming from discriminatory processes. Here, we focus on the implications of cultural difference. Prior to the 1970s, and in accordance with its assimilationist stance, Britain had not felt it necessary or appropriate in its decennial census to explore aspects of ethnic/cultural identity. This is despite the fact that countries such as the USA, Canada and Australia had for many years routinely asked people about their spoken languages, ethnic origins and/or ancestry. There was a gradual realization by civil servants, backed by a sizeable section of the social science community, that identity was becoming an important line of social cleavage and that the existing census question on birthplace was increasingly unreliable as a proxy for ethnicity. Research undertaken by the then Office for Population Censuses and Surveys (OPCS) explored various possibilities (Sillitoe, 1977).

The political project of the incoming (1979) Conservative government led by Margaret Thatcher, however, was to deny the salience of both 'race'/ethnicity and class divisions. Not surprisingly, the 'ethnic group' question was dropped from the 1981 census. There was an uneasy tolerance of the CRE, founded some three years earlier. It too had backed the inclusion of such a question, on the grounds that it would permit an assessment of the material progress of minorities following the introduction of the Race Relations Act 1976.

When a question finally received government approval (appearing in the 1991 census), it took a rather interesting form. Whilst claiming to measure ethnic self-identity, it appeared to be much more concerned with (externally) ascribed 'racial' identity. Thus, in its simplest form, it was reducible to four categories grounded in a common-sense notion of skin-colour-based phenotype: 'White', 'Black', 'Asian' and 'Other' (Ratcliffe, 1996: 8). This is illuminating in that it implicitly identifies the key impediment to the inclusive society: racism. It does, on the other hand, betray a relative lack of concern with the self-definition of ethnic and cultural difference.

Ethnic identity relates to the question of social inclusion in complex ways. Sociologists and anthropologists writing in the 1970s tended to talk about the problems of 'second generation' minorities being located, even trapped, between two cultures (Watson, 1977). This was also occasionally interpreted as a source of 'crisis' (Cashmore and Troyna, 1982). New cultural forms were thereby negated and/or pathologized. Insofar as they were acknowledged to exist, they were deemed simply to be a product of conflict between a (fixed) 'traditional culture' and a given (and also fixed) normative 'indigenous' framework. Such accounts have been replaced by more dynamic accounts of cultural transformation in the work of writers such as Back (1996) and Baumann (1996). This contemporary literature stresses the more positive implications/outcomes of cultural hybridity as well as providing an insight into new forms of 'diasporic identity' (Cohen, 1997) or 'black Atlantic culture' (P. Gilroy, 1993).

It would be a serious mistake, indeed foolish, to claim or expect that new forms of cultural hybridity have led to the elimination of historical enmities. Although rarely documented by social scientists (largely due to understandable concerns about how their material might be [mis]interpreted), conflict between sections of the various South Asian communities (and especially the younger generations thereof) has been closely monitored over recent years by Racial Equality Councils (RECs) in major cities such as Birmingham and Bradford. Much more serious than these, however, both in intensity and in terms of prospects of a socially inclusive society have been 'racially' motivated attacks on these communities by whites (Skellington, 1996).

The interpretation of inclusivity adopted in this chapter involves an acceptance of the right of any individual/community to maintain a 'minority identity' which is different/distinct (from that of 'majority society') in religious and cultural terms whilst at the same time retaining full citizenship rights, in a Marshallian sense (Marshall, 1950). But, there are two major problem areas here. First, there are difficult theoretical issues surrounding identity expression in the public and private domains (Rex, 1986). Majority society may argue, for example, that the maintenance of 'difference' in the private domain is acceptable, but otherwise adopt a philosophy of 'When in Rome . . .'. There are then a second series of concerns which stem from a recognition that 'majority society' is also culturally heterogeneous, though not necessarily reflexively so (Pajaczkowska and Young, 1992: 202–4).

The public–private dualism is also problematic primarily because it is impossible to separate the two domains in any meaningful way. When is the act of religious worship and the adherence to a particular creed solely a 'private' matter? At a simplistic level, it may be seen as private if 'it' takes places within the confines of a person's home rather than in a public place of worship. But adherence to a creed invokes collective worship, and perhaps in the case of Islam in particular involves a totalizing process guiding every aspect of a person's 'public' and 'private' life.

The notion of a 'majority identity' is problematic because, as already pointed out, it is in a literal sense meaningless. Where it can have some credence is in representing the forces of nationalism, ethnocentrism and racism(s). Thus, the idea of 'majority–minority' conflict can be a useful theoretical tool; whilst accepting the force of contra-arguments put by writers such as Modood, who have objected to theoretical representations being cast in oppositional 'Black–White' terms (thereby implicitly conflating 'Blacks' and 'Asians', among others).

Insofar as cultural heterogeneity is the norm, even majority identities raise issues for the would-be inclusive society. The question then becomes one of addressing the extent to which the inclusive society can, in policy terms, accommodate, and respond to, the needs and aspirations of such a diverse society. The crux of this question is the issue of political will; specifically, a firm commitment by the state to the notion of equality of citizenship rights in the broadest sense of the term.

Social policy and the inclusive society

The relationship between social policy and inclusivity is an extremely complex one. What follows is therefore essentially no more than an attempt to sketch out the key issues. At the risk of oversimplification, the central issues are two-fold: the elimination of discrimination and the provision of equal opportunities. The former implies an end to processes which deny access to a society's resources; human, spiritual and material: the latter, the engineering of a situation which permits the individual or group to maximize their goal fulfilment. This can only happen when societal resources reflect the needs and aspirations of the kind of culturally diverse (and changing) population typically found in the contemporary world.

Britain was slow to respond to even the first of these, as noted earlier. After many abortive attempts to introduce anti-discrimination legislation in the 1950s and early-1960s (via private member's bills) the first Race Relations Act entered the statute book in 1965. This merely outlawed discrimination against minorities (defined in terms of 'race', colour, nationality or creed) in places of public resort, however. Not until 1968 were institutional areas such as education, housing and employment covered by the legislation. It was 1976 before a potentially effective law was introduced: this Act permitting a shift from the earlier strategy based on addressing individual acts of discrimination to one where organizations could become subject to 'formal investigations' by the CRE, in cases where *prima facie* evidence of discrimination was available.

Despite some notable successes (see Karn, 1997: 265–87), however, the CRE has been hampered throughout its life, and increasingly so during the 1990s, by a lack of both adequate funds and, crucially, political will from central government. With renewed interest in sources of 'social exclusion' on the part of the incoming Labour government of Tony Blair (1997), the next few years may witness a somewhat higher profile for the CRE, but current evidence suggests otherwise. Of even more concern is that, inadequate though the British approach undoubtedly is, it goes rather further in addressing discrimination than is the norm in other EU states.

Whilst seeking to address indirect as well as direct discrimination, it nevertheless stops short of advocating positive discrimination (or affirmative action) of the sort introduced in the US and in other countries such as India. Thus, for example, whereas occupational targets are legal, quotas are not. It was always unlikely that Britain would follow the US path, given the latter's long period of retreat (since the late-1970s) under pressure from opponents in both Senate and House of Representatives and various legal challenges, principally from whites claiming that quotas had denied them access to education, jobs or services (Allen, 1994; Marable, 1995: 81–90; Oliver and Shapiro, 1997). Indeed, positive progress among some of Britain's minority groups (Modood *et al.*, 1997) may be argued to have lessened the need for such an approach. It should also be recognized that many beneficiaries of affirmative action in the US and elsewhere have felt stigmatized, not to say patronized, by the process.

In the last few years, the focus of the CRE's work in Britain has shifted towards our second core issue. Given the expense, and arguably restricted impact, of formal investigations, the emphasis of current work is on the attainment of 'equal opportunities' in employment and service delivery. Progress is assessed by performance indicators based on pre-set 'levels' or 'standards', which are related to the nature and size of a business/commercial organization or local authority. But the base criteria, in terms of ethnicity, remain intimately linked to the census categories. Whilst this is understandable given the complexity of ethnic and cultural differentiation, it tends to reify putative 'groups' and essentialize ethnic divisions. The result is, in many cases, a crude form of 'ethnic managerialism'

(Law, 1996), which can result in inter- (and indeed intra-) ethnic 'group' conflict over modes and levels of resourcing.

The rigid adherence to forms of ethnic and cultural essentialism tends to obscure cross-cutting social divisions such as class and gender: and minority identities are not fixed phenomena. As noted earlier, the significance of cultural hybridity means that 'old' categories (or even some new ones such as 'Asian-British' or 'Black-British') do not capture the essence of contemporary identities. Even in the absence of such hybridity, cultural identities change. 'Ethnic managerialism', almost by definition, relies on static conceptions about (say) 'Asian' or 'Caribbean' culture. Past experience suggests that there is often a heavy reliance on notions of 'tradition', leading to the pathologization of non-indigenous cultural forms and practices (Carby, 1982; P. Gilroy, 1987).

The question then becomes one of how, in social policy terms, this problem of 'difference' can be dealt with effectively. Indeed, is it even possible to do so? Inclusivity appears to demand that it should be. In a literal sense, it seems obvious that organizations would find it impossible to solve the myriad of problems created by diverse social identities. This is not simply a question of failing to comprehend their implications, or refusing to deal with them. The interests, aspirations and demands of different sectors of the population may genuinely be in conflict with one another. In situations where scarce resources prevail, this is almost inevitable; the result being a form of Balkanization around self-defined ethnic group constructs, or ascriptive labels. Thus, 'Hindus' may perceive a lack of concern with their interests, as compared (say) with 'Bangladeshis': local 'Whites' or 'Jamaicans' may feel that too much credence is given to the cultural or material needs/aspirations of 'Asians', and so on.

There are clearly many different, and competing, conceptualizations of Equal Opportunities Policies (EOPs), as argued by Jewson and Mason (1986) and Young (1989). The British experience suggests that many (perhaps most) organizations have failed to deal effectively with the demand for EOPs, even at a simplistic level (Jenkins and Solomos, 1989; Solomos, 1993). There has been much resistance, both on ideological grounds (EOPs being seen as an example of 'political correctness' or 'loony-left politics') and on grounds of practicality and cost (given the need for data collection and active monitoring in all matters concerned with personnel and service delivery). The best that can be hoped for is probably an increasing

awareness of the need for 'ethnicity sensitive' policies, where formulation and outcome assessment take on board the positive and
negative outcomes for different sectors of the population (Ratcliffe,
1996: 304)

Concluding thoughts: prospects for the inclusive society

The truly 'inclusive society' does not exist outside the realms of
theory. Segments of all populations invariably lose out on 'full citizenship rights' on grounds of 'race', ethnicity, religion, class, gender,
age, disability, sexual orientation, and so on. This being said, it is
instructive to ask whether the maintenance of separate 'minority
identities' is compatible with the notion of inclusion. In practice
this depends on a number of things.

We have conceptualized the inclusive society as a form of pluralist utopia, where the rights to be different are both respected and
incorporated into the polity on the basis of equality. Two core issues
were addressed: majority society's response to diverse minority identities, and the willingness and/or ability of social institutions to
reflect differing needs and aspirations. One key element of the former
is role-ascription. Irrespective of an individual's self-identity, s/he
will be subject to various external constructs of 'otherness': in this
sense a society is 'racialized' or 'ethnicized'. Certain 'socially significant' aspects of an individual's identity may be unalterable, and
hence have nothing to do with an internal desire to express a separate
minority identity; for example, phenotype characteristics such as
skin colour. Social acceptance here depends on a major social paradigm shift, whereby 'exclusionary' processes such as discrimination,
harassment and territoriality are eradicated.

The presentation of minority self-identity raises the second series
of questions for majority society (heterogeneous as this is). Insofar
as the former suggests an apparent desire to stress 'otherness' (cultural 'non-inclusion'?) for example via language, dress, religion and
customs, this will invoke in some an unwillingness to accept these
groups as fully committed to, or part of, 'the nation'. The classic,
if rather trite, example is 'Tebbit's cricket test', where the former
British Conservative Party Chairman suggested that the acid test of
the commitment of minorities to Britain lay in which national team
they supported. Global events also play a part here, not least in
the development of Islamophobia. At a more mundane, but no less
significant, day-to-day level, overt representations of 'difference' will

enhance the profile of resource competition, and potentially lead to 'ethnicized' or 'racialized' conflict. Thus, the reality of cultural pluralism may not accord with our (utopian) conceptualization.

The role of social policy in working towards the inclusive society is vital, but at the same time problematic. It clearly needs to oppose, and overtly so, the exclusionary practices noted earlier. But the removal of exclusion does not *per se* imply a policy of inclusion. The latter was seen to imply the introduction of strategies based on 'managing difference' rather than 'ethnic managerialism'. At the same time (and assuming the argument is won!), this was seen as problematic on the grounds both of multiple and changing minority identities, and of conflicting needs and aspirations. Thus, to 'include' one person may imply the 'non-inclusion' or 'exclusion' of another.

In conclusion, the most likely outcome is a form of partially inclusive society. As with the notion of 'social exclusion', inclusion is not a dichotomous entity. Levels of 'inclusion' may vary in respect of different ethnic segments, different class fractions thereof, different institutional arenas and different social milieux. These may, or may not, be linked. Success (that is, inclusion) in the labour market may not be accompanied by universal social acceptance or 'success' in terms of housing market position. But, for example, economic integration may enhance the likelihood of social integration and ultimately inclusion at the level of the 'social'. As far as Britain is concerned, there is evidence of economic progress by some, if not all, minorities (Karn, 1997; Modood *et al.*, 1997). In the USA, the experiences of minorities are massively at variance, with the African-American population increasingly bifurcated into a relatively small, but affluent, middle class and an impoverished majority (Allen, 1994; Oliver and Shapiro, 1997; Wilson, 1987), many of whom remain trapped in what have been conceptualized as 'outcast ghettos' of the poor (Marcuse, 1997).

References

Allen, W.R. (1994) 'The Dilemma Persists: Race, Class and Inequality in American Life', in P. Ratcliffe (ed.), *'Race', Ethnicity and Nation: International Perspectives on Social Conflict* (London: UCL Press), pp. 48–67.

Back, L. (1996) *New Ethnicities and Urban Culture: Racisms and Multiculture in Young Lives* (London: UCL Press).

Ballard, R. and Ballard, C. (1977) 'The Sikhs: The Development of South Asian Settlements in Britain', in J.L. Watson (ed.), *Between Two Cultures: Migrants and Minorities in Britain* (Oxford: Basil Blackwell), pp. 21–56.

Basu, D. (1997) 'Accounts of the Experiences of Middle Class South Asian Migrants in Britain', personal communication.

Baumann, G. (1996) *Contesting Culture: Discourses of Identity in Multi-ethnic London* (Cambridge: Cambridge University Press).

Bourne, J. with Sivanandan, A. (1980) 'Cheerleaders and Ombudsmen: The Sociology of Race Relations in Britain', *Race and Class*, vol. xxi(4), pp. 331–51.

Carby, H.V. (1982) 'Schooling in Babylon', in Centre for Contemporary Cultural Studies (ed.), *The Empire Strikes Back: Race and Racism in 70s Britain* (London: Hutchinson), pp. 183–211.

Cashmore, E.E. and Troyna, B. (eds) (1982) *Black Youth in Crisis* (London: Allen & Unwin).

Cohen, R. (1994) *Frontiers of Identity: The British and the Others* (Harlow: Longman).

Cohen, R. (1997) *Global Diasporas* (London: UCL Press).

CRER (1995) *Annual Report 1994–5* (Centre for Research in Ethnic Relations, Coventry: University of Warwick).

CRER (1996) *Social Integration and Exclusion: Resource Needs* (Conclusions of an ESRC Workshop) (Coventry: University of Warwick).

Dahya, B. (1974) 'The Nature of Pakistani Ethnicity in Industrial Cities in Britain', in A. Cohen (ed.), *Urban Ethnicity* (London: Tavistock), pp. 77–113.

Gillborn, D. and Gipps, C. (1996) *Recent Research on the Achievements of Ethnic Minority Pupils* (London: HMSO).

Gilroy, P. (1987) *There Ain't No Black in the Union Jack: The Cultural Politics of Race and Nation* (London: Hutchinson).

Gilroy, P. (1993) *The Black Atlantic: Modernity and Double Consciousness* (London: Verso).

Gilroy, R. (1996) 'Building Routes to Power: Lessons from Cruddas Park', *Local Economy* (November), pp. 248–58.

Jenkins, Roy (1967) *Essays and Speeches* (edited by Anthony Lester) (London: Collins).

Jenkins, Richard and Solomos, J. (eds) (1989) *Racism and Equal Opportunity Policies in the 1980s* (Cambridge: Cambridge University Press).

Jewson, N. and Mason, D. (1986) 'The Theory and Practice of Equal Opportunity Policies: Liberal and Radical', *Sociological Review*, vol. 32(2), pp. 307–34.

Karn, V. (ed.) (1997) *Employment, Education and Housing among the Ethnic Minority Population of Britain*. Ethnicity in the 1991 Census, Vol. 4 (London: HMSO).

Law, I. (1996) *Racism, Ethnicity and Social Policy* (Hemel Hempstead: Prentice Hall).

Layton-Henry, Z. (1992) *The Politics of Immigration* (Basingstoke: Macmillan).

Levitas, R. (1996) 'The Concept of Social Exclusion and the New Durkheimian Hegemony', *Critical Social Policy*, vol. 46(16), pp. 5–20.

Lewis, P. (1994) *Islamic Britain: Religion, Politics and Identity among British Muslims* (London: I. B. Taurus).

Marable, M. (1995) *Beyond Black and White: Transforming African-American Politics* (London and New York: Verso).

Marcuse, P. (1997) 'The Enclave, the Citadel and the Ghetto: What has Happened in the Post-Fordist City?', *Urban Affairs Review*, vol. 33(2), pp. 228–64.

Marshall, T.H. (1950) *Citizenship and Social Class and Other Essays* (Cambridge: Cambridge University Press).

Modood, T., Berthoud, R., Lakey, J., Nazroo, J., Virdee, S., Smith, P. and Beishon, S. (1997) *Ethnic Minorities in Britain: Diversity and Disadvantage* (London: PSI).

Morris, L. (1994) *Dangerous Classes: The Underclass and Social Citizenship* (London: Routledge).

Oliver, M.L. and Shapiro, T.M. (1997) *Black Wealth/White Wealth: A New Perspective on Racial Inequality* (New York and London: Routledge).

Pajaczkowska, C. and Young, L. (1992) 'Racism, Representation, Psychoanalysis', in J. Donald and A. Rattansi (eds) *'Race', Culture and Difference* (London: Sage/Open University Press). pp. 198–219.

Park, R.E. (1950) *Race and Culture* (Glencoe, Ill.: Free Press).

Patterson, S. (1965) *Dark Strangers: A Study of West Indians in London* (Harmondsworth: Penguin).

Peach, C. and Byron, M. (1993) 'Caribbean Tenants in Council Housing: 'Race', Class and Gender', *New Community*, vol. 19(3), pp. 407–23.

Peach, C. and Rossiter, D. (1996) 'Level and Nature of Spatial Concentration and Segregation of Minority Ethnic Populations in Britain in Great Britain, 1991', in P. Ratcliffe (ed.), *Social Geography and Ethnicity in Britain: Geographical Spread, Spatial Concentration and Internal Migration*. Ethnicity in the 1991 Census, Vol. 3 (London: HMSO), pp. 111–34.

Power, A. (1998) 'Down but Not Out in London, Manchester . . .', *Times Higher Education Supplement*, 14 August, p. 16.

Ratcliffe, P. (ed.) (1996) *Social Geography and Ethnicity in Britain: Geographical Spread, Spatial Concentration and Internal Migration*. Ethnicity in the 1991 Census, Vol. 3 (London: HMSO).

Ratcliffe, P. (1997) 'Race, Ethnicity and Housing Differentials in Britain', in V. Karn (ed.), *Employment, Education and Housing among the Ethnic Minority Population of Britain*. Ethnicity in the 1991 Census, Vol. 4 (London: HMSO).

Ratcliffe, P. (1999) 'Housing Inequality and 'Race': Some Critical Reflections on the Concept of "Social Exclusion"', *Ethnic and Racial Studies*, vol. 22(1).

Rex, J. (1986) *Race and Ethnicity* (Buckingham: Open University Press).

Runnymede Trust (1997) *Islamophobia: Its Features and Dangers: A Consultation Paper* (London: Commission on British Muslims and Islamophobia).

Sibley, D. (1995) *Geographies of Exclusion: Society and Difference in the West* (London: Routledge).

Sillitoe, K. (1977) 'Ethnic Origin: The Search for a Question', *Population Trends*, vol. 13, pp. 25–30.

Sivanandan, A. (1982) *A Different Hunger* (London: Pluto).

Skellington, R. (1996) *'Race' in Britain Today*, (2nd edn) (London: Sage/Open University Press).

Smith, S.J. (1989) *The Politics of 'Race' and Residence: Citizenship, Segregation and White Supremacy in Britain* (Cambridge: Polity Press).

Solomos, J. (1993) *Race and Racism in Britain* (Basingstoke: Macmillan).

Watson, J.L. (ed.) (1977) *Between Two Cultures: Migrants and Minorities in Britain* (Oxford: Basil Blackwell).

Wilson, W.J. (1978) *The Declining Significance of Race: Blacks and Changing American Institutions* (Chicago: University of Chicago Press).

Wilson, W.J. (1987) *The Truly Disadvantaged: The Inner City, the Underclass and Public Policy* (Chicago: University of Chicago Press).

Witte, R. (1996) 'Racist Violence in Western Europe', *New Community*, vol. 21(4), pp. 489–500.

Young, K. (1989) 'The Space Between Words: Local Authorities and the Concept of Equal Opportunities', in R. Jenkins and J. Solomos (eds), *Racism and Equal Opportunity Policies in the 1980s* (Cambridge: Cambridge University Press), pp. 93–109.

12

Associative or Communal Society? The Globalization of Media and Claims for Communality

Richard Collins

The argument stated

The globalization of media and communications has two main consequences for social identities and communities and therefore for possibilities of social inclusion. To the very large extent that modern societies have taken the form of the nation state, there has been a requirement that citizens share a culture and thereby an identity. When such national culture is eroded by globalization, social cohesion is threatened. The critical issue then becomes: Can national societies – as inclusive, communal societies thus far have mostly been – successfully metamorphose into something different – associative societies? But there is a second, ethical consequence: if there is a right to a national identity, the globalization of media is ethically objectionable because it denies the opportunity for full self-realization. Following a brief description of the globalization of media and communications, this chapter reviews the relevant arguments and indicates the requirements for modern social coherence.

Introduction

The growing interdependence of hitherto separate economies, allied to complementary trends such as the implementation of military doctrines of collective security, the pooling of sovereignty in associations such as the European Union, international agreements such as the Law of the Sea and international travel (whether voluntary tourism or involuntary migration), together constitute the phenomenon of globalization.

Globalization is particularly pronounced in information and communication. The international division of labour, on which the growth in world trade depends, requires what Weber identified as 'extremely important conditions in the fields of communication and transportation' and specifically 'the services of the railway, the telegraph and the telephone' (Weber, 1964: 339). Also, the inherent economic characteristics of information tend to make the extension of information markets, through both time and space, more pronounced than markets in other traded goods and services.

A succession of technological changes culminating in electronic transmission of sound and image have made possible successful exploitation of the highly distinctive economic characteristics of information, notably its imperishability and inexhaustibility: information does not decay and nor is it destroyed by consumption. Information can be stored, transmitted and reproduced at very low cost across time and space. It can be used many times and by many people without being exhausted. Not surprisingly, media and communications are one of the most globalized sectors of the world economy.

The internet

The internet, the most recent and striking new medium of information and communication, defies conventional statistical description and categorization and confirms the implacable globalization of media and communications. More than any other medium, the internet has decoupled distance (and often time) from price. For those with internet connections, communication with the other side of the world is as easy as communication next door. Moreover, its infrastructural architecture means the internet is an inherently international – indeed global – system which confounds established models. As Paltridge observes:

> The Internet is turning traditional point to point communication models on their head. For example, in the world of public switched telecommunication networks (PSTN) there was generally a correlation between the amount of traffic exchanged between two countries and the amount of capacity allocated by infrastructure providers for this route. For the Internet the points of origin and termination of packets of data have very little

relationship to the traffic that may be carried over any given route or to traditional PSTN traffic patterns.

(Paltridge, 1998: 4).

The internet is paradigmatic of the general integration of media and communications markets through space (and time) and represents a remarkable intensification of this long-established process. The inherently imperishable and inexhaustible (non-rival) characteristics of information, allied to technological systems of reproduction (for example printing) which have low marginal costs of production provide strong economic incentives to extend markets for 'content' media (such as printed works, films and recorded music) in time and space. In 'carriage' media, such as telephony and mail, similar considerations apply.

The globalization of media and communication, preeminently exemplified by the internet, threatens (or promises) to erode the distinctions – particularly the repertoires of symbolic distinctions – out of which societies have been constituted. *Society is not only what it includes but what it excludes.* There can be no inclusion without exclusion and globalization threatens, or promises, to dissolve difference – particularly in the symbolic domain. Difference from others keeps social groups together. Not members' difference from others in the same group but their shared difference from outsiders makes individuals members of a group. When symbolic differences erode, the integrity of established societies is weakened. Smith puts the case pithily: 'where Esperanto failed, information technology might succeed' (Smith, 1995: 17). If the symbolic bonds which engender the 'subjective feeling' which characterizes communal societies wear away, the question arises: can the inclusive society hold together as an 'associative' rather than as a 'communal' institution? Further, are members of an associative society, one distinguished by 'rationally motivated adjustments' rather than by 'subjective feeling...' (Weber, 1964 [1922]: 136), denied one of their rights (that is, their right to a collective identity in which the sentiment of affiliation with those like them can be enjoyed even if that same sentiment necessarily entails alienation from dissimilar others)?

Nationalism

Pre-globalization, the normative model of the inclusive society, was characterized by a matching, mutually reinforcing, relationship between economic structures – the character of the markets within which labour was divided, political structures – the states within which rules of law were exercised, and cultural/linguistic structures within which collective identities were sustained. These 'inclusive societies' were national societies.

The creation of national states, sovereign entities distinguished by the principle that 'the political and the national unit should be congruent', was, Gellner proposed, the midwife to industrialization and the modern era: national sentiment was necessary for the transition to modernity (Gellner, 1983: 1). Where sentiments of collective, national, identity existed, men and women could be reconciled to the traumatic exchange of the routines of the sun and seasons for those of industrial waged labour and the clock; to loss of a concrete, lived community for membership of an 'imagined' national community.

For Gellner, nationalism reenchanted the world compensating for the loss in social cohesiveness which accompanied increased logical cohesiveness (Macfarlane in Hall and Jarvie, 1992: 125). By providing an ideological glue during the intense anonymization and social stress which accompanied modernization, a sentiment of collective national identity reconciled the modernized to their lot. Nationalism, in Gellner's scheme of things, made possible modernity. It was, and is, a 'common intellectual denominator' (Hall and Jarvie, 1992: 3). Nationalism constituted the coupling of polity and culture in 'communal' societies as normative and necessary.

In spite of the importance leading contemporary theorists of nationalism have ceded to the mass media (see for example Smith, 1991 and 1995), discussion for the most part consists of a genuflection to its importance rather than a situated discussion. Central to such a discussion is the question: do contemporary international trends in media and communications threaten to make the inclusive society include too much? Addressing this question requires that we distinguish between two possible bases of social cohesion.

Associative and communal societies

Weber distinguished between 'associative' relationships characterized by 'rational free market exchange', and 'communal' relationships characterized by 'a national community' (Weber, 1964 [1922]: 136–7):

A social relationship will be called 'communal' if and so far as the orientation of social action . . . is based on a subjective feeling of the parties . . . that they belong together. A social relationship will, on the other hand, be called 'associative' if and in so far as the orientation of social action . . . rests on a rationally motivated adjustment of interests or a similarly motivated agreement . . .
(Weber, 1964 [1922]: 136)

Weber's distinction echoes Meinecke's distinction between 'cultural nations and political nations' (Meinecke, 1970: 10), reformulated by Smith (1991 *passim*) as two types of nationalism – 'civic' and 'ethnic' nationalism. It is civic, or political, nationalism which is thought to bind together states (such as Canada, Finland, India, Switzerland etc.) where citizens share neither a single linguistic/ cultural identity nor a common ethnicity.

Cultural nationalism is a doctrine of the clear necessity of congruence between culture and polity for the legitimacy and durability of societies. Social cohesion requires that societies must maintain an endogenous culture and resist exogenous cultural influence. Such an inclusive society must be made up of *people like us*. In contrast, civic nationalism emphasizes adherence to a shared body of law, social rules and conventions which are both exercized and accepted as being impartial between different ethnicities (or other social groups or collective identities). It can, potentially, deliver an inclusive society of people *unlike us* tolerant of difference, which guarantees rights independent of class, creed or colour.

The ethics of associative and communal societies

Seen from this civic perspective, the globalization of media and communications could be regarded positively, as a stage in the teleological progress towards completion of the project of modernity in which all would enjoy 'undifferentiated citizenship' as members of a global inclusive society built on associative lines (Kymlicka, 1995: 174). Viewed thus, the blocking of globalization in the name of the national – for example, impeding the development of an international division of labour; restricting the circulation of exogenous information products; reserving full political and human rights to fellow nationals; and the anathematization of difference – appears as a rejection of the project of modernity and the full realization of what Gellner (modernly) insisted is empirically, as well as epistemologically, 'one world' (Hall and Jarvie, 1992: 216).

But some have argued that associative arrangements are both pragmatically and ethically inferior to communal arrangements. For David Miller a communal society is ethically superior both because it provides for the realization of identity entitlements (the ability to fully realize ourselves through living with people like ourselves), and also because it is better adapted to the delivery of the reciprocal obligations necessary to societies carrying on carrying on. He doubts that the commitment to reciprocal obligations is robust enough in an 'associative' or 'civic' society. The principle of cohesion is too anaemic and fragile to survive extreme conditions. Only in a 'communal' society, made up of like peoples, can exacting obligations be reliably discharged. Only then will people die for each other and for society itself.

This points, of course, to a different regime for media and communications.

The ethical case for communalism

Two chief issues thus arise from the choice between associative and communal models for the inclusive society. First a pragmatic issue – can culturally discontinuous polities survive? And if so, on what basis? I have put forward the pragmatic case for associative arrangements elsewhere.[1] Second an issue of principle. Are communal societies morally superior to civic societies? Miller (and others) elaborates an ethical case for communalism and contends that there 'are strong ethical reasons for making the bounds of nationality and the bounds of the state coincide' (Miller, 1995: 73), and in consequence 'positive obligations to protect basic rights . . . fall in the first place on co-nationals' (Miller, 1995: 79 – see also Miller, 1989 *passim*).

He further states that 'in a national community . . . unconditional obligations to other members . . . arise simply by virtue of the fact that one has been born and raised in that particular community' (Miller, 1995: 42). Here Miller elaborates an argument (which Smith elsewhere names socio-biological [1995: 32]) that the 'special obligations [owed] to fellow members of my nation' are not similarly owed 'to other human beings' (Miller, 1995: 49) because of the intrinsically greater obligations owed to those to whom we are close – classically our family. This analogy does not acknowledge the importance of cases where a family is not made up of members of the same ethnic or national community, or where a family member is rightly handed over to the law. Moreover, just as the social generalization of individual volitions may be hostile to social order and the general good, so too may the generalization of what a family wishes for itself be hostile to the interests of society at large. Family commitments can (*vide* the Mafia, for which the customary synonym 'The Family' is particularly appropriate here) be hostile both to social cohesion and to others' rights. As feminism has taught us, the family is not universally recommended as a sound basis either for society or for social theory.

The family analogy starts to fray with the acknowledgement that nations can be multiethnic and that what counts is not shared descent but a 'common public culture' (Miller, 1995: 25). Shared experience may build firm bonds and social cohesion may be engendered by the common experience of being 'born and raised in [a] particular community' (Miller, 1995: 42). Multi-ethnic states may indeed share a 'common public culture'. But the difficult case, pragmatically and ethically, is not the multiethnic state but the multinational state (Kymlicka, 1995, *passim*).

Nonetheless, Miller's focus on the relatively neglected ethical issues within a sophisticated context of recognition of the complex relationships of political, historical and sentimental factors make his arguments important. He poses the stark choice between extreme viewpoints:

> At one extreme stands the view that the nation should be the supreme object of our loyalty, that every other claim should be set aside in its favour. At the other extreme stands the view that we are citizens of the world, members of a common humanity, and that we should pay no more regard to the claims of our co-nationals than to those of any other human beings regardless of where they happen to reside.
>
> (Miller, 1995: 3)[2]

Miller argues that nationalism is ethically superior to an abstract universalism because it rests 'on well established facts about human identity and human motivation' and that, accordingly, 'The onus is on the universalist to show that, in widening the scope of ethical ties to encompass equally the whole of the human species, he does not also drain them of their binding force' (Miller, 1995: 80). Miller's conclusion is rooted in his analogy: family and its bonds of sentiment and obligation model the national community. But not only is this argument less powerful than Miller supposes, but the choice Miller poses between national communities and abstract universalism is forced and false.

Doubtless there are limits beyond which the bonds of obligation which hold societies together begin to crack – societies cannot function without *some* shared values and shared communication systems – but ethics is a domain of 'oughts' rather than 'ises', a sphere of principle rather than pragmatics. Miller fails to make an ethical case for nationalism – to show that organizing political communities on national lines is how they *ought* to be. His argument that, 'Nations are communities of obligation, in the sense that their members recognize duties to meet the basic needs and protect the basic interests of other members', clearly implies that these obligations do not extend to non-members of the national community (Miller, 1995: 83). This criterion, at a time of pervasive mobility of populations, hybridization of symbolic culture and transnationalization of almost every relationship – economic, political, social and affective – that one could name, simply excludes too much – not least the empirical cases of multinational states in which 'common loyalty' derives from 'shared patriotism, not a common national identity' (Kymlicka, 1995: 13) and the claims in principle of those unlike us for the rights of 'undifferentiated citizenship' (*ibid.*: 174).[3]

For more compelling ethical – though I believe still unsatisfactory – arguments for nationalism we must go to Taylor (1994) and for a humane, practical and ethical theory of citizenship and identity politics to Kymlicka (1995). Kymlicka argues for a weaker, less normative, public culture than Miller;[4] for multinationalism and the accommodation of national identities within a single society and polity on the basis, not of a shared normative public culture, but of 'equality between groups and freedom and equality within groups' (Kymlicka, 1995: 194).[5] Accordingly, I turn now to the issues of principle implicit in rival, associative and communal, models of the inclusive society.

Considerations of principle

Whether society is to be communal or associative is not just a sociological/historical issue; it is also one of rights as, from different perspectives, Rousseau and Miller acknowledge (see also Trudeau, 1968, and Gellner, 1983: 1–2):

If, therefore, at the time of the social compact there are opponents to it, their opposition does not invalidate the contract,
but simply prevents them from being included in it; they are
foreigners dwelling among citizens. When the state is instituted,
residence is consent; to dwell in a territory is to submit to its
sovereign.

(Rousseau, 1953 [1762] Book IV Chapter II: 117)

A critically reflective person must adhere to some form of cosmopolitanism.

(Miller, 1995: 12)

These citations conveniently mark the limits of a spectrum of views
on the extent to which *difference should be acknowledged in an inclusive society*. In terms of media and communications, this issue might
be posed as: 'How far should society be organized so as to realize a
collective identity for and of its members?' The ethical case rests
on the proposition that, without a collective cultural roof under
which a distinct identity may thrive, individuals are denied their
entitlement to feel themselves. This is possible only if one feels
part of a group of like members. Central to this group sentiment
(and thus to boundary definition) is a shared language and culture,
*precisely what the globalization of media, communication and information
is transforming*. Without the ability to share membership of a group
of like people, individuals are, as Taylor argues, denied a crucial
element of self-realization. He states that a:

crucial feature of human life is its fundamental dialogical character.
We become full human agents, capable of understanding ourselves, and hence of defining our identity, through our acquisition
of rich human languages of expression.

(Taylor, 1994: 32)

And difference itself, Taylor argued, is intrinsically valuable:

Just as all must have equal civil rights, and equal voting rights,
regardless of race or culture, so all should enjoy the presumption
that their traditional culture has value.

(Taylor, 1994: 68)

Cultural rights

Similar arguments to Taylor's have been advanced in the policy domain. For example, Jacques Delors, when President of the Commission of the European Communities, stated (at the Assises de l'audiovisuel in Paris 1989) that:

> Culture is not a piece of merchandise like any other and must not be treated as such ... culture cannot flower today unless control of the relevant technologies is assured. On the first point ... we cannot treat culture the way we treat refrigerators or even cars. Laissez-faire, leaving market forces to operate freely is not enough. I would like to ask just one question of our American friends ... do we have the right to exist?
>
> (Assises de l'audiovisuel, 1989: 47–8)

Delors' arguments chime with Taylor's. Like Taylor he constitutes collective cultural identity as a *right*. Other public figures, such as Jack Lang[6] and Roberto Barzanti[7] (Barzanti, 1990) have argued in the same vein. In 1988, for example, Lang objected to the preponderance of US programmes on European screens and argued:

At a time when Europe, the cradle of Western civilization, loses control over one of the main areas in which contemporary culture is being made, the audiovisual, one can no longer react aesthetically to such liberal or ultra liberal ideologies. Reality demands that concrete steps be taken.

(Lang, 1988: 20)

Elsewhere Taylor has provided an exposition of the propositions implicit in Delors' and Lang's statements:

> The core of the modern conception of rights is that respect is owed the integrity of the human subject. This obviously entails that the human subject has a right to life, to liberty; on Lockeian assumptions, also to property. But if we add the Romantic understanding of identity, as essential to human subjecthood, then plainly there is something else here to which we have a right, namely, that the conditions of our identity be respected. If we take the nationalist thesis that these are primarily our belonging to a linguistically defined nation, we have

the beginnings of another justification of the rights of nations to political expression.

(Taylor, 1993: 48)

Taylor affirms, as intrinsic to a bundle of modern, largely individual, rights, the right to a collective identity and to the realization of that entitlement through public expression of identity. He argues that without, 'certain values, certain allegiances, a certain community. . . . I could not function as a fully human subject' (Taylor, 1993: 45).

Communal nationalism and identity entitlements

Taylor's formula chimes with Kedourie's famous statement that 'language is the means through which a man becomes conscious of his personality. Language is not only a vehicle for rational propositions, it is the outer expression of an inner experience, the outcome of a particular history, the legacy of a distinctive tradition' (Kedourie, 1966: 68). If Taylor and Kedourie are right, then multilingual states are unlikely to be friendly to the full realization of a humanity in which the experience and expression of collective cultural identity entitlements are central. Clearly, a common European culture, necessarily expressed in and through a common language, would be at the expense of the majority of the European Union's languages and cultures and devalue the 'fund of positive identification' to which Taylor (1993: 66) referred. But, paradoxically, the nearest to which Europe has come to a shared contemporary symbolic culture is in the English language media where US programmes often predominate. Moeglin observed that of 12 transnational European television channels in 1990, five transmitted in English, another used English as one of its three languages, a seventh used no language and an eighth used several languages (including English). Moreover, of 96 national and regional television channels in the European Community (at the time Moeglin wrote) 24 used English, more than used any other single language (Moeglin, 1991: 17).

The communalist doctrine of identity entitlement is hostile to the classic liberal principle of individual 'undifferentiated citizenship' (Kymlicka, 1995: 174) specifying universal equality of human rights, and does not satisfy the conditions specified by Rawls – notably difference and pluralism – which characterize 'a well-ordered society' (Rawls, 1980: 540, cited in Kymlicka, 1995: 187). Kymlicka argues that, 'Basic human rights such as freedom of speech, association, and conscience, while attributed to individuals, are typically exercised in community with others, and so provide protection for group life' (Kymlicka, 1995: 3). This is not a wholly convincing claim; at best it is a truism and, at worst, it misleadingly constructs community activity as necessarily benign – the denial of rights is typically 'exercised in community'.

It is only within a society organized on national lines of congruence between polity and culture that such collective identity rights can be realized. Not within sociopolitical structures, such as the contemporary European Union, where polity and culture are incongruent; still less within societies in which a 'they' (and globalization, migration – whether voluntary or involuntary – and a host of other factors are increasingly constituting societies as made up of different 'thems' as well as by 'us') enjoy the same rights of 'undifferentiated citizenship' (*ibid.*: 174) which are extended to 'us'.

Thus, an important aspect of contemporary media policy turns on the issue of whether collective identity entitlements can be reconciled with individual rights of 'undifferentiated citizenship' (notably to freedom of access to information emanating from *outside* the society in question). Proponents of restrictions on expression (for example, in official language laws such as France's lois Toubon and Bas-Lauriol) and on access to information and of expression (for example, the Canadian Content requirements in Canada's 1990 Broadcasting Act [Canada, 1991] and the European Union's 'Television without Frontiers' Directive [89/552/EEC amended by Directive 97/ B6/EC]), have argued for such measures on the ground that the principle of free flow of information across (and within) political boundaries is an empty principle given the unequal character of these flows and the absence of any real dialogic character to these exchanges.

Such unequal relationships do not satisfy Rawls' criteria of common citizenship: 'reasonableness and a sense of fairness, a spirit of compromise and a readiness to meet others half way' (Rawls, 1987: 21, cited in Kymlicka, 1995: 183). Moreover, they dissolve the sentimental bonds of communal societies and compromise both the durability and legitimacy of established national societies and substitute a desiccated calculation of rational self-interest for the spontaneous sentiment of social solidarity.

Kymlicka argues that the central individual 'communication' right – notably freedom of access to information and to expression – is friendly to social cohesion, but his pragmatic argument is over neat

(Kymlicka, 1995: 175). An assertion of group rights – and a right to a distinctive collective social and cultural identity in particular – is offensive to a central liberal precept, an individual's entitlement to be different without thereby incurring the fate of becoming a 'foreigner dwelling among citizens' (Rousseau, 1953: 117). Thus, neither national information exclusivity nor untrammelled openness to globalization seems to satisfy Rawls' criteria.

Recognizing some of these problems, Miller implicitly softens his case for a congruence between polity and culture, and thus for a recognition of the superior claims of those to whom we are close over those from whom we are distant, by broadening his definition of the close. He does so by arguing that a multiethnic community may be a nation. But the issue of language severely tests Miller's argument, as it does general liberal arguments for an extension of the entitlements of 'undifferentiated citizenship' to speakers of any and all languages. The realization of collective identity rights in a well-functioning society necessitates a limitation on the number of official languages recognized within a single political community. Both the principle of nationality and the principle of undifferentiated citizenship can be applied only to a limited extent.

Limits of the associative and communal models

The moral superiority of the principle of nationality is murkier than Miller claims. Kymlicka looks this problem in the face and argues that linguistic and cultural homogenization is morally and practically bankrupt. 'Globalization has made the myth of a culturally homogeneous state even more unrealistic, and has forced the majority within each state to be more open to pluralism and diversity' (Kymlicka, 1995: 9). He does argue, however, that some forms of collective rights are not hostile to individual rights. He proposes that 'collective rights could refer to the right of a group to limit the liberty of its own individual members in the name of group solidarity or cultural purity' – limits which Kymlicka (and I agree) believes to be offensive because incompatible with individual freedom – and 'it could refer to the right of a group to limit the economic or political power exercised by the larger society over the group, to ensure that the resources and institutions on which the minority depends are not vulnerable to majority decisions' which Kymlicka – and I do not agree – also believes incompatible with individual rights (Kymlicka, 1995: 7).

There are then cogent objections to the principle of nationality; so too are there to the principle of undifferentiated citizenship. Whilst there are multiethnic states (and nations), there are surely few nations or states in which a plurality of languages enjoy common currency.[8] This question of practical limits has become more and more important, as populations have become more mobile and the size of political communities has grown. The practical implementation of the principle of undifferentiated citizenship is more challenging than its proponents customarily acknowledge.

Conclusion

If there is no justification for preferring identity entitlements over entitlements to undifferentiated citizenship, how can social cohesion be secured in pluralistic inclusive societies? Is there an alternative to a common culture? The way forward seems to lie in an acceptance of the priority of different principles at different levels of social and political organization. This, in a more or less explicit and systematic way, informs the practice of some actual existing heterogeneous societies.

The official 'National Agenda for a Multicultural Australia' (Commonwealth of Australia, 1989) and in particular the section 'What is Multiculturalism?' makes the argument well. Australia's 'national agenda' proposes decoupling polity and culture and distinguishing political obligations from cultural entitlements. All Australian citizens are obligated to 'accept the basic structures and principles of Australian society – the Constitution and the rule of law, tolerance and equality, Parliamentary democracy, freedom of speech and religion, English as the national language and equality of the sexes' (Commonwealth of Australia, 1989: vii). All Australians are guaranteed 'the right . . . within carefully defined limits, to express and share their individual cultural heritage, including their language and religion' (*ibid.*).[9]

It is easy to identify the neuralgic points here, notably around language where establishing a national language clearly compromises putative rights to self-expression and public use of other languages. But the Australian model points to a practicable model for the inclusive society, one which is both communal and associative – communal at some points, associative at others. The full realization of rights is traded off against the pragmatic imperative of a society which does hang together. Australia's 'National Agenda' is a powerful testimony to a vision of a society based on universal political obligations and diverse cultural rights. It defines a basis for an inclusive society which respects rights to the maximum possible extent because it is communal and associative to different degrees at different levels.

This pragmatic striking of a balance seems inescapable. Considered in terms of communications, individual rights (for example, to freedom of information and communication) tend to conflict with collective rights (for example, to collective identities borne by language and culture). The claims of religion, and the choice between a confessional and a secular society, potentially offers an illuminating analogy. Kymlicka and Miller both observe that a seemingly irreconcilable contradiction between social cohesion (collective rights) and individual (confessional) rights was resolved by secularizing society and by making religion a private matter. (Kymlicka recognizes that secularization does not wholly solve the problem.)[10]

Globalization threatens the established basis on which inclusive societies have been constituted. It disrupts customary congruences between polity and culture that have both notionally and normatively distinguished the inclusive society of the national state. Yet, so too does the most salient principled (rather than interested) response to globalization from identity politics. For the assertion, à la Delors and Taylor, of an entitlement to collective identity is, of necessity, assertion of an exclusionary principle. To be sure, this assertion of exclusivity may be asserted to different degrees at different times and in different places (contemporary France is, for example, a very different case to contemporary Pakistan or even contemporary Malaysia). It may be argued that a modest degree of exclusion (for example, at the levels set in the national audio-visual content quotas of Canada and the European Union) is required in the interests of cultural pluralism and diversity. But it is hard to resist the conclusion that, if the inclusive society is not to exclude too much, its public culture must both be looser and more pluralistic than heretofore. *Symbolic culture embodied in the mass media can no longer be given the role of holding society together. The principle of social coherence in the inclusive society, if it is to be an ethical coherence, must be found elsewhere.* Notably in associative rather than communal social relationships, but associative relationships which acknowledge cultural diversity and difference and thus the legitimacy of claims for a realization of communalist sentiments at appropriate levels.

Notes

1 See my *Media Policy, National Identity and Citizenry in Changing Democratic Societies: The UK and Canada Compared* (Collins, forthcoming).

2 Residence, Miller's term, is of course not the issue. For the sentimental bonds we share with our co-nationals tend to endure even if we do not share a residence. Hungarians' sense of solidarity with Hungarian speakers in Romania and Slovakia; Irish Australians and Irish Americans affirm their sense of shared identity with the Irish living on the island of Ireland; Jews' solidarity with Israelis and Israel; Arabs' solidarity with Palestine and Palestinians are case in point. Moreover, the sentimental bonds of shared identity may obtain even when there is neither common citizenship nor common residence in question: the South Atlantic war of 1982 focused a sense of sentimental affiliation between many Spanish (and Italian) citizens and Argentines just as it did between many British citizens and Falklanders.

3 Miller qualifies the force of his argument later where he states: 'My claim is that in multicultural societies group and national identities should co-exist' (Miller, 1995, p. 153). However, it is hard to see how his principle that 'everyone should take part . . . on an equal footing' (Miller, 1995, p. 153) can be reconciled with his prior, and more central argument, that the principle of nationality is an organizing principle of political communities which necessitates a shared (normative) public culture.

4 Kymlicka (1995, p. 73) challenges an earlier version of Miller's arguments as assimilationist.

5 Original emphasis.

6 Lang became Minister of Culture of France in 1981, a post he held for most of the next decade: he was Minister of Culture from 1981–86 and from 1988–93 Minister of Culture and Communication. He was succeeded (as Minister of Culture) by Jacques Toubon.

7 An Italian MEP who served as Chairman of the European Parliament's Committee on Youth, Culture, Media and Sport.

8 A notable exception seems to prove the rule: South Africa, after the end of apartheid, changed its language policy from recognition of Afrikaans and English to recognition of 11 official languages. But formal recognition of 11 languages has been accompanied by the effective elimination of Afrikaans as a language of public life and a quasi-universal use of English.

9 Gellner makes a similar argument (1998, p. 79).

10 As he shows in his discussion of the Amish who secured the right to withdraw their children from public, secular schooling in the USA on the grounds that 'religious affiliation is so profoundly constitutive of who they are that their overriding interest is in protecting and advancing their identity and that they have no comparable interest in being able to stand back and assess that identity. Hence there is little or no value (and perhaps even positive harm) in teaching Amish children about the outside world' (Kymlicka, 1995, p. 163).

References

Assises de l'audiovisuel (1989) *Assises européennes de l'audiovisuel. Projet Eureka audiovisuel* (Paris: Ministère des affaires étrangères, République Française and Commission of the European Communities).

Barzanti, R. (1990) 'Audiovisual Opportunities in the Single Market', *MEDIA 92*, Newsletter of the MEDIA 92 Programme, September (Brussels), p. 1.

Beijar, K., Ekberg, H., Eriksson, S. and Tandefelt, M. (1997) *Life in Two Languages – the Finnish Experience* (Espoo: Schildts).

Blainey, G. (1966) *The Tyranny of Distance* (Melbourne: Sun Books).

Canada (1991) *Broadcasting Act*, 38–39 Elizabeth II, pp. 117–73.

Castles, S., Cope, B., Kalantzis, M. and Morrissey, M. (1988) *Mistaken Identity. Multiculturalism and the Demise of Nationalism in Australia* (Leichardt: Pluto Press).

Collins, R. (1990 and 1994) *Culture, Communication and National Identity. The Case of Canadian Television* (Toronto: University of Toronto Press).

Collins, R. (1993) 'The Internationalization of the Television Program Market: Media Imperialism or International Division of Labor? The Case of the United Kingdom', in E. Noam and J. Millonzi (eds), *The International Market in Film and Television Programs* (Norwood, NJ.: Ablex), pp. 125–46.

Collins, R. (forthcoming) 'Media Policy, National Identity and Citizenry in Changing Democratic Societies: The UK and Canada compared', in R. Boyce (ed.), *The Communications Revolution at Work: Canadian and British Perspectives on the Practical Implications of the New Information and Communications Technology* (Montreal and Kingston: McGill-Queen's University Press).

Commonwealth of Australia (1989) *National Agenda for a Multicultural Australia* (Canberra, AGPS: Department of the Prime Minster and Cabinet Office of Multicultural Affairs).

Council of the European Communities (1989) *Directive on the Co-ordination of Certain Provisions Laid Down by Law, Regulation or Administrative Action in Member States Concerning the Pursuit of Television Broadcasting Activities.* 89/552/EEC. OJ L 298 (17 October 1989), pp. 23–30.

Durkheim, E. (1964) [1893] *The Division of Labour in Society* (New York: The Free Press).

Gellner, E. (1983) *Nations and Nationalism* (Oxford: Blackwell).

Gellner, E. (1998) *Language and Solitude* (Cambridge: Cambridge University Press).

Hall, J. and Jarvie, I. (eds) (1992) *Transition to Modernity. Essays on Power, Wealth and Belief* (Cambridge: Cambridge University Press).

Hartz, L. (1964) *The Founding of New Societies: Studies in the History of the United States, Latin America, South Africa, Canada and Australia* (New York: Harcourt Brace and World).

Hoskins, C. and Mirus, R. (1988) 'Reasons for the US domination of the International Trade in Television Programmes', *Media Culture and Society*, vol. 10(4), pp. 499–516.

Kedourie, E. (1966) *Nationalism* (London: Hutchinson).

Kymlicka, W. (1995) *Multicultural Citizenship* (Oxford: Clarendon Press).

Lang, J. (1988) 'The Future of European Film and Television', *European Affairs*, vol. 2(1), pp. 12–20.

Lee, C.C. (1989) *Media Imperialism Reconsidered* (Beverley Hills: Sage).

Lijphart, A. (1977) *Democracy in Plural Societies* (New Haven: Yale University Press).

Marx, K. (1976) [1857–8] Preface and Introduction to *A Contribution to the Critique of Political Economy* (Peking: Foreign Languages Press).

Meinecke, F. (1970) [1907] *Cosmopolitanism and the National State* (Princeton, NJ: Princeton University Press).

Melich, A. (1990) *Identité Nationale et Média Contemporains* (Lausanne: Éditions Loisirs et Pédagogie).

Miller, D. (1995) *On Nationality* (Oxford: Clarendon Press).

Miller, D. (1989) *Market, State and Community: The Foundations of Market Socialism* (Oxford: Clarendon Press).

Mitrany, D. (1975) *The Functional Theory of Politics* (London: Martin Robertson).

Moeglin, P. (1991) 'Television et Europe', *Communication*, vol. 12(2), pp. 13–51.

Morphett, T. (1989) 'Television Program Standard 14: Australian Content on Commercial Television', *Australian Broadcasting Tribunal*, IP/86/11A (North Sydney), November.

Paltridge, S. (1998) *Internet Traffic Exchange: Developments and Policy*, DSTI/ICCP/TISP(98)1 (Paris: OECD).

Pool, I. de sola (1975) 'Direct Broadcast Satellites and Cultural Integrity', *Society*, vol. 12 (September–October), pp. 47–56.

Porter, J. (1965) *The Vertical Mosaic: An Analysis of Social Class and Power in Canada* (Toronto: University of Toronto Press).

Ravault, R-J. (1980) 'De l'exploitation des "dèspotes culturels" par la téléspectateur', in A. Méar (ed.), *Recherches québécoises sur la télévision* (Montréal: Albert St Martin).

Rawls, J. (1980) 'Kantian Constructivism in Moral Theory', *Journal of Philosophy*, vol. 77/9, pp. 515–72.

Rousseau, J.-J. (1953) *Political Writings*, trans. and ed. F. Watkins (Edinburgh: Nelson).

Schiller, H. (1969, 1992) *Mass Communications and American Empire* (New York: A.M. Kelley, and 2nd edn Boulder, Co.: Westview).

Schiller, H. (1989) *Culture Inc: The Corporate Takeover of Public Expression* (New York: Oxford University Press).

Smith, A. (1991) *National Identity* (London: Penguin).

Smith, A. (1995) *Nations and Nationalism in a Global Era* (Cambridge: Polity Press).

Taylor, C. (1993) *Reconciling the Solitudes. Essays on Canadian Federalism and Nationalism* (Montreal and Kingston: McGill-Queen's University Press).

Taylor, C. (1994) 'The Politics of Recognition', in A. Gutmann (ed.), *Multiculturalism. Examining the Politics of Recognition* (Princeton, NJ: Princeton University Press).

Thody, P. (1995) *Le Franglais* (London: Athlone).

Thompson, K. and Tunstall, J. (eds) (1971) *Sociological Perspectives* (Harmondsworth: Penguin).

Tongue, C. (1998) *Culture or Monoculture? The European Audiovisual Challenge* (Ilford: Office of Carole Tongue MEP).

Trudeau, P. (1968) *Federalism and the French Canadians* (New York: St Martin's Press).

Weber, M. (1964) [1922] *The Theory of Social and Economic Organization* (New York: The Free Press).

Part III
Agendas of Inclusion

13
Political Inclusion
Raymond Plant

Contrary to the beliefs of many economic liberals, some of the central characteristics of the modern world would make politics more, rather than less important. Economic liberals have frequently argued that globalization, the growth of free trade, freedom of capital movement and increasing pressure to deregulate in the search for competitive advantage in a global economy presaged a more limited role for government and politics albeit with enhanced authority within that more limited sphere. This is the relationship between more authoritative but more limited government which was so well caught by Andrew Gamble when he spoke of 'the free economy and the strong state' to use the title of one of his books on this theme. So it might be thought that worldwide free markets and limited government would be the norm, and along with this would go a decrease in the importance of politics. Such a diagnosis was also backed up by three other features of modern society. The first is the displacement of tradition as an appropriate guide to politics. Tradition has been undermined from many quarters by science, by secularization, by cultural and ethnic diversity. Those forms of politics which have served traditional values and ways of life have therefore become and will become less and less relevant.

Secondly there has been, so it is argued, a major decline in the force of ideology – particularly of communist and socialist ideologies in the modern world. The collapse of communist regimes in Eastern Europe in the late 1980s and early 1990s have led to the view that the likely trend in human development is towards free markets, and limited government with politics no longer representing a clash of ideological interests. This thesis is argued with passion and vigour by Francis Fukuyama who sees the modern world standing as at the end of history with the gradual dissipation of ideological conflict.

There is, however, another side to this in that it is possible to argue that it is precisely because of the development of global markets and the homogenizing of goods and services, and perhaps particularly cultural goods and services, that is leading to a greater emphasis in politics not so much on traditional political ideas and ideologies, but rather on a politics of identity and what is sometimes called the 'politics of presence'. I want to take a little time to explore this feature of modern politics since it connects up with many of the economic, cultural and social aspects of inclusion and exclusion. At the same time I want to come to this point somewhat indirectly.

It is frequently argued by commentators that the competitive global market produces a very great deal of insecurity in the job market. It is argued that the idea of jobs for life, and that one set of skills learned at school, college or university would equip an individual for one sort of profession or job for the rest of his/her life has disappeared. Instead of a career path we are likely to have crazy paving with many shifts and fractures along the way. This sort of insecurity has often been a feature of unskilled working class life, but is now becoming a feature of middle-class life too. It is argued (see John Gray's chapter) that the government can do little or nothing about this. The collapse of the communist economies have shown that these problems cannot be solved by planning and large-scale government intervention in the economy. Economic insecurity is going to be an endemic feature of modern life.

At the same time, it is also argued that the social democratic approach of providing not only a welfare state, but also forms of welfare and taxation that secure a degree of social justice by redistributing the 'natural' and highly unequal outcome of the market is no longer compatible with global competitiveness because the social and labour costs of the social democratic state are too high. If the welfare state is to survive at all, it is argued, it will have to be as a limited safety net and linked to welfare-to-work strategies under which the welfare state will be used to equip people with the skills and qualifications without which it will not be possible for such individuals to secure for themselves a degree of economic security not conferred by the state but by the labour market for as long as these skills are in demand.

Hence, it is argued that in the face of global competition, government has to be limited in its aspirations. Its scope has to be cut back, its aspirations curbed and its social policies directed towards improving the labour market and other supply-side techniques. Instead of social and economic citizenship being about social rights and entitlements, we shall have instead supply-side citizenship empha-sizing not so much rights but rather duties and obligations in relation to acquiring the skills necessary for the labour market. To put the point rather romantically, perhaps it could be said that the current combination of government and market cannot give to individuals a sense of belonging or a sense of being at home in the world. Insecurity is and will remain endemic and more and more will be placed on the individual to make a sense of security for him/herself as the state divests itself of more and more of its postwar social democratic role of providing a sense of security from the cradle to the grave. This is of course rather a bleak picture to those influenced by the socialist/social democratic tradition. Those who do not find it bleak are the economic liberals such as Hayek and Friedman, for these developments would in terms of the changing relationship between the state, the market and the individual correspond very largely to their own preferred economic and political vision. It is, however, a vision that should cause a degree of unease.

For the economic liberal, the market economy should be extended to cover more and more aspects of life and be used where possible to displace both public funding and public provision of goods and services. At the same time, however, they are clear sighted enough to recognize that the market cannot provide a sense of belonging, a sense of rootedness or for that matter any overall, collective moral goal or purpose. The market is *nomocratic*; governed by procedural rules, particularly in relation to contracts; not *telocratic*: that is to say pursuing certain sorts of collective goals whether these are to do with social justice or cultural identity. A sense of belonging and inclusion has to be found in private life and in private affiliation to and membership of groups of various sorts; it cannot be found in markets or in the limited politics which will be left in the globalized market. So wherein will lie the sense of legitimacy of a market order if it cannot meet some of the deepest moral and emotional attachments of people – attachments which, by their very nature, imply some kind of collective articulation and embodiment.

Hayek is interestingly ambivalent on this point. First of all he attacks such sentiments about belonging and social justice as premodern, atavistic and tribal. The legitimacy of neither the market nor government should be sought in these fields since we need to outgrow such attachments and rejoice in the anonymity of what he calls the 'great society'. The legitimacy of the market economy allied to limited government will lie in the market's ability to satisfy more effectively than anything else more and more of peoples' consumer desires and, through the 'trickle down' effect, ensure that such goods are distributed, not by government, but by the market mechanism itself to more and more groups of people. The justification of the market is essentially utilitarian: it will, more than any other system, give as many people as possible, as much as possible of whatever it is that they happen to want. Wants and preferences are to be taken as given and incorrigible. It is not the job of the government to engage in a critique of wants and preferences, so long as in pursuing my preferences my actions do not make it impossible for you to pursue yours.

At the same time, however, Hayek does argue in *The Mirage of Social Justice* that people in general do not understand that the market economy does not serve any overall or goal-based moral principles, and he does speculate on the effects of this on the market and the sense that people will have of the legitimacy of the market order. He argues that it may well be necessary for the maintenance of the market order that people actually entertain and hold to false beliefs about it – for example that the market rewards merit or secures social justice.

This should give economic liberals some pause for thought about whether the market can, as it were through its own devices, secure a sense of its own legitimacy. If not, will not a sense of that legitimacy have to come through the political side of a market society and the purposes which such governments might pursue. If this is so, then the market order will itself require a political order which can try to meet some of the attachments which cannot be satisfied by the market.

The point could be made in other ways too, ways which rather underline the claim that the market can be, so to speak, a sphere of self-contained utilitarian legitimacy with the realm of politics to do with the articulation and enforcement of the procedural aspects of market societies. The first of these has to do with the idea of nation and cultural and other forms of national identity. The global marketplace has had a highly homogenizing effect upon cultural services, with the western media, western fashion, western food – particularly fast food – making a substantial difference to cultural

identities which are often many centuries old but are, equally, being transformed at enormous speed. One of the unanticipated
consequences of the homogenizing cultural tendencies of the global economy has been to provide strong incentives for national,
local and regional identities to reassert themselves and demand an
appropriate degree of political voice and presence. This is not a
problem which is likely to be solved by more and more application
of markets and other values. These are rather *political* by products,
but ones of central importance, that have been exacerbated by the
growing homogenization of markets.

These issues of local and regional identity are also, I believe,
connected to the politics and economics of insecurity which I
mentioned earlier. As people rapidly lose a sense of status, belonging and expectation in the market economy, they are very likely to
come to value and endorse what is familiar, local and which could
give them a sense of belonging in a mass society and a mass market. It is not much use Hayek and other economic liberals condemning
these things as premodern and atavistic and urging us to embrace
the strains of civilization and its anonymity if individuals react in
quite the opposite way. There is a deep political/cultural problem
here which the global market has exacerbated and which markets,
as such, cannot solve. At the same time, however, it is not possible
in the political treatment of these problems to go back to traditional
understandings because, as I have argued, tradition has become fatally
undermined. This is the result of many factors for reasons that
should be obvious: as the result of the growth of sciences; and its
pervasiveness since the traditional is not a category of use in science;
the decline of traditional forms of religious observance given the
link between religion and the authority of tradition; and the increasing ethnic and cultural diversity of society which has undermined
the idea of a dominant homogenous tradition which could bind
society together.

Now, if some at least of this diagnosis is accurate, then it is quite
alarming. We should not, however, as I think many economic liberals
do, blind ourselves to the problem. What I am arguing is that there
are large-scale political problems to do with identity, inclusion, security
and belonging which are thrown up by the market. These cannot
be addressed or cured directly by the market. They require a political
response, but it is a response which gives to politics a role which
is not really sanctioned in free market political economy. At the
same time these political issues cannot be addressed by appealing

to a dominant political or cultural tradition since the authority and pervasiveness of these traditions have been seriously undermined.

The problem is potentially alarming because the degree of insecurity which accompanies the global economy when it is doing well poses enough problems. If, however, the world economy moves into a sustained recession at any point these problems could become very acute and give rise to some very ugly political movements to do with identity politics offering a sense of belonging and security through being a member of a particular race, tribe, religion or gender.

It seems imperative to rehabilitate the realm of politics and not to regard it as a kind of incubus on the back of the market. As I have said, there are major issues here which cannot really be addressed by markets – given that they are driven by individual consumer choices, when most of the problems are to do with collective identity – never mind being solved by them. If we want to preserve a liberal market order, not in theory but in practice, given the motivations and attachments that actually people have, not those that free market theorists would like them to have, we need to rehabilitate politics fit for a society in which individualism is strong, in which tradition has lost its authority and in which large-scale ideologies are dead – or at least in suspended animation. So we need politics to deal with such problems, but in a context in which there is not one dominant form of authority whether religious, moral, ideological or traditional.

The other feature which to an extent stands in the way of a rehabilitation of the political is the cult of the expert in modern societies. Indeed, as Alasdair MacIntyre has argued in *After Virtue*, the erosion of the idea of moral purpose in politics and society and the growth of moral subjectivism – the view that morality is a matter of subjective judgement – has left a kind of ethical vacuum at the heart of politics which has been filled by various forms of claimed expertise, for example that of the manager or the counsellor. This point can be linked to markets too. Given that the value of a consumer good is fixed by the subjective preference of the consumer – namely what he/she is willing to pay for the good – then clearly in market terms value is subjective. If this is so, and if markets come to dominate more and more areas of life, then in these wider and wider areas too value will be seen as subjective. It then becomes progressively more difficult not to think that all values are subjective.

The permeation of society by such an approach to morality leaves a good deal of space for claimed expert judgement. Issues that in the past might have been regarded as essentially moral issues to be resolved by and appeal to the shared moral values of the society are now ceded more and more to expert judgement – a good example would be the whole area of crime and punishment. We need experts to manage such areas of society's life-forces because we appear to have lost the shared moral resources that would enable us to grapple with them.

The difficulty with this reduction of the question of how we live together in society and the role of politics within that, to questions about management and expertise, is a further area in which politics needs to make a kind of re-entry. The fact is that most of these issues are not at their basis issues about expert judgement even though expert judgement is relevant to their resolution. They are moral issues, which need to be debated as moral issues and not displaced by expert views. Indeed expert judgement may in fact be rather dangerous in fields like crime and punishment where it seems clear that over the past 25 years expert judgement has led to a penal system which it appears runs seriously counter to public opinion on these matters. Expert judgement can therefore be a source of both the displacement of politics and also the creation of a degree of alienation between the government and the governed.

Nevertheless, the dilemma remains: how to create a form of politics fit for a market society, set in a highly competitive world economy, with a multicultural and multiethnic population, lacking a single authoritative moral outlook and in which, indeed, morality is seen as a matter of subjective preference. If this part of the dilemma can be resolved at all it seems to require three things. The first is that politics should be seen as dialogical and deliberative rather than tribal and ideological. That is to say, we need to look towards the development of political institutions which will facilitate people from all sectors and sections of society to have a sense that they are respected, that their views are given proper weight, within democratic frameworks within which they will have an appropriate voice. If there is no single authoritative source of judgement in politics, the resolution of political problems can only be achieved through deliberation and negotiation. In order to achieve this, other things need to be in place as part of the framework for politics.

First of all, if politics is to be restored to its proper place and if there is to be trust in political processes, then it would seem pretty clear that there is a strong case for devolved politics. This is so for several reasons. First, trust as an attitude and a virtue was initially embodied in close, face-to-face relationships and, while these cannot be replicated at a political level, it still seems likely that if and when possible political decisions are taken closer to the people affected by them they are likely to be seen as more trustworthy than decisions taken more remotely. Secondly, the economic liberals' argument about the incompetence of government in relation to large-scale economic planning (due to the diversity of knowledge, the relative lack of inspiration and the large-scale unintended consequences of large decisions) applies to a degree to the role of government outside of political economy. If more political decisions are governed by subsidiarity and taken at a more local level, then some of these issues of central competence and consequence should be easier to manage.

Furthermore, it is very important that particularly in relation to the ethnic and cultural diversity of a country, national politics should be concerned with and draw upon values which, despite the diversity, might be thought to be shared. If we are to restore trust in politics in a diverse society then political inspiration and the claim to moral authority in politics cannot be drawn from within just one culture or religious community. There is a great temptation in this postmodern world to emphasize the diversity of things, but if we are to live together and deal, as I have said, with the problems thrown up by markets but which are not susceptible to a market solution, then we have to try to negotiate an agreement about the basic procedures of political communication. Part of this, as I have argued, will be to do with devolution, but it will also involve rules for the protection of rights, privacy, freedom of expression and so forth. Diversity of opinion cannot be negotiated without agreed rules. Part of the trouble with the postmodern approach to politics emphasizing only difference and diversity, is that little or no attention is paid to how to justify and negotiate the procedural terms under which people of diverse outlooks can come to agree on the terms of political engagement. If we do not emphasize this, then politics will indeed be a type of civil war in which we disagree not only about the ends of politics, but also means and procedures. In order to achieve this, people will have to look outside the communities to which they feel attached to seek to identify values and norms about democratic politics which in many cases will go beyond the values embedded in those communities, but without which we cannot live together. There has to be a politics of shared interests and general concern and not just a politics from within cultural, ethnic and religious groups. In terms of social peace and to have any chance of dealing with the political impact of globalization, we have the strongest incentive to develop a new kind of civic politics which recognizes differences, but is not reduced to it or prevented from general action by it.

The final element relevant to a diverse and pluralistic society is the nature of representation itself. In the UK context we have become used to the idea of what has come to be called the principal/agent view of representation. In this context it means that under a First-Past-the-Post electoral system a single individual is empowered to speak on behalf of a constituency irrespective of whether that individual has anything in common with some elements in his probably quite diverse constituency. The fact of a winner-takes-all electoral system confers this legitimacy and this kind of political voice.

The other concept of representation is usually known as the microcosmic approach. On this view, it is argued that any legislative body (whether national or local) should be as far as possible a microcosm of the wider society which the assembly seeks to represent. A first-past-the-post electoral system will not approximate the election of an assembly or a microcosm of society, and therefore it is argued on the microcosmic view that one of the competing forms of proportional representation should be introduced. It is argued that this would be non-pluralistic; it would secure a place in the legislature for the voice and the presence of groups who might regard themselves as excluded on the principal/agent view of representation. Thus, it is argued, a microcosmic/proportional electoral system would be more appropriate to building political institutions for a more pluralistic society which, as I have argued, rests much more upon dialogue, deliberation and mutual respect for diversity than more traditional forms of politics. Obviously the procedural conditions of a more dialogical/deliberative approach to politics are going to be subject to considerable controversy, but whatever form these conditions take, the development of such institutions seems to be both necessary and urgent.

I have to turn to the final element of what might be seen as the procedural argument here, and that is with the citizen and in particular what does the citizen have to know in order to exercise political judgement. For two and a half thousand years, this has been a central question in political theory. The nature of knowledge and skill in politics was central to Plato and Aristotle and it is still an issue for thinking about politics in a global marketplace. The kind of more deliberative and dialogical politics which I have sought to outline as a way of rehabilitating politics in a market economy is quite demanding on the citizen. If rebuilding trust in politics has to involve bringing political decision-making closer to the people, and, if it is to be more deliberative, then people will have to be more actively involved whether in voting in more devolved elections or through other methods of testing local opinion, as for example in local referenda such as the one in Milton Keynes in the UK or procedures such as citizens' juries and focus groups.

This will require quite a lot of attention to be paid to what citizens might be expected to know, because democracy is not just about intermittent acts of electoral choice but also about judgement, and it is necessary to try to develop the capacity of judgement. Professor Crick's recent report on citizenship teaching in schools is very relevant to this as is the whole issue discussed earlier about resisting the claims of expertise.

The French Prime Minister Lionel Jospin has summed up his political philosophy as 'yes to the market economy, no to the market society'. This chapter has been an essay on the same sort of theme.

Market societies throw up intensely political problems which cannot be solved by the market order itself. Nor can they be resolved if we adopt the approach to the understanding of the role of government and politics held by free market theorists. Of course, I do not know whether the problems thrown up by the market can be resolved, but if they can it is only by politics and the first step down that road must be the rehabilitation of the sphere of politics to transform its nature to make it more capable of dealing with the circumstances of a market society.

14
Meditation on Democracy, Politics and Citizenship

Bernard Crick

'In the political tradition stemming from the Greek city states and the Roman republic, citizenship has meant involvement in public affairs . . . to take part in public debate and, directly or indirectly, in shaping the laws and decisions of a state.

'We state a case for citizenship education being a vital and distinct statutory part of the curriculum, entitlement for pupils in its own right.

'Programmes should be established to promote political discourse and understanding, as well as encouraging young people to engage in the political process.'

(From *Education for Citizenship and the Teaching of Democracy in Schools*[1])

Although a humanist, by which I think I mean a moral non-believer, I have been much attracted by the late Rheinhold Niebuhr's concept of Christian realism. We should all be aware of our capacity as men for evil as well as for goodness, or indifference and neglect of others as well as concern. Hence the imperative to be open-eyed to the short-fall in actual societies, including what we think to be good and could be at least better. This constitutes a case not for despair nor for retreat, whether to prayer alone or to the exotic academic activities of the ivory tower, but rather a case for engagement.

It behoves also to understand the world and its limitations, but never to accept that it cannot be changed, somewhat, never utterly, but to some degree for the better by combinations of thought and action.

I detest ignorant, willful action; but grow both sad and impatient how so much academic and social theory either eschews any pre-scriptive mode at all, or else in doctrinal mode set sights so unrealistically high that any short-fall is deemed defeat, any com-promise sell-out or calamity. I cannot pretend ever to have worried too much at not reaching the top of a difficult hill, so long as the view was ever so much longer and the air ever so much cleaner at some decent height.

If by 'inclusion' is meant literal equality, we chase a false hare or, if you prefer, a blue rose. But we do know the extent of the exclusion of many even in our own society, mainly by poverty, sometimes indeed by ignorance, from what in any sense, trivial or profound, could reasonably be called a good or a full life. Damn qualitative differences, and elegant quibblings about 'real needs' and 'seeming needs' ('the seeming needs of my fool-driven land', said Yeats), for life-expectancy and infant mortality tables tell a clear enough bad tale. Those of us who are comfortably off and reason-ably happy to live in our own skins in our own homes, can then indulge in depressing social theories. Globalization of economies and the market does, of course, limit more obviously than ever before the abilities of national governments to plan for inclusive societies, however defined. Firstly, there were always severe limita-tions born of economic realism; and, secondly, these limitations are no real excuse for not doing much that can be done.

The excuses can, of course, be very complex. Fear of inflation can make us accept too readily that governments cannot tax sufficiently with the obvious problems of poverty and gross underfunding in the two institutions that can do so much to enhance or limit life-chances and inclusion or exclusion: education and health services. We indulge in the specious arguments that enterprise would suffer and cease if taxation rose. Political considerations are uppermost in the restraints of government to use common resources to the common good. But are not political factors part of realism? They are, indeed, but so is the great opportunity of government to lead and educate, to shape opinion by narrative, argument and example; not sit waiting and weighing the figures in the next set of polls. Such figures are not 'givens'; they just give some indication of difficulties, or oppor-tunities, to carry people in pursuing those kind of social goals that are in the common interest. The most evident example, both grim and amusing, is the plain common need to control overuse of the motor car without which no life is thought to be complete.

Failure to achieve or not even wanting to try to achieve a more radically egalitarian society economically, is no reason for losing faith in, or failing to pursue actively rather than academically, those two historic goals and practices of democracy: inclusion and active citizenship.

Democracy is both a sacred and a promiscuous word. We all love her but she is hard to pin down. Everyone claims her but no one actually possesses her fully. A moment's thought will remind why this is so. Historically there have been four broad usages. The first is found in the Greeks, in Plato's attack on it and in Aristotle's highly qualified defence. Democracy is simply, in the Greek, *demos* (the mob, the many) and *cracy*, meaning rule. Plato attacked this as being the rule of the poor and the ignorant over the educated and the knowledgeable, ideally philosophers. His fundamental distinction was between knowledge and opinion: democracy is the rule, or rather the anarchy, of mere opinion. Aristotle modified this view rather than rejecting it utterly. Good government was a mixture of elements, the few ruling with the consent of the many.

The second usage is found in the Romans, in Machiavelli's great *Discourses*, in the seventeenth century English and Dutch republicans, and in the early American republic: that good government is mixed government, just as in Aristotle's theory, but that the democratic popular element could actually give greater power to a state. Good laws to protect all were not good enough unless subjects became active citizens making their own laws collectively. The argument was both moral and military. The moral argument is the more famous: both Roman paganism and later Protestantism had in common a view of man as an active individual, a maker and shaper of things, not just a law-abiding well-behaved acceptor or subject of a traditional order.

The third usage is found in the writings of Jean Jacques Rousseau: that everyone, regardless of education or property, has a right to make his or her will felt in matters of state; and indeed the general will or common good is better understood by any well-meaning, simple, unselfish ordinary person from their own experience and conscience than by the over-educated living amid the artificiality of high society. Now this view can have a lot to do with the liberation of a class or a nation, whether from oppression or ignorance and superstition, but it is not necessarily connected with individual liberty. The general will could have more to do with popularity than with representative or liberal institutions.

The fourth usage of democracy is found in the American constitution and in many of the new constitutions in Europe in the nineteenth century, and in the new West German and Japanese constitutions following the Second World War also in the writings of John Stuart Mill and Alexis de Tocqueville: that all can if they care take part in public life, but must respect the equal rights of fellow citizens within a regulatory legal order that defines and protects those rights.

What is most ordinarily meant today by 'democracy' is ideally a fusion, but quite often a confusion, of the idea of power of the people and the idea of legally guaranteed individual rights. The two should, indeed, be combined, but they are distinct ideas. There have been intolerant democracies and a few reasonably tolerant autocracies. Personally I do not find it helpful to call the system of government under which I live 'democratic'. To do so begs the question. I prefer to discuss how the actual system could be made more democratic. Sociologically and socially, England is still in many ways a profoundly undemocratic society, certainly when compared to the United States. Even in the United States there is little citizenship, and little positive participation in politics in the republican style of the early American Republic. Oh yes, people vote in formal elections, but between elections talk about and active participation in politics rates far, far lower as the most favoured national activity, apart from work, shopping and then sport (more often watching sport on the box).

What seems to me crucial is whether a society is prepared to educate its inhabitants to think of themselves not just as legal citizens, but as active citizens, and towards what some of us have called 'political literacy', the skills, knowledge and values that relate to the practice of citizenship, in voluntary groups and in public bodies and political parties or pressure groups. We all have something to say. Politics is too important to be left to politicians. Politicians are too busy and preoccupied with short-term advantages and actions, with winning the next election, so others must speculate and try to do their long-term thinking about civilized humanity for them. Thought and action must go together not merely if the political tradition is to be preserved, but also if it is to be extended.

By the political tradition I mean simply the activity of resolving disputes and determining policy politically, that is by public debate among free citizens. A moment's thought should remind one that this activity is one of the most important inventions of human civilization, once celebrated but now so much taken for granted or even regarded (because of the actions of particular politicians) as a debased activity. Its beneficent application is neither universally understood or, even if understood, desired. It may be the world's best hope, perhaps last hope, as we see long-term problems begin to accumulate which could destroy – the phrase does have meaning – civilization as we know it. If political solutions are not found, national and economic blocs will struggle harder and harder, more and more ruthlessly and competitively, to maintain the standard of living of at least a voting majority of their own loyal inhabitants. Two World Wars should be an adequate demonstration of this, but could yet prove an inadequate premonition of the shape of things to come. If the fear of nuclear war between the great powers has gone on to the back burner, their ability to prevent the spread of nuclear bombs to less stable regimes is now diminished almost to the point of impotence.

The invention and then the tradition of governing by means of political debate among citizens have their roots in the practices of the Greek *polis* and the ancient Roman republic. So political rule could be said to be 'Western' or 'European' in origin, yet universal in application, as much as natural science. The general ideas of both political rule and natural sciences are no longer bound to any one culture, they have spread universally, in different modulations. The West does not stand still entirely. That the concept of 'citizen' has been extended to women is no small matter; though full civic and social equality is still in the future, and the consequences of equality achieved are hard to predict.

This elevated view of politics may surprise our fellow citizens when they form their idea of 'the political' from what they read in their newspapers about the behaviour, in all respects, of actual politicians. Indeed, one must ask, are such politicians the friends or the foes of good government? Certainly they are very – to use a favourite word of Hannah Arendt's' – 'thoughtless' about the consequences in terms of public example of how they practice politics and behave themselves, which is part of politics.

More than 30 years ago I wrote a book called *In Defence of Politics*[2] which has remained in print until last year. But what has dismayed me is that during the last 30 years there has been in Britain (less so in the USA, France and Germany) a continuing decline in book publishing of serious political thinking aimed at and read by the public, despite all the troubles and unexpected opportunities of our times. Coherent political thinking can be all but abandoned by party leaders, certainly debased and too often reduced to sound-bites uttered with a coached sincerity, fragments of general principles which too often sound merely opportunistic. Profiles of personalities stand in for principles, appeals to immediate self-interest rather than to long-term mutual or public benefits. Only a few columnists and editorial writers in the broadsheets keep up the older tradition of intelligent and reasonably open-minded public debate and speculation. The standard of the popular press is a parody of the failure of the common educational system and keeps the masses from becoming citizens.

The academic discipline of political thought, however, has thrived as never before, both as the history and contextualization of ideas and as the analysis of meaning and implications of concepts in current use – say 'freedom', 'equality', 'justice', 'sovereignty', 'nation', 'individualism', 'community' and so on. But this advance has been almost wholly internalized. Most academic writing on politics and the problems of democracy can be seen, sometimes rather too generously, as contributions to the advancement of knowledge; but few authors seem interested or able to diffuse this knowledge to the public. Faults on both sides can be found. It is all too easy to make a career by writing or researching, yet for the product to remain wholly within the Ivory Tower, unknown and incomprehensible to the public. The irony of doing this for the study of politics escapes most of the denizens of the tower. They are too often like those student leaders of the 1960s who proclaimed their solidarity with the working class and 'the people' in a Marxist terminology understandable only to those among 'the people' who had a degree in social science at a new university.

In Defence of Politics argued that politics is the conciliation of naturally different interests, whether these interests are seen as material or moral, usually both. There is a famous passage in Aristotle's *Politics* where he says that the great mistake of his master Plato was in writing about ideal states as if to find a single unifying principle of righteousness. Rather:

> ... there is a point at which a polis, by advancing in unity, will cease to be a polis; but will nonetheless come near to losing its essence, and will thus be a worse polis. It is as if you were to turn harmony into mere unison, or to reduce a theme to a single beat. The truth is that the polis is an aggregate of many members.

Not all societies are organized and governed according to political principles. Most governments in history suppress public debate about policy, far preferring to encourage 'good subjects' rather than good as active citizens. But political rule existed before democratic government and is, in a very real sense, logically prior to 'democracy', unless by that term we mean rather fatuously 'everything we would like' rather than a component of good government, a concept of majority opinion and power that is not always compatible with liberty and individual rights. Some dictatorships, for instance, have been and are genuinely popular, resting on majority support and the stronger for it. Both historically and logically politics is prior to democracy. We may want to fill the cart full of good things that everyone wants and feel they need, but the horse must go out in front. Without order there can be no democracy, and without politics even democracy is unlikely to be just. Political rule is the most generally justifiable type of order.

Politics rests on two preconditions, a sociological and a moral. The sociological is that all civilized societies are complex and inherently pluralistic, even if and when (hopefully) the injustices of class, ethnic and gender discriminations will vanish or diminish. The moral aspect is that it is normally better to conciliate differing interests than to coerce and oppress them perpetually. While much political behaviour is prudential, there is always some moral context: some compromises we think it wrong to make, and some possible ways of coercion or even of defence which we think are too cruel, disproportionate or simply too uncertain. Hannah Arendt was wiser than Clausewitz and Dr Kissinger when she said that violence is the breakdown of politics not its 'continuance by other means'.

Perhaps it was too easy for me to argue that it is always better to be governed politically, if there is any choice in the matter. The thesis did not seem banal or simple-minded at a time when there was a sustained contrast, both in the text and in the world, between political rule and totalitarian rule. The simple could then appear both profound and important. But with the breakdown of Soviet power, the whole world has become more complicated, and previously existing contradictions in the so-called 'free world' have both come to the surface and grown acute. Just as totalitarian rule and ideology could break down internally, so can political rule. Political prudence can prove inadequate. I gave such situations too little serious attention when writing *In Defence*. Also, I did not consider the apparent inadequacy of the political method and of diplomatic negotiation to resolve international and global problems that genuinely threaten tragedy and even disaster. Was it, indeed, the fear of nuclear war between the USA and the USSR that diverted realists from facing up to such problems? Walking and talking in Northern Ireland for nearly 20 years has made me more eager to find a secular equivalent to Niebuhr's Christian realism. A sequel to *In Defence* would be a much darker book.

The justification of politics in terms of the negation of totalitarianism was all too easy. The mundane could be made melodramatic in terms of contrast. The 'defeat' of the USSR and the 'victory' of the West also appeared to imply the rejection and then the demise of ideology. However, political prudence and pragmatism did not take over, rather there emerged the rapid, almost wildfire spread of the belief that market forces will resolve all major problems on a global scale, or at any rate cannot be resisted.

Hannah Arendt in *The Human Condition* remarked that there have only ever been two kinds of comprehensive ideologies claiming to hold the key to history: the belief that all is determined by *race* and the belief that all is determined by *economics*. Both, racism and economicism are distinctively modern beliefs: before the late eighteenth century the world could get by without such enormous secular claims, and not even religions claimed to explain everything. Arendt pointed out that economic ideology took two rival forms, Marxism (all is class ownership) and *laissez-faire* (all is market forces). Yet their belief that there must be a *general system* linked them more than their disciples believed. The missionaries and advocates of market ideology now denounce political intervention in the economy almost as fiercely as did the old totalitarians, although fortunately they are still subject to some political restraints and a few cultural inhibitions. In a broader perspective, the degree of political restraint upon the children of Hayek, the Reagans and the Thatchers, is also remarkable. These 'innovators' have done for us, for good or ill, much less than they think they ought to have done. And that is because of 'irrational political factors', fortunately. *Man is citizen as well as consumer.*

The effects of the market can be either limited or mitigated by civic action. Some should be. New lines of demarcation and mutual influence between the polity and the economy need examining more closely. There is taxation, for instance; there is or was public and family morality, strong cultural restraints on the exercise of both economic and political power. If people see themselves purely as consumers they will lose all real control of government. Governments will then rule by bread and circuses, even if not by force; and torrents of trivial alternatives will make arbitrary and often meaningless choices pass for effective freedom. For all the absolutist rhetoric, in reality at least a degree of welcome confusion reigns. Only the two extreme positions of All-State or All-Market are untenable. There is a lot of space between for active and inclusive citizenship. Political and economic factors and principles interact with each other, limit each other; but neither can live for long without the other.

Consider, by way of contrast to even the best democratic practices of today, a passage that used to be worrying knowledge to advisers to renaissance autocrats and elites in Europe, and a source of inspiration to their opponents. Once-upon-a-time the Periclean oration would have been read by almost everyone who read books at all.

Our constitution is called a democracy because power is in the hands not of a minority but of the whole people. When it is a question of settling private disputes, everyone is equal before the law; when it is a question of putting one person before another in positions of public responsibility, what counts is not membership of a particular class, but the actual ability which the man possesses. No-one, so long as he has it in him to be of service to the state, is kept in political obscurity because of poverty.

Here each individual is interested not only in his own affairs but in the affairs of the state as well: even those who are mostly occupied with their own business are extremely well-informed on general politics – this is a peculiarity of ours: we do not say that a man who takes no interest in politics is a man who minds his own business; we say that he has no business here at all. We Athenians, in our own persons, take our decisions on policy or submit them to proper discussions: for we do not think that there is an incompatibility between words and deeds; the worst thing is to rush into action before the consequences have been properly debated . . .[6]

Yes, there is no need to remind me. Pericles was a demagogue, a kind of democratic dictator. But the point for us is what the demagogue said, the lasting ideal he invoked, not what he did or why he said it. There is no need to search far if we want to find the moral and practical basis for an inclusive society: we take seriously long understood, seldom fully acted upon, ideas of democratic citizenship. We teach them to our young and we try to hold our leaders to the meaning of the words they easily, too easily, utter.

We would fail our obligation as active citizens unless we conclude these meditations by moving from them to actual engagement as referred to at the chapter's beginning. This finds tangible expression throughout the Final Report on *Education for Citizenship and the Teaching of Democracy*, from which I quoted earlier. Here are some further key passages:

> the Education Act 1996 aims to ensure that children are not presented by their teachers with only one side of political or controversial issues. Education should not attempt to shelter our nation's children from even the harsher controversies of adult life, but should prepare them to deal with such controversies knowledgeably, sensibly, tolerantly and morally...
>
> A controversial issue is an issue about which there is no one fixed or universally held point of view...
>
> Those particular qualities of mind which we believe would be enhanced by examining controversial issues in a programme of citizenship education would include:
> * a willingness and empathy to perceive and understand the interests, beliefs and viewpoints of others;
> * a willingness and ability to apply reasoning skills to problems and to value a respect for truth and evidence in forming and holding opinions;
> * a willingness and ability to participate in decision-making, to value freedom, to choose between alternatives, and to value fairness as a basis for making and judging decisions.[7]
> * We aim at no less than a change in the political culture of the country both nationally and locally; for people to think of themselves as active citizens, willing, able and equipped to have an influence in public life and with the critical capacities to weigh evidence before speaking and acting; to build on and to extend radically to young people the best in existing traditions of public service, and to make them individually confident in finding new forms of action and involvement among themselves.[8]

Notes

1 *Education for Citizenship and the Teaching of Democracy in Schools* (London: Qualifications and Curriculum Authority, 1998), being the final report of the Advisory Group on citizenship appointed by David Blunkett and chaired by Bernard Crick.
2 Seymour Martin Lipset does not put it quite so bluntly in his masterly *American Exceptionalism: A Double-Edged Sword* (New York and London: W.W. Norton, 1996), but the figures and surveys he reports lead to this conclusion.
3 *In Defence of Politics*, 4th edition (London: Penguin, 1992), first published by Weidenfeld & Nicolson (1962), and in the USA by the University of Chicago Press.
4 Ernest Barker, (ed.), *The Politics of Aristotle* (Oxford: Clarendon Press, 1946), p. 51.
5 Hannah Arendt, *The Human Condition* (Chicago and London: University of Chicago Press, 1958), pp. 126ff.
6 Thucydides, *The Peloponnesian War* (London: Penguin, 1954), pp. 117–18.
7 *Education for Citizenship*, p. 57.
8 *Ibid.*, pp. 7–8.

15
Voluntarity: A Spark to be Nurtured

Peter Askonas

Controversy about whether and to what extent economic activity should be regulated for the sake of social cohesion, justice and fairness has been a constant preoccupation for a century and more. If there is a last word to be said, it has not yet been found. Even whilst contributors to this book are penning their case, either advocating or doubting desirability of regulatory regimes and their practicability, uncontrolled financial operations, some on a scale to cause serious upheaval, make their impact on the world economy. Take the behaviour of the major equity markets; to the detached onlooker they may well appear devoid of common sense. No convincing case can be made in support of overbidding for anticipated values of corporate balance sheets. Even less compatible with rational and responsible behaviour is exaggerated panic. It all amounts to a mix of inordinate rapacity, fear and related pressures, and over-cleverness. Governments, for their part, are signally timid to provide restraints.[1]

Take another malaise, discussed widely and also in this volume: staggering shifts of capital across the world. True, there is perpetual talk about global financial controls, stabilization pacts, rules to govern hedge funds. One recent IMF proposal would link central banks and governments by an international liaison committee; this should provide an early warning system and possibly joint regulatory action. Will this materialize? Perhaps, as on previous occasions, some structures will be cobbled together to provide a semblance of solidity – until the next time. Meanwhile, large numbers of human beings will have suffered the grave consequences of the present free-for-all. Surely, more than emergency measures are required, at least for the medium term.

Yet in the political economy debate the counter-arguments, not least those which stress the wealth-generating effects of deregulated free-flowing capital are well-rehearsed. How many times have we heard about not to kill the golden-egg-laying goose. How many times have we been told that regulation will always be circumvented. These assumptions, together with enormous pressures by economic power centres, and not least uncritical acceptance of neo-liberal doctrine continue to influence policy-making. What is so wrong, it is asked, with a political philosophy which asserts that unrestricted personal initiative, stimulated or 'regulated' by market forces only, corresponds as nearly as possible to the human condition? You can say, if you are unashamedly exclusive, that this non-system gets results; better results for some, than those of dirigist regimes. Indeed, on its own terms this position has something going for it. That is if you ignore the growing disparities between wealth and poverty, or the financial fiascoes which several contributors to this book describe.

In any case, those who hold political power are usually allergic to taking chances by interfering with the game of the market. Note that usually the players are presented as being moderately sensible and responsible. In the marketplace's everyday scenario, though, sensibility and rationality are manifestly absent; even in persons who, were we to meet them in their or our homes, might appear sensible, rational and responsible. Not so in the 'real' world of un-reasonableness. Usually unforeseen events are more effective in enforcing solutions without which civilized living could become precarious. Temporary solutions they will be, of course. Beyond that, the neo-liberal formula and its derivatives lead to less responsibility and greater human self-centredness, whether that be in personal or group behaviour. The very opposite to the disposition which addresses inclusiveness seriously.

In that light, the need for regulatory regimes still outweighs its negative effects. The alternative dirigist formula, especially in its radical enactments and despite all its benefits by generating wealth and thus softening one kind of exclusion – acute deprivation – has been seen to result in exclusion of another kind – violence and degradation. It seems to hold little promise of solving the dilemma. If in Eastern Europe 'the state has withered away', it was not because it had accomplished its task, but because the citizenry found its restraints too oppressive and its economic benefits inadequate. We have to look elsewhere to advance inclusiveness, together with human dignity and freedom.

Is, then, benevolent intervention – preferably minimalist – the alternative on which the Good Society,[2] or a somewhat better society, can be constructed? Or is this merely a less-unattractive option? Pragmatically, regulatory measures are necessary; responses to urgent problems from which we cannot walk away. They are forced on us because if the present lack of restraint continues, more and more people on the globe will find their lot intolerable, with prospects of new totalitarian visitations, in so far unknown fearful shapes. But is this the best at which to aim?

One can see regulation as an aspect of order, the kind of order essential for human flourishing. The question is: who should regulate? Self-regulation at the institutional level has so far proved to be a blunt instrument, and in many cases a sham. The state? To assign the function primarily to the state is in the long run unsatisfactory. Those who exercise state power are usually too tied to pursuing their political advantage to serve the common good wholeheartedly. Let us not rely on the state except as the second-best.

The over-arching principle for a political philosophy with a humane direction is something quite other. I envisage the foundation of sociopolitical behaviour and ultimately the primary regulator to be neither state nor market but The Person, the 'I' orientated towards and informed by the community.

Evidently this high-toned statement can make sense only when qualified. First, the project is a long-term one. 'Climatic' change and evolution of human disposition require large time frames. These are problematic when we have to deal with immediate political needs. Moreover, a huge act of faith in that 'I' is demanded. In the world of day-to-day experience the 'I' surrendering itself to communal needs is conspicuously rare; and perhaps is getting rarer still in a postmodern environment. Nevertheless, I will try to show that, far from being fanciful, my assertion corresponds to a primary mode of existence which functions beyond many layers of accident, disruptiveness and disorder; and that it finds expression here and now in practical initiatives with an ordering, regulatory influence. Yet, prior to telling their stories, it should help to analyse my proposition reflexively.

Why we need something more fundamental than regulation

'Person', 'Self', 'I', 'Ego'; these words are given many meanings in the different disciplines which use them. There is ambiguity too about 'mind' and 'consciousness'. Even more at variance are perceptions of 'person' in the light of an ultimate direction. And, not least, how to relate 'person' and 'individual' gives rise to constant misunderstanding. Though all these words are part of daily discourse, we share no common dictionary to agree their contents. Experientially we can grasp the reality of 'this person'; but to encapsulate it in verbal communication within the limitations of analytical rationality tends to be a frustrating exercise.

I restrict myself here to extremely simplified interpretations. They express, rather than define, what the person is. A person's being reveals itself extensively by what he/she does, by the way that he/she relates. The consequence of relating is 'becoming more by being less'. The more I give, the more I surrender my 'self' to the 'other', the more I am. In simpler language: the more I am committed to others, say by service, the more I grow in authenticity, in personhood. Oddly enough, the process is often invisible. Thus many truly 'great persons' are the unnoticed ones.

Contrast this notion of person with that of the individual; and consequently with individualism. These indicate separateness, autonomy for its own sake, a mode of self-assertion where the self is an end in itself.

Again, person and personality are commonly seen as closely related concepts. But the linguistic parentage hides a profound functional difference. Personality, colloquially, may designate the tycoon, the political dictator, the popular idol. Usually their ilk are anything but dedicated to those around them. Even so, who would *a priori* deny their personhood? Some are larger-than-life persons, and in special instances humanity would be much the poorer without their contribution. Sometimes their mark on history is indelible – happily or disastrously so. Like every paradox, this one defies simplistic explanations. Carl Jung offers a psychological insight: personality can be conceived as 'the shadow' of personhood;[3] the aggregate of the person's aspirations; or else their negative expression.

*   *   *

We turn now to the person and its relation to community as the basis for political models. Returning to political thought. It is illuminating to juxtapose passages from four great seekers of our century. First, Frederick von Hayek:

Society can thus only exist if by a process of selection rules have evolved which lead individuals [sic] to behave in a manner which makes social life possible ... the responses of the individual to the events in their environment need be similar only in certain abstract aspect to ensure that a determinate overall order will result.[4] In all free societies ... the coordination of the activities of all those organisations, as well as of separate individuals, is brought about by the forces making for a spontaneous order ... growth of the mind can direct ... the more comprehensive order within which organisations function. [It] rests on adaptation to the unforeseeable ... The only possibility of transcending the capacity of individual minds is to rely on those super-personal 'self-organising' forces which create spontaneous order.[5]

For contrast, I turn to Nicholas Berdyaev. Perhaps less widely known he has laid the foundations of contemporary philosophical personalism:

Personality signifies interiority to self ... By the very fact that each of us is a person and expresses himself to himself, each of us requires communication with the other and with others in the order of knowledge and love ... *Personality*, of its essence, asks for a dialogue in which souls really communicate. Such communication is rarely possible. This is why personality in man seems bound to the experience of affliction.[6]

The theme is amplified by Jacques Maritain:

Personality signifies interiority to self ... my act is simultaneously the act of myself as an individual and as a *person* ... by the fact that it is free and engages my whole being, each act is linked in a movement towards the supreme centre.[7]

And here is Charles Taylor:

That our relations are of a certain kind is not just the combinations of a fact about me, say my disposition, and a fact about you. What this decomposition leaves out is the crucial factor ... that we have some common understanding about this ... Common understandings are undecomposable. This is because it essential to their being what they are that they be not just for me and for you, but for us.[8]

At first sight we may be struck by what looks like synergy linking these writers. All see individual and person (personality) as key concepts. Both seem to have in mind some mode of convergence of human beings, leading to order which elsewhere they will show to be the prerequisite of cohesion. All, though this is not explicit in the quotations, are conscious of the precariousness of the kind of order in question. All are prompted by awareness of a continuous longing for convergence. But when it comes to substance they inhabit alien worlds. Their perceptions of the individual and the person, of the ontological grounding and the end towards which he/she moves, clash.

Hayek's 'spontaneous order' and the 'emergent possibilities' from which this arises in an unpredictable environment are orientated towards utility. The individual in such a setting is an 'I for itself' for whom maximalization of achievement (economic achievement) is the natural term of reference. Notwithstanding Hayek's passionate commitment to the idea of liberty and human dignity, he does not seem to see that his model must, in view of its determining premises and mechanisms, end in the undoing of dignity. The human being becomes an object in the movement towards spontaneously emerging socioeconomic patterns and subsequent orders. These orders, presumably numberlessly succeeding one another, are ends in themselves. It hardly needs underscoring how profoundly this thinking influences not only contemporary socioeconomic reasoning, but the modern world view at large.

A social personalism in terms of a wider world-view

Awareness of the interaction self–the other–self–the community is not a twentieth century preoccupation. A long chain links discernments which we owe to thinkers of the classic period to phenomenological and existential analysis of recent time. Within this continuity increasing emphasis is given to a realization that we cannot understand ourselves, nor bear the weight of existence, unless within the context of relationship. In our often maligned century we encounter an astonishing number of fertile minds who are creatively exploring different facets of interaction between self and other as the basis of a beneficent praxis.

Karl Barth describes three modes of I–Thou relationships: that of God within Himself; that between God and Man; and that between man and man (n.b. feminism had not yet assumed prominence when he availed himself of the male pronoun). 'If God for man is the eternal covenant . . . there arises a relationship which . . . is natural to Him. God repeats Himself in this relationship 'at extra'. . . he makes a copy [image] of His own nature'.[9] Barth speaks of 'the plurality inherent in the I–Thou relationship'. He goes on: '[if] God lives in togetherness with Himself . . . then men live in togetherness with one another.'[10]

Some would object: these propositions might be meaningful for the believing person, especially for the person with a belief in a Trinitarian, relational deity. What has this line of thought to offer the agnostic, the disbeliever? Peter Vardy, philosopher and pedagogue reminds us that 'the person who lives a life of responsibility and care for others, of denial of self, and of compassion may be found closer to God than the "believer", whose beliefs do not radically affect his or her life'.[11]

Barth is at his most penetrating when discoursing on 'humanity' (better translated by human-ness): 'Man as the Being-With-the Other'. Barth offers an analysis of the 'I' as 'I am' in encounter with the other . . . leading to 'I am as Thou art'. Lastly: 'Being in encounter consists in the fact that we render mutual assistance in the act of being'.[12]

On to Martin Buber who will blend Jewish and Christian wisdom: 'The one primary word is the combination I–Thou' . . . 'Primary words intimate relations'. This primacy develops: 'Just as the individual becomes a person, a "fact of existence", insofar as he steps in a living relation with other individuals, so does a social aggregate become a community insofar as it is built from . . . units of relation'. 'The true community does not arise through people having feelings (though indeed not without it), but through their taking their stand in living relation with a living Centre, and in living in mutual relation with each other'.[13]

Lastly, I turn to a thinker who, though not easy to follow, adds significantly to the understanding of selfhood and relationship, Paul Ricoeur. Strikingly, he identifies the Other not as separate but as part of the Self. As I understand it, he can identify within this nuclear relationship – I and the other within myself – a dialectic which can serve as prototype for the functioning of all relationship. He refers to 'the fact that otherness is not added on to selfhood from outside, but . . . belongs instead to the ontological constitution of selfhood . . . [and] with the full force of the expression *oneself as another'.*[14] The other as constituent of the self points analogically to the other as the necessary constituent of the community, and to a similar dialectic within communal relationship. That dialectic is one of inescapable tension and pain. Ricoeur encapsulates this dialectic in the concept of *thrownness*. Let this word reverberate in the mind to fathom how it expresses what is virtually unsayable. (It is worth noting that *thrownness* is also a constituent of Vaclav Havel's thought-system. Perhaps it indicates the philosopher–president's awareness of an unresolvable tension at the heart of his, and indeed of every available political vision.) 'The notion of a thrown-project carries to the level of strangeness our human finiteness ... [and] the burdensome character of the task of having to be'[15]

This insight safeguards against the false optimism which colours twentieth century individualism. Tension, pain, becoming – with the counter-part of solidarity and fulfilment: we can recognize essential constituents of personhood and of relationship. Hence the insight that I am compelled, knowingly or otherwise, to respond to the uniqueness of the other, not because of his/her particular achievements or of any specific character trait, but because he/she is vulnerable – and so am I; he/she is subjected to the pain of the world – so am I; and because he/she yearns to relate, to receive and give joy – so do I.

The profusion of material on this subject published by sociologists, psychologists and many others indicates the challenge of grasping what is at issue. Attention must be drawn, also, to yet another linguistic double-meaning. The concept of the other in all passages quoted here hints at affinity, yet it is also used extensively in an antinomous sense: the other is the alien, the threatening hostile one whom we must defeat lest he defeats us. We tend to wish away otherness of this kind, not only to escape implicit tension, but because of the painful demands on self-knowledge by two opposing – dare I say contrapuntal – needs: for the complementary and the antagonistic other.

A community orientated personalism

If the perception of personhood which will have emerged from these quotations approximates how things are, it legitimizes not only an outward-directed personalism, but one with the capacity to shape social policy. The person is then recognized as the primary and immediate agent, with the potential to bring about restraint in

conformity to principles of justice and fairness. **It follows that –
at least in principle – agency of that order should not be subjected to inordinate outside restraint which will inhibit his/her
spontaneous creativity.**

This set of concepts and its effectiveness will be challenged: utopian and out-of-touch with reality it will be called. Let me be the
first challenger. I would then point to the pain-ridden history of
humankind and of perennial exclusion by exploitative structures,
to the persistence of self-aggrandizement, to disregard of the other
as the norm of political behaviour. I would assert that this an unalterable feature of our species. I would cite as an example in recent
political history the apparent failure of Vaclav Havel's vision of
mutual 'civility'. I would show how the steamroller of ever-increasing
concentration of economic entities is progressing constantly and
makes a mock of humanness. Jargon, like 'people's companies' and
'customer choice' is empty, even deceitful. I would refer to the
dismantling of the large mutual enterprises, the withering away of
the cooperative movement, the unquestioning priority status given
to shareholder value. To this list could be added the persistence of
national tribalism in our own quasi-liberated post-enlightened milieu, and not least the divisiveness caused by fundamentalist faiths.
Lastly, I would register doubt about the relevance of academic philosophical and sociological utterances on the subject, because 'the
person' in these accounts is 'a' person, some kind of abstraction,
not 'The Person', alive and unique.

Moreover, personhood is over and over again overwhelmed by
structural and individual inhumanness. (One does not have to scratch
much of the surface to discover this in one's own make-up.) And
even more devastatingly by indifference, the facelessness of mass
non-culture, of downgrading what is of value. Zygmunt Bauman
castigates this trend in an earlier chapter. Indifference, the blank
face of the individual unresponsive to others increasingly makes a
mockery of aspirations to inclusiveness.

Yet, in advocacy of a community-orientated personalism, I can
mount a counter-challenge. I will then say: yes, we are confronted
by deep-rooted discontinuity. To achieve political structures based
on personal responsibility and civility may sound like an unrealistic project, but this is a one-sided view. We can recognize, on the
contrary, that inclusiveness, far from being a preoccupation of the
few, has moved towards the centre of serious political agendas.
Inclusiveness has become respectable – let us hope not too respect-

able We can also discern, at least in outline, that dispositions towards communality have not only the potential for becoming normative. They are worked out here and now in multiple shapes.

*   *   *

From principles to praxis, and from grand designs to ordinariness

From philosophy a plunge into praxis. Here are a few considerations of how persons can be instruments of human flourishing by their interaction with other persons; and how this should lead to a growing sense of inclusiveness. I will relate stories about comparatively humble initiatives, where the participants play their parts primarily not for their own but for each other's benefit. When necessary they take on 'Goliath'. Little fear there, even of massive and global economic units and of those who control them, only their own advantage in mind.

'The East London Communities Organization', and 'Community Organizing' TELCO operates in East London and connects with six affiliated organizations through over 150 local associations, religious congregations and schools. This broad-based 'people's organization' has sprung up during the 1990s to kindle awareness in local citizens of their potential for civic action and mutuality. It concentrates on the most neglected areas of Britain, wishing to contribute to 'reweaving the fabric of UK society'. Let them speak for themselves:

> Our organisations are fuelled by thousands of volunteer hours of talented people in local communities. Each organisation works on a range of issues, including fighting to stop factories polluting neighbourhoods, making roads safe for children, tackling drug dens, persuading public transport companies to change policies which threaten neighbourhood centres, seeking closer relations with the police to tackle crime, seeking mutually beneficial working relationships with elected politicians. We are not expecting a leader to do it all for us. We value the principle of both rotating and collective leadership. We employ small teams of professional organisers, to keep us together, to agitate us and stop us falling out of relationship with each other. We are assisted by sympathetic foundations and some businesses which see the necessity of investing in this country's 'Social Capital'. Our iron rule: never

do for others what they can do for themselves. We believe in building for power which is fundamentally reciprocal allowing mutual respect. We organize out of love and stubbornness, out of joy and despair, and sometimes because we do not see who else will do what needs to be done.[16]

Direction of this mix of loosely integrated yet internally intimately bonded networks is in the hands of Neil Jamieson, a Quaker. He believes that the most fertile background for communal action are faith communities: the East London Mosque, the local Synagogue, the parish churches of different denominations. Beyond that, the network is extended to other 'empowerment centres' such as social clubs and schools. Seemingly unsurmountable barriers are overcome and common resources are mobilized. Civic action is the common denominator. Jamieson sees voluntarity as a road to empowerment. The volunteer is an 'I', she/he has shed their anonymity and finds authenticity by submerging that 'I' in others (and he recognizes that potentially the 'I' is also an ego who engages in civic relationships for the sake of self-assertion). He considers that some 10 per cent of those making up various communities can be mobilized; and that this is sufficient to bring about effective action. Ten per cent of relatively small numbers face-to-face with large and highly efficient bodies. A testimony to the efficacy of personal commitment.

Community Organizing is only one of an astonishingly substantial number of groupings who promote inclusiveness at grass roots level. They function as regulators, if you like. Typically, in close vicinity to TELCO are found Community Links ('never to do things for people, but to guide and support, to train and enable, to simply inspire'). This grouping concentrates on young people at risk. Last year more than 2500 persons benefited from projects run by over 450 volunteers in 60 key sites.

The number and variety of kindred initiatives up and down the land abounds. To get the broad picture we can look at the statistic of the Third Sector. For example there is extensive information under the heading Narrow Voluntary Sector, a term used by welfare economists to cover 'not-for-profit' organizations other than political parties and religious institutions.[17] Thus, in 1998 the sector included 135 000 charities in the UK, with some 485 000 staff and over 2 million active volunteers (the majority part-time). This means very large sums of money (though still only 2.2 per cent of GNP). In 1995, 36 per cent of the UK Third Sector revenues resulted from donations; 19 per cent were self-generated by charities, and 45 per cent came from government for services performed on behalf of some of its departments. (This latter figure demonstrates a trend, initiated by Conservative ideology and perpetuated by New Labour, to off-load responsibilities previously associated with the Welfare State.) These data are impressive, but they do not even comprise another important component of voluntarity: the large numbers of persons who take the initiative in activating or leading common-interest groups with a particular communal target. Take, for example, those springing into action when service-user interests are threatened; or officers of road associations, or political grassroots activists; these make up vast numbers of persons generating networks and relationships.

Still, though all the generosity mobilized by the Third Sector is inspiring, basic social needs exceed available resources by far. For example, we are only belatedly acknowledging – alas impotently – the financial challenge of old age provisions and care. Plant and human resources provided by the state are, with few exceptions, a disgrace, and it is well-known that private sector facilities are still worse. Voluntary bodies like Age Concern and Help The Aged, for all their fine work, cannot provide sufficient home-care let alone accommodation of quantity and dignifying quality. Most privately owned 'homes' are a blot on our society.

The Third Sector must get substantially increased support in terms of donated time and funds from whatever source to fill the gap ignored by governments preoccupied with restraint on public expenditure. This requires a transformation of the civic ethos to make normative an expanded level of sharing and caring, notably by the better-off in response to moral and social pressures. An unlikely development? It can happen only step by step and will require much imagination. Phrases like, 'it cannot be done' will need discarding. Consider, for example, nationwide contributions – *voluntary but made near-compulsory by social and moral pressure* – to fund fresh care initiatives. Such resources would be expected at a progressive rate, from those with upper and high incomes. The odium attached to statutory taxation could be reduced if such programmes would reward the donor/payee by adding visibly to his/her civic standing. Of course not everyone will play the game. Much depends on genuineness in presentation, on transparency, and on firing people's imaginations by the project's boldness. The result would have more meaning than mere alleviation of misery; it could constitute a move away from regulation to civil concern through voluntarity.

Current steps towards generating civic responsibility are signalled by the People's Panel set up under the aegis of the Cabinet Office.[18] This aims to assess citizens' expectations on a wide variety of public issues. The initiators claim that it will enable government to provide the services that people want and simultaneously stimulate the sense of 'I count'. Five thousand persons are being consulted. Personal contact is emphasized. Findings are fed back to central or local government and other concerned bodies, and will – so goes the claim – influence decision-making. By early 1999 two 'waves' of consultation on standards and delivery of public services have taken place. Here is a sample of typical questions and findings:

Health and Care
Q: Which two or three health-related issues for possible Government campaigns do you think are the most important?
A: drug misuse 52%, cancer 37%, heart disease and stroke 32%.
Electronic Government
Q: Which devices for dealing with Government would you use?
A: telephone 72%, personal computer 35%, interactive TV 16%, none of those 14%.
Satisfaction with Public Services
50% think these are what they would expect, but 40% think they fall slightly or a long way short of expectations.

Other consultations on modernizing government and local democracy are now taking place. And so are Focus Groups – normally eight to ten persons led by a trained facilitator in a one-off discussion where participants bounce ideas off one another – and Citizens' Juries – a structured process for obtaining detailed views on particular issues. Judicious formulation of questions can make citizens conscious of the implications of their responsibility for others.

Some will say that these undertakings are peripheral. It might also be argued that such initiatives in the hands of a political agency, namely government, tend to become mere public-relations exercises; even means of manipulation. The risk is there, but so is the possibility of developing genuine instruments for expanding self-awareness, for facilitating initiative, and for allowing persons to see their own choices in relation to communal needs. Informed opinion rather than emotive attitudes are a precondition to constructive responses. Here is the rub. Not that there is a lack of information; on the contrary, we are exposed to over-information.

Take as example the printed matter which is sent out by local councils and public services; or data to be accessed electronically. Even the experienced user finds it difficult to absorb what is essential or to distinguish this from the peripheral. Yet, simultaneously, we are frequently underinformed regarding issues which require responsible action. An example is the actual cost of personal consumption of health services: it might make a substantial difference to attitudes towards public spending and related taxation if each citizen had an annual statement of direct expenditure on his/her behalf. Another piece of paper? Or an eye-opener? Whether, by whom, and according to what norms selectivity can be promoted is so problematic that no one in a democratic environment dares to talk about it seriously. Yet sooner or later such talking will become imperative.

The 10 per cent regulator

To draw out some practicable principles from these selected stories it is best to go back to Neil Jamieson and his formula – the ten per cent segment of a constituency as a driving force. Ten per cent, who relate to others in a way which effects transformation. Ten per cent who bring into being a network of dissenting, activating and correcting relationships. If we are pessimistic about this figure, then say 5 per cent, say 1 per cent; then look at history: it has always been this core of humanity who have provided the impulse for paradigmatic change – sometimes for worse, sometimes for a move ahead. At face value, it will be objected, this is a recipe for exclusion. Not necessarily. Surely it is not the few, the 10 per cent, the nuclei of dedicated persons who downgrade communal values, who make inclusion meaningless, who necessitate regulation, but the aimless crowds in the hands of manipulators.[19] Thus the Latin American Liberation Theologian Juan Louis Segundo: '. . . *authentic minorities – i.e. ones that are not merely elitist behaviour patterns based on every man for himself – are cognizant of their conditioning by the mass and are deeply concerned about elevating it on a mass level. At the same time they are concerned about salvaging from the mass all minority lines of conduct that are possible . . .*' I would add a reminder that in Judeo-Christian consciousness it is the one single Person who is expected to realize, or has indeed realized, what mass movements then and now fail to achieve.

It may be argued that the unspectacular achievement of a few persons' service and giving is unlikely to satisfy norms for cost-effective performance which are *de rigeur* for postmodern institutions. True, judging superficially, what is achieved and its costs may be out of proportion to what is seen as the overall aim. Progress, if any, is bound to be impeded by *tohu-va-bohu*[20] and human incongruousness; at least for a while.

Those of us who find themselves comfortably included may not be greatly disturbed by such uncertainty. We might sit back in our libraries and speculate about society's gradual development and prospects for the inclusive model. On the excluded who need to have their conditions bettered now, not later, slow-motion progress towards inclusiveness will be hard. Hence there is no excuse for delay. To invent, refine, multiply and support more and more enabling initiatives is shown to be feasible. Voluntarity is the significant catalyst. When nurtured with conviction, voluntarity gradually takes over from compulsion. This will help to support the establishment of the right proportion between regulation and responsible freedom, including the issue of who can regulate and how. I hope that this brief sketch shows that both in theory as in praxis, it is within our capability to nurture personhood and self-identity and thereby bring inclusiveness closer.

Notes

1 There are solid reasons for inducing soundness into equity pricing by variable taxation: punitive for very short-term gains ranging down to a negative tax on realization of very long-term gains (indexation was an initial step in that direction, but much more ought to be done).
2 Careful! 'The Good Life' – 'The Good Society'. These terms have been used, since Aristotle, with so many nuances that their contents and the value judgements they imply are in the words of Riceour 'nebulous'.
3 A recurring theme with Jung and his followers. See 'Aion' in *Collected Works*, 1970.
4 von Hayek 1982, sec. II.
5 *Ibid.*
6 Berdyayev (1943) chap. I. This now little known thinker (1874–1948) deserves to be read more widely. His ideas go to the heart of the postmodern malaise.
7 Maritain (1948).
8 Taylor (1995) chap. 12.
9 Barth (n.d.) *Kirchliche Dogmatik* (Church Dogmatics, trans. Macquarrie) III. iii, sec. 50.
10 *Ibid.*
11 Vardy in Askonas and Frowen (1997).
12 Barth, *op. cit.*

13 Buber (1956) 'I and Thou'.
14 Ricoeur (1992).
15 *Ibid.*
16 TELCO (1994) from Statement of Aims and Objectives.
17 Kendall (1998).
18 The People's Panel. Cabinet Office in conjunction with Mori.
19 Sobrino (1947), Conclusions.
20 A Jewish word which has become a colloquialism; from the Hebrew 'tohu', that is, chaos.

References

Askonas, P. and Frowen, S. (eds) (1997) *Welfare and Values* (Basingstoke: Macmillan).

Barth, K. (n.d.) *Kirchliche Dogmatik* (Church Dogmatics, transl. Macquarrie).

Berdyayev, N. (1943) *Slavery and Freedom* (Geoffrey Bless).

Buber, M. (1956) *Selected Writings*, ed. Will Herberg (New York: Meridian Books).

Hayek, F.A. von (1982) *Law, Legislation and Liberty* (London: Routledge & Kegan Paul).

Jung, C. (1970) *Collected Works* (London: Routledge).

Kendall, J. with Almond, S. (1998) *The UK Voluntary (Third) Sector.* Personal Social Services Research Unit (University of Kent).

Maritain, J. (1948) *Les Degrés du Savoir* (Paris: Desclees).

Ricoeur, P. (1992) *Oneself as Another* (Chicago: University of Chicago Press).

Sobrino, J. (1947) *Evolution and Guilt*, trnsl. J. Dury (New York: Maryknoll).

Taylor, C. (1995) *Philosophical Arguments* (Cambridge, Mass.: Harvard University Press).

16
Inclusion in the Workplace: The Stakeholder Debate

Diana Winstanley and Christopher Stoney

Introduction

An inclusive approach to managing people within the workplace has been promoted over a number of years in a variety of different ways. In this chapter the concept of inclusiveness in the context of work organizations will be explored and the attack on its legitimacy outlined. We conclude by considering what needs to be done to salvage and bolster the inclusiveness project.

The making of inclusion: key components

There is no unequivocal set of principles and features of inclusiveness in the workplace to which any company claiming to be inclusive would have to conform. The Centre for Tomorrow's Company investigation into 'inclusiveness' (RSA, 1995) found that the lack of established criteria made it difficult to identify companies practising or working towards 'inclusiveness'. It seems sensible, then, to begin by hypothesizing what the core principles of inclusiveness might be. The relevant concepts are drawn from three areas, humanistic psychology, ethical theory and work on structural and process components. These are summarized in Table 16–1.

Humanistic psychology

Theories of child development suggest that one of the primary influences on social beings is their experience of attachment to the primary caregiver and then, as the social world develops, to significant others (Bowlby, 1979). Where initial experience involves repeated

Table 16.1 Key components in the making of inclusion

Values from Humanistic Psychology and Quality of Working Life Movement

- Attachment and reciprocity
- Security
- Acceptance
- Congruence
- Self-actualization and meaningfulness

Ethical Constructs

- Kantian respect for persons as ends in themselves
- Gilligan's ethic of care
- Etzioni's community of care

Structural and Process Components

- Diversity (versus unity of vision)
- Equitable resource distribution
- Voice and involvement in decision-making

separation, detachment and loss, individuals may later experience difficulties in forming secure fulfilling relationships, experience feelings of lack of worth and isolation and often high levels of depression and anxiety.

There is much to suggest that these processes can exist in working life. As many organizations have undergone competitive tendering and outsourcing in the public sector, and downsizing, heightened competition and globalization in the private sector, as well as significant changes to the psychological and explicit work contract, the experience of attachment has been significantly weakened and distorted. Increasing responsibilities are placed on individuals but, at the same time, more of the risks faced by the organization are placed on them (Heery, 1999). This implies a move away from attachment and reciprocal contracts to a more market-based model of employment.

Attachment and reciprocity form the basis from which individuals can become committed to membership of a community. Without some commitment of the organization to its members, or enabling of its workforce to become members in the first place, it is difficult for individuals to form the reciprocal bonds which constitute inclusive communities. The breaking of organizational bonds may lead to atavistic egoistic individuals, where the only real attachment is based on treating others instrumentally as means to our ends.

The lack of reciprocity and detachment of individuals from organizations also leads to insecurity. Although organizational membership has never been guaranteed, the increasingly precarious and temporal nature of the employment contract has led to increased risk and anxiety (Rubery, 1996; Stanworth, 1999). For those who lose work, loss of income, social prestige and feelings of self-worth can be great; for those in work, the insecurity can lead to 'playing it safe', staying in unsatisfying jobs because the alternative may be worse, guilt at having a job at all and fear lest one should lose it. It can lead to over-dependency on the organization, which can lead to disempowerment and even an abuse of that dependent role by the employer. Although some risk can be energizing, too much insecurity and risk can be debilitating to health and performance. The Involvement and Participation Association (IPA, Coupar and Stevens, 1998) and many trade union leaders (Monks, 1998) have argued that the inclusive partnership organization can only generate commitment and mutuality from its members if there is also some commitment to job security. Processes of globalization (Legge, 1999) make this an invidious task.

Another process vital to individual growth within an inclusive community is that of acceptance (Rogers, 1967). Where children grow with unconditional acceptance of their own intrinsic self-worth, they develop a strong sense of self. Too strong conditions of worth can lead the individual to become alienated from their true self, lacking an internal locus of control, leading to feelings of anxiety, hopelessness and meaninglessness. In contemporary work organizations the cult of performance management and evaluation leads to individuals constantly being graded, classified and appraised through processes of selection, promotion and performance assessment (Townley, 1994). Where these processes become too strong, they undermine attempts to enable the individual to develop, grow and actualize within the work context.

Greater acceptance also requires the ability for individuals to behave consistently across their lives. A lack of congruence leads to cognitive dissonance and internal stress. If an individual has to behave in one way at work and a radically different way in other settings, this can cause further splitting of the self. Where an organization has gone through a culture and values change, with the new set being imposed from above, attitudes, values and manifestations of these in norms and practices are slow to change but this process can become even more unhealthy when the new set are at odds with strongly held values an individual holds in the rest of their lives. An inclusive organization does not deny these value differences or ride roughshod over an individual's value system. The notion of an inclusive work organization requires some acceptance of the individual, their own uniqueness, valuing their difference from others (see the discussion of diversity below). Otherwise what is being included is only contingent on organizational values of success, and parts of the self are excluded and denied.

The human relations movement, epitomized by writers such as Maslow (1970) and Herzberg (1968) and propounded by the Quality of Working Life (QWL) group, advocated more emphasis on humanizing work, enabling more opportunities for involvement, variety, autonomy, decision-making and self-actualization. As Terkel (1972) poignantly wrote:

> [work] is about a search for daily meaning as well as daily bread, for recognition as well as cash, for astonishment rather than torpor, in short, for a sort of life rather than a Monday to Friday sort of dying.

The values of self-actualization and meaningfulness of work may also enable the building of commitment and inclusion.

Ethical constructs

Three ethical frameworks enable us to conceptualize a community of care which would facilitate the inclusiveness project: Kant's respect for person, Gilligan's ethics of care, and Etzioni and the communitarian movement. The first two emphasize the importance of seeing individuals as ends in themselves, each with their own unique perspective and view of self-actualization; the third locates this ethics of care in the context of caring communities.

A theme evolved from the work of Kant is the notion of respect for the person and their intrinsic value, producing a deontological perspective from which many have built the notion of rights, embracing issues such as the fundamental right to life and safety, the human rights of privacy, freedom of conscience, speech and to hold private property. Kant's first categorical imperative suggests that one should follow the principle that what is right for one person is right for everyone, and thus it is important to do unto others as you would be done by – the criteria of universality and reversibility.

The second is the principle of respect for persons whereby people should be treated as ends in themselves, never as means to an end. Elements of contemporary workplaces suggest that the utilitarian and instrumental view of individuals has blinded us to some of the real consequences for people who are treated as contingent commodities. Some suggest a move back to identifying individual rights in the workplace as a way of including people and their needs more explicitly. For example, in specific areas of human resource management, Winstanley and Woodall (1999) draw together a number of examples where this approach can be applied, such as in relation to selection interviewing, occupational testing, equal opportunities and diversity management, flexible employment contracts and working time, 'whistleblowing' and even employee reward and development. Staff charters are also suggested as one inclusive way forward to balance rights with responsibilities.

Much ethical debate in the area of managing the employment relationship has viewed feelings, intuitions and senses as dysfunctional to ethical judgement and to be purged from ethical reasoning. However, Gilligan's work *In a Different Voice* (1982) has shown that more subjective and intuitive approaches in ethical reasoning takes us back to a more humanistic basis for managing people. Moral judgements need to be sensitive to both the needs of the situation and other individuals. Being impartial makes it difficult to imagine oneself in the other's position, and thus adequately understand the other's perspective (Carse, 1996: 86). For Gilligan, moral reasoning involves empathy, responsiveness and responsibility, where moral choices are made in relationship with others, not in isolation. This incorporation of a place for feeling and emotion in organizational life supports some of those principles from humanistic psychology mentioned above, namely empathy, acceptance, genuineness and congruence.

Communitarianism as advocated by Etzioni (1995) in the USA and Tam (1998) in the UK discusses organizations as moral communities of purpose which incorporate much of the reciprocity of rights and responsibilities in organizational life, combined with the features of ethics of care. Etzioni (1995) suggests that the unbridled liberal defence of freedom is a fallacy; we are all members of overlapping communities. The workplace is one such community of purpose, with the potential for shared values, belonging and inclusiveness.

Although it appears appealing to draw on communitarian principles as a way forward for inclusiveness, there are dangers and problems. While appeal to mutuality is currently very strong on the part of employers, the overall balance of rights and responsibilities appears to be in their favour. Heery (1999) illustrates this through the way that new payment systems expect employees to assume more responsibility and risk; similarly, Simpson (1999) has pointed to the persistence and extension of long-hours cultures for managers and professionals, despite European Union directives on working hours. Arguments that stress 'community' and mutuality focus upon achieving harmony and consensus. The danger is that all too often the equilibrium of a community of purpose can be disturbed by 'greedy' employers (Coser, 1974) concerned to push for more, be it by means of 'stretch' targets and variable pay or in their appetite to 'shape' employee values, beliefs and corporate cultures. A community of purpose is always in danger of becoming too paternalistic and narrow in its perspective, which can present problems for ensuring that values of diversity and difference are able to flourish and grow. There is a huge difference between a paternalistic employer that cares for the welfare of employees, from a paternal 'parent knows best' approach, foisting values and morals on the workforce (as in the case of the early Quaker-based businesses), and one which is more compatible with the inclusiveness project by putting into practice structural components to allow for more equitable power distribution, open communication and voice, features discussed below.

Structural and process components

Many work organizations perpetuate membership through forms of homogeneity, such as recruiting in the self-image, consensus-seeking behaviour and group-think, where individuals voicing different views are scapegoated and marginalized. A truly inclusive organization accommodates a pluralist model of the organization, assumes that some conflict and disagreement will be inherent and develops approaches to identify the plurality of views and ways of synthesizing these. Here critics highlight the inadequacies of the inclusive model – whose views are upheld and whose are denied in this mass of self-actualizing individuals and groups? Some even suggest that the concept of diversity as it has evolved in the 1980s and 1990s has gained credence through its association with business performance – to encourage diversity is to become more successful and competitive as everyone's talents can be harnessed to the needs of the work organization. The problem is whether this has developed at the expense of equal opportunities – the concept which had a stronger basis in individual rights irrespective of its impact on success. There also continues to be a paradox in inclusiveness in its requirements for the development of unity and the tolerance of diversity.

Implicit in the notion of inclusiveness is an assumption that the workplace is not divided into two camps of 'haves' and 'have-nots'. At the bottom end of resource distribution, it assumes that individuals' basic needs are met, they have rewards that sustain a reasonable standard of living, accompanied by non-pecuniary benefits for enhancement and growth such as training, development and reasonable working conditions, working hours and holidays. An inclusive company should perform well on indicators of training and reward. As well as basic and actualization needs, we would also expect some equity in the perceived reward relationship. Two main issues arise here. One is that such companies would have a lower than average differentiation between the rewards gained by those at the top of the organization and those at the bottom. Commonly cited here is the example of Ben and Jerry, the ice-cream company, where there is a maximum ratio set for this distribution. One would also not expect such organizations to provide the 'fat cat' top executive salaries which appear regularly in the press in relation to privatized utilities. Huge inequities of this type have an undermining effect on inclusiveness, where some in the organization are doing much better than others, and not always for reasons of performance. Likewise, where surpluses and profits are generated, inclusive companies are likely to be cited as having systems for profit-sharing so that all those included in the creation of the profit are also the recipients of the reward.

For individuals to be truly included, their voice has to be heard through authentic processes for involvement and participation in decision-making. The industrial democracy movements sought representation and codetermination in management structures. Concepts such as empowerment, participation, and involvement all emphasize processes for including the views of employees in decision-making. We have already mentioned the work of the IPA, but two other sources are also useful here, Hirschman's work on voice and the burgeoning literature on stakeholding.

Hirschman (1970) suggests that there are three things an individual can do if they are not happy with their situation, whether at work or in another context. They can merely accept with loyalty and a form of passive unassertiveness and fatalism, that what will be will be; they can exit, and vote with their feet, such as by quitting their job or the organization; or they can voice their concerns. Hirschman suggests that the last is the most desirable, both for the individual and for organizational survival. For an organization to be truly inclusive, they need to facilitate the process of voice, both in culture and in mechanisms and procedures.

Stakeholding is another way to describe involvement. We can identify two levels of stakeholder theory. Level one suggests that organizations should ascertain the needs of their key stakeholder groups and identify ways in which their needs can be met (Freeman, 1984). Some go further to suggest a challenge on the mission and objectives of the work organization, where its primary objective is to meet these other stakeholder needs, not just to create profit for shareholders. Level two stakeholding suggests this is not just a question of meeting needs, *but a redistribution of power, to allow stakeholders a voice in decision-making*. For example, the work of Goodpaster (1993) makes the distinction between stakeholder *analysis*, where stakeholder views are solicited to inform decision-making, and stakeholder *synthesis* where stakeholders are more fully incorporated into decision-making processes, implying a more radical attempt at power sharing. A number of organizations are experimenting with more innovative and inclusive types of participation, for example the social audit process conducted by the Body Shop (Sillanpaa and Jackson, 1999).

It is over this last aspect of inclusion, that of voice and stakeholding, that the most virulent attacks have been made on the inclusive model.

An attack on inclusion and stakeholding at work

The legitimacy of the inclusiveness project is challenged from many different sides. The central conflict appears to be between the human and the economic model of the work organization, proponents of each perspective being described by the other as utopians or economic fatalists respectively.

This critique of inclusiveness is mounted from three directions: from those on the right who uphold the shareholder rather than stakeholder view of the firm, and who see stakeholding and inclusion as a burden on competitiveness; and from those on the left who see it as utopian in the face of economic determinism and its inability in the face of global economic forces; and finally from those who discuss the problems of implementation.

The view from the right: the shareholder view of the firm and stakeholding's burden on competitiveness

Since it represents a potential challenge to the existing order of organizational and societal relations, the stakeholder or inclusiveness concept has unsurprisingly been criticized more by the political and intellectual right than it has by the left. The arguments of writers such as Argenti (1993), and Sternberg (1997) build on Milton Friedman's ideas (1962) that each company should have a clear sense of its own purpose and responsibility:

> There is one and only one social responsibility of business – to use its resources and engage in activities designed to increase its profits so long as it stays within the rules of the game, which is to say, engage in open and free competition, without deception or fraud.
>
> (Friedman, 1962: 74)

Argenti (1993) asserts that organizations that try to be all things to all people or to benefit all stakeholders 'are not only at a huge competitive disadvantage, they are also . . . literally unmanageable' (Argenti, 1993: 36–37). His basic premise is that stakeholding theory is an oxymoron that in practice will obfuscate and compromise a company's main goal, which is to maximize profits and dividends to shareholders. Sternberg (1997) similarly claims that those who support stakeholder theory 'seek to do away with business as it has traditionally been understood', and 'seek to subvert essential features of business accountability'. The basis of her criticism lies in her belief that it is an unworkable objective, incompatible with corporate governance. It undermines private property, agency and wealth, so that:

> In the spurious expectation of achieving vaguely 'nicer' business behaviour, the stakeholder approach would sacrifice not only property rights and accountability, but also the wealth-creating capabilities of business strictly understood
>
> (Sternberg, 1997: 23)

There are three main responses to this: First, Sternberg's argument only works if we take a maximalist view of stakeholding and inclusion, that it challenges the organization's purpose. This only works for shareholding organizations; it does not apply so much to public sector, not-for-profit and social businesses whose main aim is not profit maximization. Secondly, there are those who would suggest that the state or international community can and should contain the excesses of capitalism in the interests of society and its members. The third response disputes the argument that inclusiveness would be a burden on competitiveness.

Stakeholder and inclusiveness advocates realize that its ability to enhance shareholder value will be crucial to success, and many take the 'enlightened self-interest' view that capitalist businesses can be more successful in the long run if they do pay attention to their members' needs and interests. Kay (1997), Plender (1997) the Tomorrow's Company Report (RSA, 1995), and the report of the CTC into inclusiveness and organizational performance (CTC, 1998), all cite internal and external stakeholder alliances as the primary source of competitive advantage. They maintain that companies having flexibility and trust in their stakeholder relationships can generate synergies of cooperation and information which help adapt more quickly to the changing business environment. As Williamson (1997: 167) states, 'it is through long-term, committed relationships with their stakeholders that companies will equip themselves for the competitive challenges of the global marketplace.' Likewise MORI found that nearly three-quarters of the business leaders questioned in their 'Captains of Industry' survey thought that a business services its shareholders by also catering for the needs of its employees, customers, suppliers and the wider community. Only 9 per cent of the 88 respondents agreed that a business loses out if it pays attention to interested parties other than shareholders (Merrick, 1997).

For this argument to be tenable research needs to demonstrate the success of the inclusiveness or stakeholding approach, through hard evidence rather than rhetoric and opinion. One survey by Strategic Compensation Associates (SCA) did find that there was a strong and positive link between how well a company serves shareholders and how it serves stakeholders, but with a very limited sample (Lynn, 1997). What is needed is research with larger samples and more comprehensive indicators of inclusiveness to demonstrate the link with shareholder value. The main problems concern the difficulty of establishing numerical measures that can be applied across industries to companies of varying size.

Some stakeholder advocates suggest that the success of present-day stakeholder-run companies should stand as testament to the theory. Wheeler and Sillanpaa (1997), for example, identify Marks and Spencer, Glaxo-Welcome, Toyota, the Body Shop and British Airways as companies which exercise best practice towards particular groups of stakeholders. Although each of the companies has enjoyed a high degree of success financially and in terms of market share, there are obvious problems with selecting such companies as evidence of stakeholder effectiveness. First, commercial success can be transient (the Body Shop and Marks and Spencer, for example, have recently run into commercial problems). Second, given the lack of consensus about what constitutes an inclusive organization, it is at best contentious to present the above companies as exemplary. Third, even if these are examples of successful inclusive companies, there is no certainty that inclusiveness is a major factor in their success. Finally, there is the related question of causality; in other words, are these companies successful because they subscribe to inclusiveness or do they subscribe to inclusiveness because they are successful?

Faced with the difficulties of selecting individual companies to illustrate that stakeholding can improve performance and add shareholder value, several writers have used Germany and Japan as exemplars of stakeholder-based economies and pointed to their sustained postwar success as further evidence of the merits of an inclusive approach. However, their recent decline in economic performance means that it is by no means clear that capitalism can be regulated in this way without compromising productivity, competitiveness and growth.

A view from the left: a flawed epistemology and a cynical form of worker control

From the left's perspective, stakeholding and inclusive work societies can be interpreted both as a model of society based on an inaccurate and flawed epistemology, and as a cynical exercise in worker control and co-option, part of management's continuing attempt to manage the contradictions endemic to the employment relationship. Whereas a Marxist analysis implicates a dualistic model of capitalist society in which the interests of capital and labour are dialectically opposed, the inclusiveness model is developed around a pluralist framework of communities of care with acceptance of diversity. Here, a multitude of groups with often diverse and conflicting interests are seen to compete for influence and resources within society and organizations respectively. Crucially, however, such conflict is assumed to be a tractable feature of modern societies with governments and managers empowered to assess interests and allocate resources accordingly, and to promote the terms mentioned above of reciprocity, acceptance, diversity and voice.

Three Marxist criticisms of pluralism are of particular relevance here: first, the pluralists' limited explanation of how different interests arise and are generated within society – the contradictory interest of capital and labour for example; second, the conceptualization of power as a commodity that can be observed, measured and negotiated through democratic and institutional processes; third, contrary to the standard pluralist view that economic and political processes remain to an important degree separate from one another, they are conjoined in a complex set of social and historical relationships (McLennan, 1984).

The pluralists' tendency to conceptualize society and organizations as constellations of competing interest groups (or stakeholders), and inclusionists' assumption that the formation of communities of care is possible, is considered by the left to be unrealistic and naïve. Williams *et al.* (1996), for example, suggest:

> There is not and cannot be a plan for getting from exclusion to inclusion when the vision rests on a political fantasy about general benefits for all stakeholders and their economic analysis does not confront the structural reality of redistributive conflict between stakeholders.
>
> (Williams *et al.*, 1996: 120)

Despite the claims of some that it provides an attempt to socialize the capitalist enterprise and empower those individuals and groups whose interests and rights have traditionally been subjected by those of shareholders (Freeman, 1984; Handy, 1993; Hutton, 1995; Plender, 1997), it is possible from a more radical perspective to interpret stakeholder theory and the inclusive model as being the latest in a long line of management strategies to control and coopt the workforce. It is seen as having parallels with concepts such as empowerment, human resource management, total quality management and business process re-engineering. Each of these initiatives encourage management to conceive of employees as individuals and to resist the promotion of collective rights through workplace trade unions.

From this perspective, stakeholder theory can be interpreted as a cynical 'divide and rule' control strategy that presents a further threat to collective bargaining as trade unions are circumvented or reclassified as merely one of many interest groups. Consequently, for trade unions and individual workers the stakeholder model may pose an added threat to their already declining influence rather than as a means towards their longer-term salvation. It is surely more than pure coincidence that as trade union membership and recognition have declined, the power and influence of other stakeholder groups – in particular, customers – appear to have flourished. (The latest workplace employee relations survey (WERS, 1998) found that 47 per cent of workplaces had no union members at all in 1998, compared to a figure of 37 per cent in 1990; only 2 per cent had all employees as union members, down from 7 per cent in 1990; and 45 per cent of workplaces recognize one or more trade unions for collective bargaining purposes, down from 53 per cent in 1990, and 66 per cent in 1984.)

The inclusiveness model does appear to have major differences with earlier attempts to build industrial democracy and co-determination during the 1960s and 70s. During this period the unions negotiated from a position of relative economic and political strength, whereas today, by contrast, they no longer possess sufficient powers to negotiate a commensurate stake in the running and decision-making of business.

Both radical and neo-classical perspectives acknowledge the problem of global market forces. Legge (1999) discusses the very real difficulties faced by those trying to attempt any ethical action, not just actions for inclusiveness, where the spatial displacement and internationalization of trade and the search for competitive advantage on a global scale may create obstacles. Issues related to the international differentiation of the labour market, the mobility of foreign investment and the emergence of more flexible and temporal organizational forms, suggest that inclusiveness may just be a luxury for very scarce, core workers. Is the stakeholder model therefore realistic and workable in a capitalist economy?

Both analysis and experience suggest that it is naïve to believe that stakeholder theory or theories of social inclusion could make significant changes to the balance of power and interests within the firm. As Gamble and Kelly (1996: 28) acknowledge, 'those who at present own and control assets are unlikely to concede even a share in that control without a prolonged struggle'. Unlike the right, who argued normatively that one shouldn't challenge the current economic orthodoxy concerning the purpose of modern corporations, the left argue more analytically that it would not be feasible to so do.

Problems of implementation

One of the main criticisms of the inclusive approach concerns overgenerality and lack of conceptual precision – who exactly is being included, what are they being included in, and how does this inclusion take place? The myriad of interpretations, generalizations and definitions of the term gives it a martini label of being for 'anytime, any place, anywhere'. It is unclear as to whether it is being used merely to inform company mission statements, to guide changes in corporate governance practices, or to initiate a wholescale transformation of modern capitalism.

Employers and managers can be encouraged to move in the direction of inclusiveness voluntarily or can be forced through legislative and other means. Legislation is certainly being used to promote inclusion. The Fairness at Work bill (1998) includes a commitment to statutory trade union recognition, individual rights with relation to unfair dismissal and other collective rights at work, and family-friendly practices with relation to improvements to maternity and paternity leave. This is in the context of other recent reforms from European directives, such as regulation of working time and limitations on excessive working hours and night working, rights to rest breaks and annual leave, the introduction of the national minimum wage, and works councils to enable more employee participation in decision-making.

Gamble and Kelly (1996: 24) argue that initiatives such as Investors in People (IIP) and Employee Share-Ownership Schemes (ESOS) offer opportunities for inclusiveness to permeate the corporate sector. They also suggest (*ibid.*: 28–29) that an ethos of inclusiveness is required to inform policy-making at various levels – global, national and local. They believe that only by promoting this will New Labour in the UK be able to provide a framework for stakeholder capitalism and ensure the basis for new forms of corporate governance. Against this, Campbell (1997: 448) argues that management and markets must be left to determine these factors and adds that firms will only have a choice when they operate at a surplus. Furthermore, he suggests that management should merely be expected to make these factors explicit so that 'stakeholders can decide whether they want to commit to a relationship with that company'.

The RSA's Inquiry into *Tomorrow's Company* (RSA, 1995) has attempted to take the notion of inclusion as a 'philosophy' a stage further by exhorting business leaders to develop an 'inclusive' approach to managing organizations. The inquiry's research continues in an attempt to illustrate that companies organized around stakeholder principles are more likely to succeed than more traditional, shareholder-based companies. Despite this, those behind the report remain firmly opposed to the national or international legislation of stakeholder rights and practices, mainly objecting that companies operate in different industries and markets and face widely different pressures and circumstances.

There is clearly a major contradiction contained in reasoning that the inclusive approach is ultimately more profitable and sustainable, but any attempt to legislate its introduction will cause many companies to fail. This paradoxical reasoning appears to confirm the view that voluntary self-regulation is unlikely to work in a highly competitive market.

Others, notably Hutton (1995), contend that making the business enterprise more representative of stakeholder interests will require a more radical transformation of national and international institutions and regulations. Hutton identifies the short-termism of UK financial institutions as a major barrier to creating sustainable long-term relationships between stakeholders in the workplace. Thus, the UK signing up to the social chapter is seen as an important step in establishing the rights of workers and communities where livelihoods might otherwise be threatened by exploitative wage rates and by capital flight. Hutton believes that through such regulation national governments and international bodies such as the EC can play a significant part in creating a more patient and sustainable capitalism.

A similar emphasis on institutional restructuring is found in Bailey and Clancy's (1997: 49) advocacy of inclusion through the reformation of corporate governance structures, in which the main instrument would be the establishment of a number of regional development banks which would lay down a number of conditions in exchange for long-term funding (Bailey and Clancy, 1997: 52).

Conclusion

As a concept, the inclusiveness project appears to be in its adolescence. It still has an identity crisis as to what in fact it really means which is revealed in these paradoxes: the tension between unity and diversity, competing interests, and unitary and pluralist models of the organization. Does inclusiveness lead to heightened business performance, are there methods for resolving conflict, can voluntary and legislative approaches make an impact on practice? To grow further in maturity requires a great deal of support, which it is getting from legislative and voluntary change. But the project also faces much opposition. Our perspective as writers differs as between humanistic and Marxian standpoints, but we share a commitment to a humanistic ideal, and awareness of the limitations of how far this can be achieved. Large-scale organizational change is unrealistic – it would constitute the triumph of hope over experience. There, remains however, the possibility that some of the undesirable features of contemporary work organizations can be challenged through analysis and practical implementation of the inclusiveness project.

References

Argenti, J. (1993) *Your Organization: What is it For?* (New York: Macmillan).

Bailey, D. and Clancy, J. (1997) 'Stakeholder Capitalism via Socialism', *Renewal*, vol. 5(2), pp. 49–60.

Bowlby, J. (1979) *The Making and Breaking of Affectional Bonds* (London: Tavistock).

Campbell, A. (1997) 'Stakeholders: The Case in Favour', *Long Range Planning*, vol. 30(3), pp. 442–49.

Carse, A. (1996) 'Facing up to Moral Perils: The Virtues of Care in Bioethics', in S. Gordon, P. Benner and N. Noddings (eds), *Caregiving: Readings in Knowledge, Practice, Ethics and Politics* (Philadelphia: University of Pennsylvania Press).

Centre for Tomorrow's Company (1998) *The Inclusive Approach and Business Success* (London: CTC).

Coser, L.A. (1974) *Greedy Institutions: Patterns of Undivided Commitment* (New York and London: Free Press/Collier Macmillan).

Coupar, W. and Stevens, B. (1998) 'Towards a New Model of Industrial Partnership: Beyond the "HRM versus Industrial Relations" argument', in P. Sparrow and M. Marchington (eds), *Human Resource Management: The New Agenda* (London: Financial Times/Pitman Publishing), pp. 145–59.

Etzioni, A. (ed.), (1995) *Thinking New Communitarian: Persons, Virtues, Institutions and Communities* (Virginia: University Press of Virginia).

Freeman, E. (1984) *Strategic Management: A Stakeholder Approach* (London: Pitman).

Friedman, M. (1962) *Capitalism and Freedom* (Chicago: The University of Chicago Press).

Gamble, A. and Kelly, G. (1996) 'Stakeholder Capitalism and One Nation Socialism', *Renewal*, vol. 4(1) (January), pp. 23–32.

Gilligan, C. (1982) *In a Different Voice: Psychological Theory and Women's Development* (Cambridge, Mass.: Harvard University Press).

Goodpaster, K. (1993) 'Business Ethics and Stakeholder Analysis', in E.R. Winkler and J.R. Coombs (eds), *Applied Ethics: A Reader* (Cambridge, Mass.: Blackwell).

Handy, C. (1993) 'What is a Company For?' *Corporate Governance: An International Review*, vol. 1(1), pp. 14–16.

Heery, E. (1999) 'The New Pay: Risk and Representation at Work', in D. Winstanley and J. Woodall (eds), *Ethics and Contemporary Human Resource Management* (Hampshire: Macmillan).

Herzberg, F. (1968) 'One More Time: How Do You Motivate Employees?' *Harvard Business Review*, vol. 46(1), pp. 53–62.

Hirschman, A. (1970) *Exit, Voice, and Loyalty: Responses to Decline in Firms, Organizations, and States* (Cambridge, Mass.: Harvard University Press).

Hutton, W. (1997) *The State We're In* (London: Jonathan Cape/Random House).

Kay, J. (1997) 'The Stakeholder Corporation', in G. Kelly (ed), *Stakeholder Capitalism* (Hampshire: Macmillan), pp. 125–42.

Legge, K. (1999) 'The Ethical Context of HRM: The Ethical Organization in the Boundaryless World', in D. Winstanley. and J. Woodall (eds), *Ethical Issues in Contemporary Human Resource Management* (Hampshire: Macmillan).

Lynn, M. (1997) 'How Partnerships Pay Dividends', News From the Centre, *The Journal from the Centre for Tomorrow's Company* (January), p. 5.

McLennan, G. (1984) 'Capitalist State or Democratic Polity', in G. MacLennan, D. Held and S. Halls (eds), *The Idea of the Modern State* (Milton Keynes: The Open University Press).

Maslow, A. (1970) *Motivation and Personality*, 2nd edn (New York: Harper & Row).

Merrick, N. (1997) 'Business Chiefs Take to Stakeholding Ideal', *People Management*, vol. 3(9), pp. 12–13.

Monks, J. (1998) 'Trade Unions, Enterprise and the Future', in P. Sparrow and M. Marchington (eds), *Human Resource Management: The New Agenda* (London: Financial Times/Pitman Publishing), pp. 171–8.

Plender, J. (1997) *A Stake in the Future: The Stakeholding Solution* (London: Nicholas Brearley).

Royal Society for Arts (RSA) (1995) *Tomorrow's Company: The Role of Business in a Changing World*, Final report of the RSA Inquiry (London: RSA) (otherwise known as 'the Tomorrow's Company Report').

Rogers, C. (1967) *On Becoming a Person: A Therapist's View of Psychotherapy* (London: Constable).

Rubery, J. (1996) 'The Labour Market Outlook and the Outlook for Labour Market Analysis', in R. Crompton, D. Gallie and F. Purcell (eds), *Changing Forms of Employment, Organizations, Skills and Gender*, (London: Routledge).

Sadles, P. (1998) *The Inclusive Approach and Business Success* (London: Centre for Tomorrow's Company).

Sillanpaa, M. and Jackson, C. (1999) 'Conducting a Social Audit: Lessons from the Body Shop experience', in D. Winstanley and J. Woodall (eds), *Ethics and Contemporary Human Resource Management* (Hampshire: Macmillan).

Simpson, R. (1999) 'Presenteeism and the Impact of Long Working Hours on Managers', in D. Winstanley and J. Woodall (eds), *Ethics and Contemporary Human Resource Management* (Hampshire: Macmillan).

Stanworth, C. (1999) 'Flexible Working Patterns', in D. Winstanley and J. Woodall (eds), *Ethics and Contemporary Human Resource Management*, (Hampshire: Macmillan).

Sternberg, E. (1997) 'The Defects of Stakeholder Theory', *Corporate Governance: An International Review*, vol. 5(1), pp. 3–10.

Tam, H. (1998) *Communitarianism: A New Agenda for Politics and Citizenship* (Hampshire: Macmillan).

Terkel, S. (1972) *Working* (New York: Avon Books).

Townley, B. (1994) *Reframing Human Resource Management: Power, Ethics and the Subject at Work* (London: Sage).

WERS (1998) *The 1998 Workplace Employee Relations Survey: First Findings* London: ESRC/ACAS/DTI) (M. Cully, A. O' Reilly, N. Millward, J. Forth, S. Woodland, G. Dix and A. Bryson).

Wheeler, D. and Sillanpaa, M. (1997) *The Stakeholder Corporation: A Blueprint for Maximizing Stakeholder Value* (London: Pitman).

Williams, K, *et al.* (1996) 'Stakeholder Economy? From Utility to New Labour', *Capital and Class*, vol. 60 (Autumn), pp. 119–34.

Williamson, J. (1997) 'Your Stake at Work: The TUC's agenda', in G. Kelly (ed.), *Stakeholder Capitalism* (Hampshire: Macmillan), pp. 155–68.

Winstanley, D. and Woodall, J. (1999) (eds), *Ethics and Contemporary Human Resource Management* (Hampshire: Macmillan).

17
Company Law: An Instrument for Inclusion – Regulating Stakeholder Relations in Takeover Situations

Giles Slinger and Simon Deakin[1]

A company's stakeholders are those whose relations to the enterprise cannot be completely contracted for, but upon whose cooperation and creativity it depends for its survival and prosperity.

Introduction

A company's stakeholders make up a web of relationships both with and within the company. The company depends on the continuing health of these relationships for its survival and prosperity. In many cases, a process of bargaining or mutual adjustment between the different stakeholders may be sufficient to ensure that the health of these relationships is maintained. Contracts, explicit and implicit, can allocate risks and rewards in such a way as to maximize returns on the investments made by all the parties. However, the terms upon which bargaining takes place do not always result in mutually beneficial outcomes. Contracts are affected by uneven access to information, and hence to bargaining power. This in turn results in the imperfect allocation of risks and rewards and hence to lost opportunities for all concerned.

In this chapter, we consider a number of potential justifications for regulatory intervention aimed at overcoming what we may call 'contractual failure' in stakeholder relations. We identify two distinct functions of stakeholding which we characterize in terms of 'contract' and 'innovation'. We then show how these are linked to two distinct approaches to the regulation of stakeholder relations, one based on 'rights' and the other on 'cooperation'. After exploring

the areas of takeovers and company reporting, we conclude by suggesting that the effectiveness of regulation will depend on the capacity
of legal rules and procedures to promote cooperation within stakeholder relations, in particular by generating markets for information.

The role of regulation

A common theme running through the different formulations of
the stakeholder concept is their emphasis upon inclusion. The idea
that many groups, and not simply the shareholders, have 'something
directly at stake' in a company is given increasing importance
in contemporary debate. Why does 'inclusion' in a corporate context call for regulation of relations between different groups of
stakeholders? The stakeholder approach, whatever its moral justification, has always required an economic justification consisting of
net benefits to the group or society that adopted it. From this point
of view, we will suggest that a space for regulation exists because
cooperation between the different stakeholders, which is the foundation of the company's success, cannot be completely contracted
for. Law and regulation are needed to shape the bargaining process
in ways that foster the well-being both of the company and, in the
final analysis, of society too.

There are two broad economic justifications for basing regulation
on the stakeholder concept. The first is an argument at the level of
contract. In long-term economic relations, high transaction costs
(including the costs of negotiating, monitoring and enforcing express
contracts) may impede the formation of contracts that would provide for an efficient sharing of risks and information between the
parties. Where this is the case, the contractual interests of certain
parties are under-protected.[2] Here, the provision of legal rights for
stakeholder groups could be seen as completing the terms of the
'incomplete contracts' which the parties arrive at through autonomous bargaining. By such means, the contractarian model of
stakeholder relations can give rise to a rights-based conception of
the role of legal regulation. The definition of stakeholders is narrowed to 'those whose rights are affected by the firm' and the
definition focuses upon what is 'due to' stakeholders because the
firm imposes upon them costs or risks which cannot effectively be
contracted for.

The second justification rests upon an argument orientated towards innovation. A growing body of research attests to the

importance of close collaboration between firms, and between management and labour within firms, as a prerequisite for innovation.[3] Because innovation requires planning for the long term, but at the same time involves radical uncertainty over the future, the success of collaborative ventures depends upon the willingness of both sides to respond flexibly to changing circumstances. As a result, contractual relations are inevitably 'incomplete', so giving rise to a role for the law in supporting long-term cooperation.[4] However, rather than seeing the role of the law in terms of the 'completion' or 'perfection' of incomplete contracts, its purpose now is to encourage incompleteness: to encourage a flow of information and cooperation which goes beyond the terms of any express or implied contract. The basis for this form of extra-contractual cooperation has been usefully termed 'goodwill trust'.[5] While not ruling out space for a rights-based discourse, the emphasis instead is on procedural rules whose aim is to foster learning and creativity within stakeholder relations, rather than simply on redistributive measures which purport to create an optimal incentive structure for contracting.

If a company's stakeholders were simply understood as the 'affected parties', or 'those who can affect the firm', then a contract-based approach would be sufficient to govern their relations. However, the fact that stakeholder relations have the potential for innovation has very important implications. In particular, it provides a link to inclusion, since inclusion is a means by which cooperation may be enhanced. Inclusion may sometimes require regulating the form that contracts and markets can take. It does not mean that stakeholders should always or automatically have absolute rights to information or control. Rather, because of their importance to the productive process, it means that it makes sense for markets, information systems and contracts to be designed in ways that help all stakeholders to give of their best. Our working definition of a company's stakeholders, then, is

> A company's stakeholders are those whose relations to the enterprise cannot be completely contracted for, but upon whose cooperation and creativity it depends for its survival and prosperity.

Our definition of stakeholding has implications for company law. The legal system provides a framework within which the contractual and innovation-based models of stakeholder relations are continuously tested. UK company law, like that of most other common law systems (such as those of north America and the Commonwealth), provides important rights to shareholders as the 'residual claimants' of the company, but currently provides relatively few such rights to other stakeholder groups. The question we wish to examine here is whether the exclusion of stakeholders who are not shareholders from participation in corporate decision-making can be justified on economic grounds.

A highly influential view of the company sees it as the focal point of a set of contracts or bargains, of varying degrees of explicitness, through which the wishes of all the stakeholders are expressed. According to this point of view, the interests of the different stakeholder groups are best represented (and reconciled) through bargaining. Company law plays a role in reducing transaction costs by supplying legal rules which operate as a kind of standard form contract, which the parties can modify or adjust to their own particular needs, but which rarely constrain or prohibit private contractual solutions. A principal focus for legal rules of this kind is to reduce the agency costs that arise from the separation of ownership (by shareholders) and control (by managers). In this view, corporate governance is largely a matter of addressing the difficulties which shareholders have in controlling managers whose interests and information may diverge from their own. These difficulties are limited wherever institutional investors are willing to intervene to demand changes in management policy, or where the market can use an outside disciplinary mechanism, such as the hostile takeover. Hence a number of mechanisms – some legal, some extra-legal – are available for promoting efficient bargaining solutions.

Similarly, this line of thought argues that the wider stakeholders – employees, long-term customers and suppliers – are best protected by contractual mechanisms or, where bargaining is not feasible, by certain statutory provisions which control the exercise of contractual power (such as employment protection laws, in the case of employees, or laws governing late payment, in the case of commercial suppliers). What is not appropriate is to give such groups ownership or control rights within the framework of the company. To do this, it is said, would be to undermine the position of the shareholders as 'residual claimants', that is to say, as those who bear the ultimate risk of the company's failure and who, conversely, stand to gain most if the company succeeds.[6]

Were the monitoring role of shareholders to be diluted, or shared with the other stakeholders, it is argued that the effect would simply be to entrench corporate managers against scrutiny of their behaviour. As we shall see in further detail below, this is the basis for the view that the introduction of controls over hostile takeover bids would reduce the effectiveness of shareholder scrutiny of managerial behaviour, thereby leading to a loss in overall efficiency. But even so, from this perspective, the issue confronting policy-makers in the area of corporate governance is: how should the company be regulated so as to enhance its effectiveness as a mechanism for enhancing the overall wealth or well-being of all stakeholders?

The regulation of hostile takeovers in the UK

The nature of the task facing policy-makers can be illustrated by considering the arguments for and against hostile takeovers. In other work, we have argued that the system currently operating in the UK exposes non-shareholder stakeholders in listed companies to undue risk in two ways.[7] Firstly, it places the interests of target shareholders above those of other stakeholder groups, to a greater extent than is warranted by the general law on directors' duties. As a result, the current law contributes to a system of incentives which encourages managers to favour the short-term financial interests of shareholders when faced with a hostile bid. Secondly, the law hampers the ability of potential target firms to put in place anti-takeover defences. This helps to perpetuate a situation in which virtually all publicly quoted companies are 'in play', or subject to the market for corporate control, and hence to pressures on managers to retain the confidence of the market at all times.

Is this situation conducive with economic efficiency? In one view, the benefit of hostile takeovers is not only that they can directly alter practices of corporate underachievers, but that they can also encourage better performance in those companies which, as a result of the threat, improve their performance and hence never have to face a bid. As the 'great white shark' of the corporate world, hostile takeovers encourage 'all the fish in the ocean to swim a little quicker'.[8]

The contrasting argument, made at least since the mid-1980s,[9] is that hostile takeovers can undermine relations of goodwill trust between a company and its stakeholders. In addition to damage to the internal relations of the firm, a number of negative externalities may also be imposed on third parties. The publicity attracted by one hostile takeover bid can cause employees in other companies to place less faith in the value of their own implicit contracts. Where local communities are highly dependent on a particular employer, the costs of restructuring, which tend to follow on from takeovers, may fall unevenly on such groups. This is a kind of 'social pollution' whereby institutions beneficial to many, such as implicit contracts, are damaged by the privately interested actions of the few. Hence one company's emphasis on maximizing returns to shareholders at the expense of the under-protected, 'implicit' interests of other stakeholders, has effects beyond the individual takeover situation, and is corrosive to the productive potential of many other, similarly-situated companies.

In addition, the hostile takeover mechanism, it is argued, operates through a relatively inefficient market. The relentless pressure of quarterly performance assessments for fund managers means that they cannot afford to take a long view of investment decisions. The balance of the econometric evidence is that the market assesses takeovers – in particular agreed bids – inefficiently, making consistent and sizeable errors in valuations of the bidder company, and not selecting the most poorly performing candidates for bids.[10] As a result, managers may be best advised to seek greater size, or to reduce long-term investment, to preserve their positions.[11] This gives greater credence to the argument that employees may be wary about making long-term investments (such as those involved in acquiring firm-specific skills) in their relationship with the company. For all the reasons above, arguments are advanced for restrictions on hostile takeover bids.[12]

Arguments that regulations should be imposed, however, are often criticized by those most closely involved in the operation of the takeover system. In the course of our research on the takeover process, market professionals said to us:

I am very strongly against the idea of requiring a positive proof of public interest. To whom would the proof be given? What standard of proof would be required? It would allow political intervention and it is dangerous to allow politicians to start to make this kind of decision.

I am absolutely against any blanket ban on takeovers – think of the comparison with your own personal property, and the government forbidding you the right to buy or sell it. The suggestion of requiring 75% approval for control change is rubbish – try applying it to Parliament! In any case, shareholders can vote for this kind of change if they so wish. Sand-in-the-works? I would not expect increasing transactions costs by putting 'sand in the works' to have any effect on the takeover business.[13]

Those we spoke to believed that takeovers permitted flexibility in reorganizing economic arrangements. There was a belief that a bureaucratic assessment of costs and benefits would not offer the same thing. The chairman of a large UK plc said to us:

The overall takeover process is extremely healthy. It does keep open the one serious option for change. I would if anything like to see more M&A [merger and acquisition] activity ... and I would actually have a shorter version of the [takeover] process. Sixty days is too long. Proof of positive public interest? This would be very difficult to prove, and to win the argument. It would block the capitalist process.[14]

The argument here is not whether any regulation should be imposed. Regulation shapes the entire market from corporate control, from company law, through the Takeover Code, to the rights of employees under employment protection and (now) minimum wage legislation. The question is not whether, but how, and to what extent contractual arrangements between companies and others should be shaped by regulation, and to what extent they should be left open. It is on this issue that the difference between understanding stakeholders as rights-holders and understanding stakeholders as creative innovators becomes important.

If stakeholders are 'those whose rights are damaged', the aim would be the identification of damage, and compensation. Yet if stakeholders are 'potentially creative innovators', the aim would be to maximize the gains from innovation, and to share any gains in a way that continued to encourage innovation. From this point of view, the argument as to whether the disciplinary function of takeovers outweighs the disruption and short-termism which they are said to cause, should not be settled solely in terms of rights to compensation. Regulation of stakeholder relations should strike a balance between accounting for past costs and benefits, and emphasizing learning and adaptation for an uncertain future. For this reason, we should be wary of any particular distributive solution that is proposed for stakeholder relations. Instead, we should seek to create frameworks that can permit cooperative and innovative solutions to be found. A purely contractarian view of stakeholder relations – even a 'sophisticated' one which takes account of implicit contracts – is not capable of capturing the dynamic role of innovation within stakeholder relations.

Reforming takeover regulation

A number of proposals have been made at various times for protecting stakeholders from company takeovers. Some of them involve strengthening employee rights in general, and are not specific to takeover activity; for example, there is a strong case for granting employees protection against the abuse of pension funds. This issue has been addressed by recent pensions legislation[15] which has gone part of the way to giving employee representatives a clearer monitoring role in respect of pension fund management. Of greater interest for present purposes are proposals which relate directly to the balance of power between managers, shareholders and other stakeholders within corporate governance. Here, in the face of arguments that would give the market for corporate control free rein, stakeholder proponents have argued for drawing it back sharply: allowing more anti-takeover defences, including permitting cross-shareholdings; judging takeovers by the public interest criterion, with a greater role for the Monopolies and Mergers Commission; and creating a tax differential to encourage long-term retention of shareholdings. In response, it has been suggested that those regulatory changes that impose a particular redistributive solution may distort existing markets, increasing costs without generating sufficiently large benefits by way of compensation. It is also argued that the UK is not an abstracted contracting environment, on to which solutions from other countries' systems (for example) can simply be grafted. The regulatory options, it is argued, have to be considered within an existing commercial culture.[16]

In our view, these objections are properly understood as arguments against certain forms of regulation, and not against regulation as such. We defined stakeholders above as those affected by the firm in ways which cannot completely be contracted for, yet who could potentially interact with the firm in cooperative, creative, mutually beneficial ways. This approach implies a need for a framework of rules to provide incentives for the sharing of risk and information and to foster long-term cooperation based on trust, rather than one that seeks to impose a particular solution on the contracting parties. What would such an approach imply in practice for the regulation of takeovers in the UK?

A theme running through the analysis of hostile takeovers is that both managers and shareholders make decisions on the basis of incomplete information. The best counter, then, to market and managerial myopia is the provision of a wider range, and a higher quality, of information about the company's activities. The criticism levelled by Richard Roll's 'hubris hypothesis',[17] for example, was not just that companies cut investment, but that they did so because of failures in the market for information. Companies make heavy investments in the human capital of their employees despite being unable to identify clear returns; companies announcing large-scale retraining programmes have been known to suffer immediate share price declines.[18] By contrast, it has become accepted wisdom in the City that companies in difficulty can restore share prices by instituting large-scale redundancies, thereby forfeiting potential longer-term gains based on previous investments in skills and training. With better information of the effect of training cuts on staff morale, customer opinions, and retention ratios of both, the market would be able to allocate its capital more efficiently, and fewer myopic decisions would be made by both managers and by the representatives of institutional shareholders.

The role of advisers' incentives might also be considered here. Econometric studies show that expert advisers are involved in a business that, on average, loses money for the shareholders of the bidding firms, in particular in the case of agreed bids.[19] Even when agreed and hostile bids are analysed separately, mergers resulting from hostile bids lead, on the whole, to performance which is no better than the average performance in the industries in question. Viewed from this perspective, the failure of the market for corporate control to evaluate effectively the longer-term effects of mergers and takeovers is a clear instance of the reality of agency costs: those who own shares in bidder firms appear to be incapable of exercising adequate control over the managers who prepare and plan takeover bids.

How should shareholder representatives in potential bidder companies respond? Their options include (1) demanding better justifications from the companies they invest in for any takeover bids made; and (2) encouraging the introduction of incentive fees based in whole or in part on the long-term relative stock market performance of the bidding company. On the evidence of past practice, however, the capacity of shareholders to perform this monitoring role must be in doubt. For whatever reason, there are few signs that UK institutions are prepared to counter this form of managerial myopia.

Under such circumstances, it is legitimate to question the widespread view that shareholders are, because of their role as 'residual claimants', best placed to perform the role of monitoring corporate managers. At the very least, we may be sceptical of the idea that the shareholders alone of all the stakeholder groups should play a significant monitoring role. Attention then turns to giving non-shareholder stakeholders a more prominent role in order to balance the information arriving at the decision-making level.

As the situation stands, the nature and content of directors' fiduciary duties is a central issue. The interaction between the overlapping regulatory systems of the Takeover Code, the Companies Acts and the common law results in a situation in which directors of target companies, faced with a bid, place the interests of shareholders clearly ahead of those other stakeholders. Although they have an obligation to act with regard to the interests of the company as a whole, directors find themselves owing specific duties to the shareholders, for example concerning the accuracy of information concerning the bid.

One option for reform is to clarify the law so that directors enjoy greater autonomy from shareholder pressure during takeover bids. There are models for such reform in the 'stakeholder' statutes passed by many US state jurisdictions in the late 1980s and early 1990s.[20] Similarly, the draft EC Directive on takeover bids (the 'Thirteenth Directive') requires the board of a target company to 'act in the interests of all the company, including employment' when responding to a bid.[21] Indeed, section 309 of the UK Companies Act 1985 requires directors to take the interests of the company's employees into account when discharging their duties to the company. In this vein, the Takeover Code could be amended so as to reflect more completely this provision of the Companies Act. However, changing the law relating to directors' duties is unlikely to have much practical effect in the absence of any moves to give other stakeholders, such as employees, legal standing to challenge decisions of boards. Nor would reformulating directors' duties in the way suggested help boards to decide how to resolve conflicts which may arise between the interests of the different stakeholder groups.

A more concrete proposal that has been made from time to time in the protracted debate over the draft Thirteenth Directive is to require both the bidder and the target companies to engage in a process of consultation with employee representatives during the course of the bid. Rule 24.1 of the Takeover Code merely requires the bidder company to state its intentions with regard to future relations with employees. Offer documents issued by bidders under the rules of the Code nearly always contain a statement to the effect that existing rights of employees will be fully respected. This says nothing more than that the bidder company will respect the company's prior legal obligations to its employees; it has become a formality, which is represented in offer documentation by the use of a standard 'boilerplate' formula.[22] It says nothing about the protection of implicit but legally unprotected obligations.

Granting clearer protection to employee expectations (an 'implicit contract' approach) is one option open to legal reformers; in some US jurisdictions, rights of employees to employment protection are statutorily enhanced following a takeover (so-called 'tin parachute' rights).[23] Employees whose firms are subject to takeover are better protected than other similarly placed workers. The effect may be to deter certain types of 'breach of trust' by takeover bidders, but even then the best such laws can normally achieve is higher levels of compensation for those who lose their jobs in the aftermath of a change of management. In the UK, in contrast to the USA, it is normal for employees to qualify for some form of compensation if they are made redundant whether or not their companies are taken over. This does not seem to have deterred takeover bidders to any degree.

The proposal for consultation with employee representatives in the course of the bid could have a much more wide-ranging effect on the process of managerial decision-making. The legal meaning of consultation, in this context, requires the parties to consult with a view to making an agreement.[24] Statutory rights to information and consultation already exist in respect of decisions for large-scale redundancies,[25] and where a business is sold from one employer to another through a 'transfer of undertakings';[26] however, these rights do not extend to changes of control by share transfer.[27] The closure of this anomaly (for this is what it is, viewed from the vantage point of employment law) would help to provide a basis for the monitoring of managerial conduct by employees. In recent drafts of the Thirteenth Directive, however, concerns about the possibility of lengthy and costly disruptions to bids led to the deletion of any references to employees' consultation rights. The only requirement, as under rule 24.1 of the Takeover Code, was that bidders should state their intentions with regard to the future treatment of employees.[28] These concerns about hampering bids appear overstated. That a requirement to consult with employee representatives would hamper certain bids is not, in itself, a good reason to oppose consultation. On the contrary, requiring bids to pass the threshold of consultation with employees could usefully deter precisely those bids whose financial *raison d'être* lies in expropriating rents from stakeholders who are not shareholders.[29]

Consultation during bids would be most effective if it were coupled with a general obligation to provide wider information about the treatment of employees. Here, a relevant model may be found in the 'balanced business scorecard' approach to company reporting. This recommends that companies should report on measures for customer satisfaction, dealer satisfaction, employee morale and empowerment, and environmental responsibility, alongside more traditional measures of financial performance.[30] In the context of a takeover bid, the impact of the bid on other stakeholders – on customers, employees, suppliers, and possibly the local community – is arguably highly relevant to an assessment of its merits. The decisions of these constituencies will determine the company's long-term prospects. Both during takeover bids and more generally, it therefore seems legitimate to suggest that the reporting duties of both the target and the bidder company should be broadened to include a description of the identification and monitoring systems in place, auditors' evaluation of their effectiveness, and the company's performance to date in meeting the identified interests of its various stakeholders. Such an obligation could supplement the present duty to provide information to shareholders in the annual reports, and would provide content for consultation with employee representatives during bid situations.

Conclusion

In this paper, we have suggested that regulation has a role in enhancing cooperation in stakeholder relations, and we have suggested how a modest reform to the current law governing takeover bids could mitigate some of the more disruptive effects of hostile bids.

We argued that the interaction of law and regulation strongly protects target shareholders, leaving both bidder shareholders and, particularly, wider stakeholders relatively exposed to risk. At the same time, the takeover mechanism was strongly praised by some of our interviewees for its encouragement to corporate efficiency. Our general approach to takeovers has therefore been to identify interactions between legal and economic regulatory systems that produce damaging effects, and to address failures in those systems. We noted the dangers opened up by payments to advisers and managers that did not fully correlate their long-term interests with those of shareholders; and rules on communication by managers that focused their attention on shareholders during bids, dissuading them from communicating effectively with other stakeholders, particularly employees. All of these had consequences in takeover situations that could be addressed by reforms aimed at limiting the numbers of bids, but, equally, their effects in bid situations could be addressed by reforms aimed at enhancing the flow of information about and to non-shareholder stakeholders.

Particular solutions to the issue of stakeholder relations can be imposed on companies. Such imposed solutions might settle the contracting arrangements once and for all. But they also leave themselves open to problems arising from the evolution within the economic environment. Emphasizing rights at the expense of co-operation, they encourage a conflictual approach to dividing gains from the firm. The particular solutions might be appropriate at one time, but are vulnerable to change.

The reluctance to impose fixed solutions in the context of a changing and open-ended environment was the drive behind the argument for a greater range of information to be communicated to shareholders and stakeholders, and thereby into the public domain, on the question of stakeholder relations. The information approach allows space for the creation of local contracting arrangements, and emphasizes the productive potential of cooperation between stakeholders. We have also argued for laws that promote consultative arrangements between companies and their wider stakeholders. The aim of such reforms would be to allow inclusive solutions to be sought. This seems to us to be the best way of expressing through a regulatory approach the essentially cooperative and creative concept of stakeholding.

Notes

1 This work draws on research on takeover regulation carried out by the authors under the Corporate Governance Programme of the ESRC Centre for Business Research (CBR). The support of the Economic and Social Research Council is gratefully acknowledged.
2 Shleifer and Summers in Auerbach (1988), p. 33; Winter, in Blair (1993), p. 55.
3 See Deakin and Wilkinson in Campbell and Vincent-Jones (1996).
4 See Deakin, Lane and Wilkinson (1994).
5 Sako (1992).
6 See Macey and Miller (1993).
7 Deakin and Slinger (1997).
8 A market professional, interviewed by the authors for the ESRC Centre for Business Research (CBR) project on takeover regulation, 1995–96.
9 Shleifer and Summers (1988).
10 The extensive literature is summarized in Deakin and Slinger (1997); Mueller and Sirower (1998).
11 See Roll (1986).
12 See Hutton (1995); Plender (1997), at p. 260. For a contrary view, see Commission on Public Policy and British Business (1997) at p. 110.
13 A City financier, interviewed by the authors for the CBR research project on takeover regulation, 1995–96.
14 Interviewed by the authors for the CBR research project on takeover regulation, 1995–96.
15 In particular the Pensions Act 1995.
16 See Manser (1990), where the arguments for and against takeover regulation are rehearsed, the author coming down strongly in favour of the latter.
17 Roll (1986).
18 See the example of Marks and Spencer plc in the summer of 1998.
19 See Mueller and Sirower (1998).
20 *Ibid.*
21 Article 5(1)(c). See *Official Journal of the European Communities*, C 378, 13 December 1997.
22 See Deakin and Slinger (1997).
23 *Ibid.*
24 See Deakin and Morris (1998) at pp. 786–8.
25 This legislation dates back to 1975 and is currently contained in the Trade Union and Labour Relations (Consolidation) Act 1992. It is supported by a number of EC directives (in particular Directive 75/129 on Collective Redundancies).
26 The Transfer of Undertakings (Protection of Employment) Regulations 1981, implementing EC Directive 77/187 (the 'Acquired Rights Directive').
27 There is a provision for there to be annual consultation over merger plans between company representatives and representatives of employees in the Annex to the European Works Councils directive (Directive 94/45). However, this is unlikely to lead to significant employee participation in decision-making on mergers: see Wheeler (1997).

28 The amended proposal is published in the *Official Journal of the European Communities*, 1997, C 378, 13 December 1997. The background to the proposal is explained in Commission document COM (97) 565 final. See also House of Lords Select Committee on the European Communities, *Takeover Bids*, 13th Report, HL Paper 100, Session 1995–96.
29 For reasons of space we have to pass over here some important issues concerning the precise scope of a duty to consult as proposed in the text, and the remedies which the law should make available for a failure to consult.
30 Kaplan and Norton (1992, 1993, 1996).

References

Commission on Public Policy and British Business (1997) *Promoting Prosperity: A Business Agenda for Britain* (London: Vintage).

Deakin, S., Lane, C. and Wilkinson, F. (1994) '"Trust" or Law? Towards an Integrated Theory of Contractual Relations between Firms', *Journal of Law and Society*, vol. 21, pp. 329–49.

Deakin, S. and Morris, G. (1998) *Labour Law*, 2nd edn (London Butterworth).

Deakin, S. and Slinger, G. (1997) 'Hostile Takeovers, Corporate Law and the Theory of the Firm', *Journal of Law and Society*, vol. 24, pp. 124–51.

Deakin, S. and Wilkinson, F. (1996) 'Contracts, Co-operation and Trust: The Role of the Institutional Framework', in D. Campbell and P. Vincent-Jones (eds), *Contract and Economic Organisation: Socio-Legal Initiatives* (Aldershot: Dartmouth Press).

Hutton, W. (1995) *The State We're In* (1995) (Harmondsworth: Penguin).

Kaplan, R. and Norton, D. (1992) 'The Balanced Scorecard: Measures that Drive Performance', *Harvard Business Review* (January–February), pp. 71–9.

Kaplan, R. and Norton, D. (1993) 'Putting the Balanced Scorecard to Work', *Harvard Business Review* (September–October), pp. 134–47.

Kaplan, R. and Norton, D. (1996) 'Using the Balanced Scorecard as a Strategic Management System', *Harvard Business Review* (January–February), pp. 75–85.

Macey, J. and Miller, G. (1993) 'Corporate Stakeholders: A Contractual Perspective', *University of Toronto Law Journal*, vol. 43, pp. 401–23.

Manser, W.P. (1990) *The UK Panel on Takeovers and Mergers: An Appraisal* (Edinburgh: David Hume Institute).

Mueller, D. and Sirower, M. (1998) 'The Causes of Mergers: Tests Based on the Gains to Acquiring Firms' Shareholders and the Size of Premia', mimeo (Cambridge: ESRC Centre for Business Research).

Official Journal of the European Communities, Article 5(1)(c), C 378 (13 December 1997).

Plender, J. (1997) *A Stake in the Future: The Stakeholding Solution* (London: Nicholas Brealey).

Roll, R. (1986) 'The Hubris Hypothesis of Corporate Takeovers', *Journal of Business*, vol. 59, pp. 197–216.

Sako, M. *Prices, Quality and Trust: Inter-firm Relations in Britain and Japan* (Cambridge, Cambridge University Press).

Shleifer, A. and Summers, L. (1988) 'Breach of Trust in Hostile Takeovers', in A. Auerbach (ed.), *Corporate Takeovers: Causes and Consequences* (Chicago: University of Chicago Press).

Wheeler, S. (1997) 'Works Councils: Towards Stakeholding?', *Journal of Law and Society*, vol. 24, pp. 44–64.

Winter, S. (1993) 'Routines, Cash-Flows and Unconventional Assets: Corporate Change in the 1980s' in M. Blair (ed.), *The Deal Decade* (Washington: Brookings Institution).

18
Work and Social Inclusion

Richard Sennett

A portent of adult life came to me as an adolescent, walking once through a Chicago neighbourhood with my uncle. A judge of the strictest probity, my uncle was also an amateur of the city, familiar as a botanist would be with every human outcropping in its steel and cement landscape. On this particular walk, which took us through a slum, we passed a voting station outside which rather forbidding men in poorly-pressed suits handed envelopes to the citizens about to enter and vote.

I asked my uncle what they were doing. 'Bribing voters', he replied. I expected a homily to follow this observation, but none came. 'It's illegal', I prodded, but earned only a look of mild disgust. 'Don't the people taking the envelopes feel demeaned?' At last I goaded him into speech: 'the money is only a few bucks, and it makes them part of the community.' This was my introduction to the issue of social inclusion.

Social inclusion is not a subject which reformers think through well. We tend to focus on exclusion, assuming that if we diminish racial discrimination, class inequality or sexual prejudice, then a more socially cohesive society will inevitably result. But inclusion has its own logic. Inclusion, be it in a small-scale project or in a nation, requires mutual recognition; people must signal that they are aware of each other as legitimately involved together in a common enterprise. The sociologist Norbert Elias called such mutual recognition a matter of 'social honour'; this rather grand phrase denotes simply that members of a group feel that they are noticed and heard, that they have what the law calls 'standing'.

In this essay, I shall try to show how the conditions of contemporary capitalism diminish social inclusion, by denying to individuals, in their work lives, that experience of mattering to others.

The chemistry of inclusion

Simply sharing a belief is not enough to generate social inclusion. We may all believe in universal human rights or in democracy, but these convictions are empty if they lack corresponding practices. At least three elements are necessary for people to practice social inclusion. There must be mutual exchange; the exchange must involve elements of ritual; and the ritual must generate witnesses who serve as judges of the behaviour of individuals.

The envelopes changing hands at the Chicago voting stations are an instance of mutual exchange. While students of political corruption tend to treat votes traded for cash as akin to a business deal, my uncle's observation – 'the money is only a few bucks' – suggests an exchange which is less materialistic. Practically, the ward bosses of Chicago ruled in the 1950s without challenge; still they offered symbolic dollars to each voter: the bribe redeemed raw subjection. Moreover, it would be naive to say that the Chicago ward bosses had 'corrupted' their voters. Offspring of immigrant families from European villages, these poor citizens expected their rulers to make gestures of recognition and obligation. Their expectation highlights an important fact about a code of honour: if it must be mutual, it does not require that the recognition be among equals.

A second element of social inclusion is its realization through ritual. If anthropology has taught us anything about ourselves, it is that ritual is society's strongest cement, its very chemistry of inclusion. But – if you will forgive the mixing of metaphors – ritual is not simply the oil of the social machine; ritual values are not crudely functional. The nineteenth century diplomat Talleyrand gives a striking instance of why this is so in describing his aunt, a countess living in a country chateau, who each month in an elaborate ceremony in her best drawing room doled out medicines from her herb gardens to the servants and peasants on her estate. Few people were cured by these potions, but that wasn't the point. The formal room, the words of encouragement, the directions the countess wrote with her own hand on each bottle – such seemingly trivial details of the ritual established a mutual bond, if useless in promoting health.

The third element of inclusion is that there be witnesses to one's behaviour. The philosopher Paul Ricoeur portrays the act of witness as follows: 'Because someone is counting on me, I am accountable for my action before another.' There is more to this statement than meets the eye. It argues that because someone else depends on you, he or she has a right to judge you. We usually think that judges are superior to those whom they judge; Ricoeur, like Emanuel Levinas, wants to reverse these roles. Witnessing of the sort these philosophers have in mind occurs in religious rituals, as when congregations hold priests or rabbis accountable for conducting properly their offices. But this concept of witness seems very far away from the offices of accountants. And indeed that absence defines my theme: in the modern world of work we see less and less those kinds of mutual, symbolic exchanges which signal that employees are noticed and heard by the corporations for which they work; the fraternal rituals which bind worker to worker are diminishing; employers eschew being subjects of witness, accountable to those who depend upon them. It is for these reasons that social inclusion is weak in the realm of work.

In one way, this weakness should astonish us. In terms of shared beliefs, the horizon of inclusion is far broader in modern society than in the *ancien régime* world of Talleyrand's aunt; we believe in universal human rights which proclaim all human beings to have an equal and inherent dignity. Modern society wants to be far more tolerant; by 'democracy' we intend that every citizen recognize the worth of those with contrary opinions, differing needs or interests. Of course capitalism has long claimed its place in this expanded horizon of inclusion – from the 'carrières ouvertes aux talents' of the first eighteenth century exponents of free labour to the celebrants of upward mobility in the industrial era, to the celebrations of small-company entrepreneurship in the present age. Today, at least, the gap between promise and practice makes the experience of labour foreign to the pursuit of inclusiveness in modern law or politics.

Flexibility

To understand the weak chemistry of inclusion in labour we need to understand its structural organization. A great revolution is currently underway in the way work is organized. It challenges the burgeoning bureaucracies which Max Weber studied a century ago. He compared the capitalist institutions of his time to armies: both corporations and armies could rationalize their operations, he saw, by becoming efficient pyramids of power; positions in the corporate hierarchy were to become elaborately defined and stable, orders passed down intact from the top to the bottom. And, in fact, after the Second World War the pyramid of power structured those giant multinational firms which ruled the mid-century.

Today, the managers of modern corporations have revolted against the pyramid of power. They are doing so because businesses thick with bureaucratic layers are seen to respond too sluggishly to changing conditions in the global market. Modern managers want networks instead of pyramids; the networks are to contain semi-autonomous cells or teams of workers. Management claims this is both more responsive and democratic a form of bureaucracy – and the latter claim is only half false. Production and profit targets are set at the top; the workers in teams and cells are left to their own devices to meet these commands.

More salient is the flexibility of this kind of organization: it can be constantly reorganized, 'reengineered' in Management-Speak, as market conditions change, with large numbers of workers shed or added short-term. Modern production and information technologies make possible the redesign of workplaces quickly and comprehensively; flexible response is unthinkable without the computer.

In manufacturing, the General Motors operations like the Willow Run plant exemplified during the 1950s the Weberian pyramid; the Toyota plants in Toyota City today operate as a flexible network. In services, the Aetna Insurance company still embodies the Weberian model, while the German Allianz insurance empire represents the newer work world; in high-tech, IBM before 1993 represented the old way, IBM after a cataclysmic corporate makeover in 1993 now works in the new way, its engineers and programmers coming and going as the computer giant's operations rotate as in a kaleidoscope.

It might seem that flexible bureaucracy is simply a return to the instabilities of an earlier, anarchic, Balzacian capitalism, but that is not quite correct. In the convulsive conditions of nineteenth century capitalism, investors like J.P. Morgan or Rockefeller looked for ways to make corporate activity predictable; stability was the goal of monopoly capital. Today, finance capital tends to gravitate to those corporations willing to reengineer or reinvent themselves; businesses plunged in the flux of unpredictable change, like internet companies, are more attractive to investors than stable corporations, even if these latter are more profitable – they promise nothing new.

Finally, the bureaucratic revolution in modern capitalism is a portent of things to come rather than already consummated. Most firms do not operate directly in the global economy, nor are they purely flexible in form. Flexibility represents a desire, a model: few investors or managers dream of creating new pyramids of power thick with bureaucratic layers; rather, they search for ways to take such institutions apart.

My argument is simply that social inclusion falls victim to flexibility. In one way, this argument is hardly a revelation.

In the last decade it has become all too evident that chameleon businesses have enormous problems in arousing corporate commitment and loyalty among their employees. How could someone reasonably feel loyal to an organization which makes no binding commitments to them? A recent study of one flexible business found, for instance, that only 6 per cent of its employees thought their bosses would fight to protect their jobs. The loss of faith in institutions is, to be sure, broader than the realm of work. For the last 20 years, throughout Western Europe and North America, trust in government has steadily declined. But as workers the voters have good cause to trust government less: neo-liberal governments are loath to intervene in the internal affairs of businesses, so ordinary workers face the strains of flexibility ever more alone.

Consultants who orchestrate corporate life attempt to make a virtue out of this loss of social cohesion at work. They repeat over and over the mantra that loyalty is a virtue whose time has passed in corporate life; the sociologist Gary Becker says that the instabilities of flexible organization make explicit the purely contractual character of work, freed of any paternalistic taint. We should expect no social cohesion through labour, Friedreich Hayek long ago argued; we should look elsewhere for it, in families or local communities. However, work is the single activity in which most men and women today spend most of their waking hours. These views amount to the claim that the social contract, particularly those exchanges which create mutual obligation between the strong and the weak, will and should occupy only a small corner of human consciousness as measured in time.

The question of time in work itself raises issues about social cohesion which are perhaps less familiar.

Flexible bureaucracy is oriented to the short term. Its structure aims to be provisional rather than durable; the labour process is organized as a set of time-limited tasks and projects. In IBM, for instance, a team may typically work for a period of six to eight months on a particular effort, then the group dissolves and the workers recombine when a new effort starts. There is indeed a real virtue to a short, flexible time frame in work; it relieves the boredom of fixed, routine labour; it promises to stimulate workers by variety and new opportunities. But this very time frame can inhibit social inclusion.

'It's only temporary' is hardly an invitation to invest passion or commitment in any situation. Nor are mutual commitments instant. You can command someone 'trust me!' but he or she probably will not immediately feel it; social bonds like trust take time to develop. Informal trust also takes time; in a crisis, you need to have worked long enough with others to know who will go to pieces and whom you can rely on. Put another way, the exchanges which lie at the heart of social inclusion have a time dimension: they require duration in social relations – not permanence, but sufficient time for unfolding, repeated interaction to give an experiential meaning to formal commitments. Yet in flexible bureaucracy, time is short.

Repeated action in time, of course, gives a ritual its structure; a person learns what to do and what to expect. An important function of ritual, the anthropologist Clifford Geertz observes, is to discipline time. Work rituals, however, can have a different character than the rite of the countess' pharmacy. They can be used as tools of resistance.

In a back office of one large credit-card company, I watched, for instance, a group of file clerks 'cover' for a fellow worker who was in the throes of divorce; the clerks lied convincingly to different supervisors to explain why she was not at her desk. Had this been a one-off act of deception it would not have qualified as ritual; however, the file-clerks developed an almost balletic rhythm about who would answer the young woman's phone while she spent a week crying her eyes out in the lavatory, and what each would say. This rhythmic deception required institutional time: the file clerks needed to have known each supervisor long enough, for instance, to understand what he would find a creditable absence; they needed to have known each other long enough to care to make the effort, one dangerous for their own jobs.

It is just this 'ingrown' character of labour which flexible companies oriented to the short term wish to erode. When I first began studying industrial labour 30 years ago, I found rituals of resistance like the one I've described rife in manufacturing plants; they bound workers together, not only against employers but also against those union bosses who frequently failed to protect ordinary employees.

Today these rituals seem – though I can cite only my own ramblings – much less in evidence in flexible organizations. Work under these conditions has ceased to be ingrown, with an attendant loss of solidarity. The desire for solidarity certainly exists; the structural conditions to realize it do not.

So far I have argued that, both in its form and its time structure, the current capitalist regimes challenge social inclusion. Symbolic exchanges involving mutual obligation and commitment are eschewed; rituals of solidarity are aborted. Yet the relation of labour and social inclusion could not be left at this, which is a story of Demon Capitalism; stories with villains and heroes are best left to Hollywood.

Dependency

The political economy which rules us seeks to put another source of honour in place of social inclusion. That value is autonomy. We would be very poor analysts of ourselves to reject this replacement out of hand, for autonomy is a fundamental modern value; someone in control of him or herself commands respect. But it is impossible to understand autonomy without its shadow, dependency.

To avoid abstraction, let me summon once more the scene I witnessed in Chicago. Urban reformers have attacked it and its countless kin by invoking the virtue of autonomy. In America, the Progressive Movement early in this century aimed to purge American cities of the feudal habits of the immigrant European villagers; the Progressives hoped for citizens who practised independent judgement rather than blind fealty. Today, in taking aim at the supposed corruptions of the welfare state, an unabashed modernizer like Tony Blair in the UK aims for more self-reliant citizens. Neither American Progressives nor European adherents of the 'Third Way' are apostles of selfishness; the politics of autonomy arise instead from a horror of dependency, the root cause of fealty. Dependency seems demeaning, a source of social dishonour.

Horror of dependency is lodged deep in modern consciousness; for instance, in the writings of Locke. In arguing against Filmer, an exponent of paternalism, Locke declared that the dependent person lacks, as we would today put it, an identity of his or her own, instead relying on others to confer it. In making this argument, Locke affirmed the value of free and open, rather than determined, experience: our religious values must, for instance, be tested by risking doubt in God. For Locke, life has the character of an experiment, and honour resides in conducting that experiment fearlessly. Whereas dependence on others simply borrows their experience, like their religious faith, as one's own.

Or again, closer to the present, the horror of dependency informs the writings of Nietzsche, as when he works out the idea of the needy person as a cunning parasite. 'I am weak, and so I need you': by playing on my unworthiness and neediness, I am trying to manipulate you, to make you do something which, had I declared 'I am strong enough' I would not dream of asking you – I want you to relieve my fear of suffering, to take responsibility for my pain.

Or yet again, in our own time we might think of Freud, who combines in his concept of ego-strength something of Locke's experimentalism and Nietzsche's resolute insistence on taking responsibility for one's own suffering. None of these thinkers equates autonomy with indifference to others; no more is isolation the goal of those political reformers seeking to destroy habits of dependence. Instead, they have tried to affirm the dignity of a life lived without guarantees, and to emphasize personal agency and self-responsibility within that context. These views suppose that mutual respect will arise as persons recognize and honour in each other the attempt to construct life as an experiment.

Self-sufficiency, however, is more than a state of mind; it requires money, status and education. American Progressives and European exponents of the 'Third Way' indeed believe that to create a self-sufficient and independently-minded polity, you must make more people middle-class. But one of the peculiar consequences of the regime of flexible capitalism is to disorient middle-class life, particularly the middle-class experience of autonomy.

Let me give a prosaic example of how Locke's experiment in living is conducted in a flexible organization. This example concerns changing jobs. For all members of a flexible business, taking the risk of changing jobs is indeed a plunge into the unknown. There is no fixed organization chart, with clear categories of higher or lower jobs, such as Weber studied in the steel mills of America and armies of Prussia; the chameleon activities of the modern corporation do not lead to such precise divisions of standing. Nor does the short time-frame help individuals make good predictions about what they might gain or lose in changing jobs; in two years, conditions in the new job may be nothing like what they appeared at the time a person chose to move. From a strategic point of view, flexible bureaucracies are illegible.

The managerial elite usually has enough human capital to survive a job experiment gone wrong. The illegibility of a business may matter little to people at the bottom: flexible capitalism has benefited, for example, immigrants who in the past were shut out of closed unions and fixed corporations. The illegible character of flexible institutions does not daunt those young workers in their twenties who carry little personal baggage with them.

However, middle-ranking employees with children, mortgages and ties to community find their inability to read an institution both disorienting and disquieting when they change jobs. No one responsible for others wants to take risks in the dark; I found in interviews with such employees, therefore, that they are much more focused on what they are likely to lose than to gain. And rationally so: data on voluntary job-change show such mid-level workers are as likely to lose income in three years time as to gain it; in terms of corporate structure, most make lateral moves of an ambiguous character. As one accountant who switched companies remarked to me, 'Did I grow my career? To tell the truth, I just can't measure that.'

Current managerial ideology frames job-change as seizing an opportunity, work as a commodity, a 'brand' in Third-Way speak, to be repackaged continually through the course of a lifetime. Self-management of this sort is one definition of autonomous behaviour. Most of my interviewees accept this view, rather than yearn for the past. But they also find it difficult to manage risk in the dark. They believe in opportunity, but don't know how to behave strategically.

A miner who heard me talk about middle-class uncertainty remarked 'why are these people complaining? Each day I go down in the pits I don't know if I'll come up alive.' The illegible character of job-change, however, points to something more substantial than cowardice among accountants. It offers a clue as to why modern corporations can actively pursue policies which destroy internal social cohesion.

Very few horizontal corporate networks, their layers of bureaucracy thinned out, are in fact flat playing fields. Indeed, the current revolution in bureaucratic structure is centralizing power in an elite-technical managerial class. Thanks to the way information technologies are currently deployed, it is possible to transmit orders from this inner elite core quickly and comprehensively, with less mediation and mid-rank interpretation than occurred in old-style pyramidal bureaucracies. Reckoning of results is also instant, thanks to the computerization of corporate information. Dependency thus does not disappear in flexible bureaucracies; in some ways it has become more naked and absolute.

However, flexible bureaucracies split their command function from their response function. An inner core will set production or profit targets, give orders for reorganization of particular activities, then leave the isolated cells or teams in the network to meet these directives as best each group can. Those outside the elite corps are told what to achieve, but not how to achieve it. High-tech 'mental-work' corporations like Microsoft practice this division, as do flexibilized 'low-tech' industries like Allied Signal. The economist Bennett Harrison characterizes this split as a concentration of command without centralization of response.

Flexible institutions suffer from high degrees of operational chaos especially at those turning points when management or outside consultants decide to reorganize a business plan; this was the experience of low-level programmers at Microsoft who were suddenly told, in 1995, 'think Internet', without much indication of what 'think Internet' might practically entail. This command expresses an intention rather than an action; it is difficult to explain; like job-change institutional change is often illegible.

Just because the split between command and response denies workers an answer about how to do their jobs or how to meet core demands, corporations may try to draw on the belief that the need for answers from those about is a shameful sign of dependency. I found that many middle-level employees half believe this; they want to be free to work as they wish, but that supposed freedom to respond becomes an exercise in frustration. If an interviewer avoids the word 'dependence' and asks people, 'do you want guidance or direction in coping with an ambiguous assignment?', they are not at all embarrassed in affirming that they do. Since the commands were not of their own making, they feel in fact that it is only just for those who command to specify what they expect.

The realities of dependence, and the need for social cohesion between people of unequal power, appear exactly at such moments of flux. Of course, the need for direction appears in all kinds of organizations. In flexible ones, the split between command and response functions serves a special function. It protects those who issue commands from bearing responsibility for their consequences; in the sports metaphor which dominates current management ideology, the boss becomes a team-leader who simply coaches others to perform. As players, they are on their own.

We might at this point recall Paul Ricouer's definition of witness: 'Because someone is counting on me, I am accountable before another'. Quite reasonably, many of the mid-level employees I interviewed tended to view their superiors as frauds, since the bosses issue orders without any idea of how to make them operational. This can occur, of course, in armies, old-fashioned firms, or in politics. What's distinctive about flexibility is, first, that the person in power does not witness the very work-time he commands. Moreover, the flexible response to being held accountable does not refuse outright, as when a person called to account responds, just do what I say! don't ask questions! Rather it evades being called to account by manipulating absence, which is a much more sophisticated form of evasion. 'Now you are on your own' is a way to manipulate those to whom one issues commands; it deflects them from focusing on the legitimacy of the commands to dwelling upon their own status, upon their own conundrum of autonomy.

But again, we risk a version of Demon Capitalism if matters are left at this. In the context of modern labour, the value we place on autonomy raises troubling questions about the ultimate element of social inclusion, that of one person serving as a witness, a judge, of the behaviour of some one else. For Nietzsche, the fact that individuals must cope with situations not of their own making is part and parcel of the human condition. 'We are all victims of time and place', a consultant remarked, observing the chaos of a business in the throes of reorganization. Of course, in saying this he ducked being held personally accountable. But in another way he is a corporate Nietzsche; his act of witness consists in establishing the limits of personal responsibility.

What has most struck me as an observer of modern work organizations is that the failures, betrayals and inadequacies people experience in their dealings with one another serve as reasons for mutual withdrawal rather than for coming together – as though insufficiency is like a negative magnetic charge. You see that negative charge in lapses of fraternity among workers, as when dismissed employees are shunned by their former colleagues as though the downsized are deceased, or likely to make unanswerable appeals for pity. That negative charge adheres also in the very disposition to see the management elite as consciously bent upon harm, rather than caught itself by the demands of investors who want a short-term rise in stock prices at the expense of a well-run company generating long-term profits. The weakness of social cohesion under such flexible conditions is structural, rather than psychological. The operative model of work is the single entrepreneurial transaction rather than sustained business relationships. Judgements which totalize failure, inadequacy and lack of control are appropriate for entrepreneurial transactions; they are not appropriate for sustained relationships.

Perhaps I can make this clearer by reverting, for the last time, to the scene with which I began. Puritanical to a fault in his own affairs, as a citizen my uncle put that code aside. He accepted limits and impurity in the conduct of others as inhering in the symbolic exchanges which had created a sense of community in the Chicago slum. Modern workplaces have no such interest in community of this sort. As Japanese and West German productivity figures make clear, strong work communities can return good economic results, but by profit criteria which are divorced from the standards of current entrepreneurial investment. All communal activity is an impure mixture of different strengths and weaknesses, virtues and vices; because flexible workplaces are not viable communities, they are not forgiving.

I raise this issue to give a more balanced picture of accountability in the modern workplace. On the one hand, the flexible business differs from Weber's model of the military chain of command: when officers who issue commands then remain on the field of battle to carry them out, they earn the intense respect of their fighting troops. The trend in modern management is to command and then to depart; it sacrifices authority and leadership to protect itself. On the other hand, flexible businesses in their very structure place little value on collective survival, for the long term. Both authority and fraternity wither when the onus of survival shifts to individuals.

* * *

I've made heavy weather of the issue of autonomy and dependence because work experience today has distorted, in my view, the realities of mutual need which bind people together. A lover who declares, 'Don't worry, I can take care of myself, I will never be a burden on you', will soon be shown the door: why should you care about someone who feels no need of you? A child who fears depending on his or her parents is a damaged human being. Drawing a line around friendship so as to exclude those who are sick or old impoverishes the value of friendship itself. Yet in the current political economy dependence is considered degrading. People cannot sustain themselves alone. Yet in the modern political economy, that fact is treated as shameful.

The horror of dependence has negative consequences in work. It puts the burden of making practical sense of flexible organizations on those who are at the receiving end of power – a difficult challenge given the chameleon and illegible character of such organizations. If we deny people the right to depend on others, we diminish their capacity to hold others accountable. In a flexible institution the horror of dependence helps legitimate the divorce of power from authority. The argument I have made applies to the welfare state as much as to the world of work. Today, welfare-state bureaucracies – health services, schools, unemployment agencies, old-age homes – are being challenged to operate more like flexible businesses, focusing on the short term, making no guarantees, weaning people from dependency. As I say, we do not inherently lose our dignity by needing guidance when young, help when old or sick, when we are in love, making friends, or seeking education. Yet the reformers of the welfare state cannot easily imagine the place of bureaucracy in these experiences; instead, reformers tend to view durable and secure organization as debasing them into parasitic neediness.

In conclusion, I'd like to return to Norbert Elias' observation that social cohesion depends on what he calls 'social honour'. Social cohesion is diminishing in the workplace in large part, I believe, because the social honour which attaches to being an employee is diminishing. Honourable work is now symbolized by the entrepreneur rather than the employee. In brute fact, far fewer people work as entrepreneurs than as employees, and most entrepreneurial efforts fail – in the United States, home of the self-made man, over 90 per cent of new small businesses go bankrupt within a three-year period. Most of us are destined to be employees, which means we will need to depend on organizations, and within organizations, upon people with more power. This reality is fundamentally out of joint with the culture of social honour which pervades modern capitalism. And it is for this reason that I believe the fundamental task of social reform today lies in reestablishing the dignity of men and women as workers.

Part IV
Concluding Thoughts

19
Social Inclusion: A Radical Agenda?

Angus Stewart

We are all familiar with the widespread claim that the discourse of social inclusion represents the modernization of previous radical traditions, preserving their vision of social change while updating their analysis and consequent prescription. We are equally aware of the cynical response that such arguments frequently and easily produce, a response grounded in the realities of growing inequality, insecurity and political abnegation in the face of economic 'realities'. Against that background, my purpose in these concluding remarks is to consider the extent to which the term social inclusion can provide a meaningful focus for a radical political and social perspective. I organize this discussion around a consideration of several major issues raised by the discussion of social inclusion.

The proposed division between inclusion and equality

At one level, this division seems unproblematic. As a matter of historical record, in the development of New Labour discourse in the UK, discussions of social inclusion have replaced discussions of equality. In the course of this development, the operative political agenda continues to be highly individualized in that the principal focus of political discussion and governmental intervention is the individual, whether as worker, consumer, citizen, unemployed person, lone parent or whatever. The priorities of this agendum are those of business efficiency, functional adaption to the dynamic of market forces and social cohesion. (In the assessment of this 'efficiency', business tends to act as judge and jury, disregarding, discounting or socializing the many hidden costs.) In this discourse, the focus of political action moves from issues of equality to questions of equality of opportunity.

As Ruth Lister points out, such an emphasis on equality of opportunity can offer the basis for a potentially wide agenda of social inclusion, provided a sufficiently broad account is taken of the diverse social obstacles to be addressed in the creation of such equality of opportunity. Such accounting requires debate and decision over how best to negotiate the chronic tensions that characterize relations between economic processes and other social values and practices. For government to fail to acknowledge the frequent reality of enforced 'choice' between participation in the labour market and responsible and committed parenting is merely to generate social exclusion in the name of social inclusion.

Given the reality of structurally generated inequalities, the creation of a genuine equality of opportunity – the goal of which is individual and social well-being – will necessarily require redistributionary measures. This is not to argue for a collectivist levelling imposed by an overweening state. It is to assert that what is hidden by the 'hidden hand' of liberal market theory are processes of systematic social exclusion which must be addressed if equality of opportunity is to be meaningfully pursued.

Political inclusiveness as opposed to the politics of inclusion

If the question of the relationship between inclusion and equality allows no formulaic resolution, the distinction between political inclusiveness and a politics of inclusion can and should be recognized as more clear cut. Those perspectives on inclusion which focus primarily upon questions of value-integration and social cohesion have a potential to advance the possibility of a singular vision of the truth and, consequently, for a particular set of policy implications. It is a stance, moreover, powerfully fuelled by a stultifying and exclusionary 'politics of contentment' in which political 'leadership' becomes solely a matter of electoral calculation. Such a stance denies the inescapable reality of the pluralism of the modern world, of a diversity of interests, material and real, and for the requirement of that politics of negotiation powerfully articulated by Bernard Crick as the necessary and desirable mechanism of the inclusive society whatever its geographical boundaries.

The alternative is a political inclusiveness which, whatever its lip service to diversity, pluralism and dialogue, fundamentally and operatively understands difference and dissent as deviance. This alternative takes many forms in late modernity: the most familiar and obvious are the various reactive fundamentalisms of religion and nationalism which explosively haunt the persecutory fantasies of Western societies. These are significant – but as much for the symbolic role they play in fostering an escalating xenophobia, intolerance and state authoritarianism as for the realistic threat they pose to a culture of diversity and inclusion. Of equal importance is a hegemonic culture of populist political inclusiveness, involving an admixture of posturing moral self-righteousness, as against a constructive admission of limitation and fallibility, the control and spin-doctoring of information as opposed to the recognition of information as the essential ingredient of a free and inclusive society and the marginalization of opposition as delinquent and malcontent rather than the occasion for debate, dialogue and negotiation.

Central to the conflict between political inclusiveness and a politics of inclusion is the problem of difference, the problem of the other: the two represent opposed strategies for dealing with difference, one by denying and suppressing it, the other by accepting and engaging with it.

Determinism vs contingency

Running through the diverse discussions of social inclusion is a thematic disagreement about what possibilities there are for purposive political change in late modern societies. One focus for such disagreement is discussions of globalization – its nature, scope and amenability to regulation, whether at the level of the national state or through international agreement. One position views the dominant structures and processes of late modernity as largely beyond control. An alternative, while not denying the complexity of economic and social processes, nevertheless emphasizes their politically constructed character, seeing them as consequently accessible to political intervention. Such intervention is a matter of political will and leadership.

Social dislocation vs democratic participation

Inclusion used in the sense of a device for dealing with the consequences of social dislocation as opposed to inclusion as referring to the never-ending pursuit of the democratic regulation of public affairs in a world of pluralistic difference. Whereas the social dislocation stance is largely fatalistic about the possibility of addressing the causes of such dislocation – the stance is ameliorative rather than proactive – the project of democratic inclusion prioritizes process, participation and representative accountability as the key values of immanent communities of inclusion. (Several of the preceding contributions explore both the complexity and the necessity of this task, emphasizing the exclusionary potential of inclusionary democratic mechanisms.) Arguments about citizenship are of central relevance here, with the proviso that in late modernity the possibility exists of detaching citizenship from the singular context of the national state. The potential – already to some degree an actuality – of multiple political identities anchored in multiple political contexts exists in both federalism and regionalism, but also in political struggles to democratize the European Union.

A common thread running through many of the above contributions concerns the relational character and quality of social inclusion. In thinking and practicing social inclusion, we have to give equal weight to both the noun and the adjective. Further, social inclusion requires the maximization of opportunities for meaningful participation both as an intrinsic good and the necessary source of legitimacy in modern societies. In the endless pursuit of the inclusive society, we have to address any and all inequalities of power which clearly impede such agency whether with respect to class, gender, race or religion. In this task, the realities of power relations in late modernity require the generation and use of collective and effective political instruments, whether locally, nationally or internationally.

20
What Kind of Hope for our Future

Peter Askonas

To have watched the gestation of this book has been akin to observing contemporary social and political development projected on the small screen. Even whilst the chapters were written, events with significant structural impact appeared and disappeared. Familiar questions were given new significance; new ones emerged. Inclusiveness became more tangible, at least in some settings; whilst in others it seemed more than ever utopian.

Simultaneously the 'feel' of the book became modified. We set out recognizing the importance of our subject, recognizing also the obstacles, but, in spite of the latter, intending to project cautious optimism. As contributions arrived, a considerably darker book has taken shape. The desirability of a truly inclusive society remained a widely shared ideal; its feasibility raises serious question marks. Is social thought today more permeated by the pain of the world, more lucid *vis-à-vis* chaos than previous political analyses? However we reply, the sobriety which runs throughout most chapters of the book does away with facile assessments and prescriptions.

Our contributors here considered inclusion and exclusion from two angles. Some thought about the Inclusive Society in principle terms. Others focused on ways to make inclusion happen. Another distinction emerged. We are presented not with a single story but with two. One tells of social inclusion as an instrument, the other, about the Inclusive Society, as the end; at least as a preliminary end. The former relates to concerns for here and now. The latter assesses a long-term project. On that view: even when some of the components of an Inclusive Society are in place, the end may be attained only in time, perhaps even only beyond time. Moreover, some specific inclusive systems and instruments can be made operational in their own right, yet in isolation they are insufficient to constitute a truly inclusive society.

Implicit in much of what the various chapters say is the question: 'Inclusiveness, why?' It is to the end that this 'why-question' applies. What end? Accomplishment of a supreme value, 'something worth dying for', to use the words of Anthony Giddens in his 1999 Reith Lectures. Going even further, I see that end as comprehending – and, indeed, transcending – the gamut of targets such as the Inclusive Society. A worthwhile end is the harmonizing of differences in such a way as to achieve the richest possible synthesis. Whichever answer we have in mind (and it must be accepted that in the days of pluralism there is more than one answer) achievement hinges on being clear about the specific end. In ordinary political transactions this is often not so.

A related question needs reiteration: 'Inclusiveness – concrete possibility, or purely an ideal?' Anyone's response will be shaped not just by reason but by intuition. Readers will bring along their own response. I opt for 'possibility'. Even in minimalist terms, such as possibility is an ineluctable good. Without it, human aspirations are ensconced in futility. Worse than that, they are bound to be self-destructive. Some would have it, though, that this confidence is no more than psychologically necessitated self-delusion. But on this reckoning the concept of an Inclusive Society is a value-deprived one. Some may see this confidence as a function of utility. Yet others still, those who are motivated by a belief that all existence derives its being from an ultimate source, experience confidence of this order as concrete expression of their belief. I suggest that for all of us confidence, trust and hope in the realization of the type of society we here call 'inclusive' contains an admixture of something intangible, something that goes beyond rational proof. We might call it alertness to vision. We may recognize it without being able to articulate it adequately. It is this vision – beyond proof – which imparts the primary impact to the creation of an Inclusive Society. Without it 'the people perish' (Book of Proverbs, 600 BC approx.).

Enriching the scope of our reflections

Most chapters have examined the subject in economic, sociological or political perspectives. However we would have fallen short of contributing seriously to the debate if we did not introduce other elements crucial for designing a promising model. These comprise modes of inward experience, and of reflexivity; not least those concerned with intellectual inclusion and exclusion. Design as sophisticated political institutions as you will, unless you can overcome *a priori* exclusion of ideas and intellectual dispositions, the Inclusive Society remains a myth. For example, exclusion which erects unpassable barriers between different disciplines and professions is pernicious. When it conflicts with a wide compass of orientation, the project of inclusiveness is bound for an impasse. Heidegger's dead-end – *Holzweg* – is an apt description. Listening and conversing with 'aliens', in academia as elsewhere, is all too rare. It must be cultivated.

Inclusiveness and truth-assertions

Convictions and insights almost inevitably cause conflict. The most paradoxical example is that of differing beliefs, notably those of primary faith-truths. These imply (must they not?) the claim to possess something that is more true than the truth of others – and thereby exclude the other's truth. The other might be welcome to be 'included' when sharing *my* truth on *my* terms. A perennial dilemma: eliminate the deep conviction that *my* truth is *the* truth, that truth becomes enfeebled. We know painfully where this acceptance of plurality can ultimately lead us.

Charles Taylor (1997) offers a clue, at least at the level of conflicting social and political beliefs, by introducing the concept of Irreducible Social Goods. He confronts the apparently unresovable polarity between what for different persons is their particular irreducible truth:

> Understanding the other undistortively, without being led to deprecate or relativize the goods one still subscribes to, this can confer an important benefit. Most . . . world views are bound up with a deprecatory view of others. . . . These stories form part of the support systems for faith everywhere. The contrasts are real;

and so to understand the views against which one's own is defined, and hence to see its spiritual force, must bring about a profound change. The deprecatory story is then no longer credible . . . Where the faith was nourished exclusively by the story, it will wither. But where not, it will be free to nourish itself on better food, on something like the intrinsic power of whatever the faith or vision points us toward.

(*Philosophical Arguments*, ch. 8,
'Comparison, History, Truth')

Self-exclusion must also enter our equation. There are times when I must insist, radically even, that my belief and I set me apart, and make me assume a distinctive stance. It might be a divisive one. Accommodation for convenience's sake is not 'on'. I refer here not, for example, to facile political posturing but to dissidence. Nor do I bother with opting out when this is a fad. The dissident who, paradoxically, functions as a source for inclusion is the one who goes his/her way with integrity. Remember Havel and 'Charter 77'; remember also their transforming impact.

To be remembered, moreover, is the impact of persons, or of small communities, who stand aside 'from the world' – out of step with correctness; highly suspect! Call them hermits in the very middle of the 'world': seen as eccentrics by some, as source of strength by others; usually not the most comfortable of personalities, but people by whose existence the rest of us can be the better. Exclusive they might appear; but it is an exclusiveness wide open to embracing those who are similarly open. Or call them fools; and what is so wrong with folly? A world in total thrall to rationality would be all the better for loving folly. Recall the holy fool, much revered in Slavonik lore and literature.

We may well have to learn that in this phase of history which is under the spell of growing bigger and bigger, small is not only beautiful but essential. Aggregates exist as functions of particles. So, the big changes and the big revolutions, inevitable though they are, will not generate new meaningful social structures without the hunger for justice and consequent deeds of the microcosms of persons and small communities. I am speaking of the hunger for convergence, for something that unifies, for meaning beyond now.

So, back to the theme of tensions which has been running throughout the book. In high modernity, darkness and contradiction may be the appropriate medium for a maturing of Inclusiveness. So must be acknowledgement of almost irreconcilable differences and reaching out, beyond almost. So must be listening, replacing compromise by openness. Foremost, and more effective than debate and formulation of concepts, is the mediation of the inclusive act. It is summed up perfectly by: *Go, and do likewise.*

Index

Note: figures and tables are indicated by *f* and *t*.